New Directions in Market Design

NATIONAL BUREAU *of* ECONOMIC RESEARCH

National Bureau of Economic Research
Conference Report

NBER
NATIONAL BUREAU *of* ECONOMIC RESEARCH

New Directions in Market Design

Edited by **Irene Lo, Michael Ostrovsky, and Parag A. Pathak**

The University of Chicago Press

Chicago and London

The University of Chicago Press, Chicago 60637
The University of Chicago Press, Ltd., London

Published 2026
Printed in the United States of America

35 34 33 32 31 30 29 28 27 26 1 2 3 4 5

ISBN-13: 978-0-226-84659-0 (cloth)
ISBN-13: 978-0-226-84661-3 (ebook)
DOI: https://doi.org/10.7208/chicago/9780226846613.001.0001

Library of Congress Cataloging-in-Publication Data

Names: Lo, Irene, editor. | Ostrovsky, Michael, editor. | Pathak, Parag A., editor.
Title: New directions in market design / edited by Irene Yuan Lo, Michael Ostrovsky, and Parag A. Pathak
Other titles: National Bureau of Economic Research conference report.
Description: Chicago : The University of Chicago Press, 2026. | Series: National Bureau of Economic Research conference report | Papers from a conference held May 11–12, 2023 in Washington D.C. | Includes bibliographical references and index.
Identifiers: LCCN 2025034997 | ISBN 9780226846590 (cloth) | ISBN 9780226846613 (ebook)
Subjects: LCSH: Auctions—Congresses. | Markets—Congresses. | Microeconomics—Congresses. | LCGFT: Conference papers and proceedings.
Classification: LCC HF5476 .N49 2026
LC record available at https://lccn.loc.gov/2025034997

♾ This paper meets the requirements of ANSI/NISO Z39.48-1992 (Permanence of Paper).

Authorized Representative for EU General Product Safety Regulation (GPSR) queries: **Easy Access System Europe**—Mustamäe tee 50, 10621 Tallinn, Estonia, gpsr.requests@easproject.com
Any other queries: https://press.uchicago.edu/press/contact.html

Relation of the Directors to the Work and Publications of the NBER

1. The object of the NBER is to ascertain and present to the economics profession, and to the public more generally, important economic facts and their interpretation in a scientific manner without policy recommendations. The Board of Directors is charged with the responsibility of ensuring that the work of the NBER is carried on in strict conformity with this object.

2. The President shall establish an internal review process to ensure that book manuscripts proposed for publication DO NOT contain policy recommendations. This shall apply both to the proceedings of conferences and to manuscripts by a single author or by one or more co-authors but shall not apply to authors of comments at NBER conferences who are not NBER affiliates.

3. No book manuscript reporting research shall be published by the NBER until the President has sent to each member of the Board a notice that a manuscript is recommended for publication and that in the President's opinion it is suitable for publication in accordance with the above principles of the NBER. Such notification will include a table of contents and an abstract or summary of the manuscript's content, a list of contributors if applicable, and a response form for use by Directors who desire a copy of the manuscript for review. Each manuscript shall contain a summary drawing attention to the nature and treatment of the problem studied and the main conclusions reached.

4. No volume shall be published until forty-five days have elapsed from the above notification of intention to publish it. During this period a copy shall be sent to any Director requesting it, and if any Director objects to publication on the grounds that the manuscript contains policy recommendations, the objection will be presented to the author(s) or editor(s). In case of dispute, all members of the Board shall be notified, and the President shall appoint an ad hoc committee of the Board to decide the matter; thirty days additional shall be granted for this purpose.

5. The President shall present annually to the Board a report describing the internal manuscript review process, any objections made by Directors before publication or by anyone after publication, any disputes about such matters, and how they were handled.

6. Publications of the NBER issued for informational purposes concerning the work of the Bureau, or issued to inform the public of the activities at the Bureau, including but not limited to the NBER Digest and Reporter, shall be consistent with the object stated in paragraph 1. They shall contain a specific disclaimer noting that they have not passed through the review procedures required in this resolution. The Executive Committee of the Board is charged with the review of all such publications from time to time.

7. NBER working papers and manuscripts distributed on the Bureau's web site are not deemed to be publications for the purpose of this resolution, but they shall be consistent with the object stated in paragraph 1. Working papers shall contain a specific disclaimer noting that they have not passed through the review procedures required in this resolution. The NBER's web site shall contain a similar disclaimer. The President shall establish an internal review process to ensure that the working papers and the web site do not contain policy recommendations, and shall report annually to the Board on this process and any concerns raised in connection with it.

8. Unless otherwise determined by the Board or exempted by the terms of paragraphs 6 and 7, a copy of this resolution shall be printed in each NBER publication as described in paragraph 2 above.

Contents

Introduction

Irene Lo, Michael Ostrovsky, and Parag A. Pathak

Introduction

The first FCC spectrum auction, designed with substantial input from academic economists and subsequently recognized with the 2020 Nobel Memorial Prize in Economic Sciences (awarded to Paul Milgrom and Robert Wilson "for improvements to auction theory and inventions of new auction formats"), took place 30 years ago in 1994. In the years since then, an extensive body of research has focused on improving auction design, and many countries worldwide have followed the United States in using economic tools to design their spectrum auctions. The speed at which new insights moved from the research frontier to policy design was very short in the case of spectrum auctions. Some of the innovations that were applied in the 1994 FCC auction were developed just a decade earlier.

Irene Lo is an assistant professor of Management Science and Engineering at Stanford University.

Michael Ostrovsky is the Fred H. Merrill Professor of Economics at the Stanford Graduate School of Business and a research associate and codirector of the Market Design Working group at the National Bureau of Economic Research.

Parag A. Pathak is the Class of 1922 Professor of Economics at the Massachusetts Institute of Technology, and a research associate and codirector of the Market Design Working group at the National Bureau of Economic Research.

This volume and the conference on which it is based were made possible by a generous grant from Schmidt Futures to the National Bureau of Economic Research. We are grateful to Thomas Kalil of Schmidt Futures for his interest in and support for this project. Helena Fitz-Patrick provided outstanding assistance in the editorial process, Denis Healy expertly managed the Schmidt Futures grant, Rob Shannon skillfully administered the conference, and James Poterba steadfastly supported this project. For acknowledgments, sources of research support, and disclosure of the authors material financial relationships, if any, please see https://www.nber.org/books-and-chapters/new-directions-market-design/introduction-new-directions-market-design.

In parallel, in 1995 the National Residency Matching Program commissioned a report to develop a new clearinghouse algorithm for the medical match, with particular emphasis on outcomes for married couples. The recommendations of that report drew on some existing research but also broke new conceptual ground in addressing multi-agent matching problems. The report's recommendations were adopted by the medical profession in 1997 and have been widely viewed as very successful. This project was featured prominently in the 2012 Nobel Memorial Prize in Economic Sciences (awarded to Lloyd Shapley and Alvin Roth "for the theory of stable allocations and the practice of market design"). Just as in the case of the FCC spectrum auctions, collaboration between academics and practitioners was essential for developing practical solutions to market design problems.

In recognition of these two nearly coincident 30-year anniversaries, the NBER's Market Design Working Group organized a two-day conference in Washington, DC, on May 11–12, 2023. The conference combined a retrospective assessment of key discoveries and advances in market design over the past three decades with prospective analyses of the most promising directions for future applications. One unique feature that made this conference special was extensive engagement from both academic researchers and practitioners in a number of sectors of the economy: government, industry, and NGOs.[1]

This volume contains a selection of contributions based on the talks presented at the conference. These contributions provide different approaches and topic areas for market design research, illustrating the wide variety of different applications that can benefit from the market design viewpoint as well as the broad diversity of methodological techniques.

We now briefly summarize the chapters in this book, drawing also on portions of the lectures.

Alvin Roth, "Market Design and Maintenance"

From matching medical residents to saving lives through kidney exchanges, economists have evolved from theorists to hands-on market designers. In a chapter on the evolution of economists' involvement, Alvin Roth traces this transformation over the past quarter-century. Though markets have been designed since antiquity, economists' role as active architects is relatively modern. Three cases illustrate this evolution. The American medical residency matching system, established in the 1950s, required significant retooling in the 1990s to accommodate the surge of women doctors and couples seeking joint placements. Today, the system struggles under the weight of electronic applications, creating a new form of congestion. Proposals to introduce preference signals and caps on applications are being explored.

1. The agenda of the conference, along with video recordings of many of the talks, is available at https://www.nber.org/conferences/new-directions-market-design-spring-2023.

The economics PhD job market faces its own disorders. As interviews and offers become increasingly scattered across the calendar, the market risks "unraveling"—a phenomenon where hiring decisions are made prematurely, to the detriment of all. Without better coordination, the possibility of market breakdown looms. A third case is kidney exchange. Since America's first kidney swap in 2000, economists have helped craft increasingly sophisticated matching systems across hospital networks. Innovation has flourished: "donor chains," initiated by altruistic donors, have multiplied the number of life-saving transplants. Yet with diabetes driving up kidney failure rates, demand continues to outstrip supply. Cross-border exchanges show promise, though regulatory and logistical hurdles persist. Roth observes that markets, like buildings, require constant maintenance.

Estelle Cantillon and Aurélie Slechten, "Market Design for the Environment"

Can market forces be harnessed to save the planet? Estelle Cantillon and Aurélie Slechten examine the promise—and pitfalls—of environmental market design, with particular attention to carbon trading schemes and voluntary offset markets. The fundamental challenge is the familiar tragedy of the commons. Clean air, pristine waters, and thriving ecosystems suffer from a market failure—their benefits are shared by all, but their costs are borne by none. Traditional remedies have evolved from simple auctions of resource rights to sophisticated cap-and-trade mechanisms and markets for ecosystem services. The European Union's Emissions Trading System serves as a case study. Europe's flagship carbon market has weathered storms of price volatility that have threatened to undermine investment in clean technology. The sources of volatility include overlapping green policies, financial speculation, and rigid market architecture. Proposed solutions range from price floors to dynamic supply adjustments. Perhaps most intriguing are voluntary carbon markets, where companies seek to offset their potential contributions to global warming through emissions-reduction projects. According to Cantillon and Slechten, this nascent marketplace is plagued by credibility problems. "Greenwashing" scandals and dubious carbon credits have prompted calls for stricter oversight. The debate now centers on the trade-offs between decentralized innovation or centralized regulation. Cantillon and Slechten argue that the success of environmental markets ultimately hinges on careful institutional design but are optimistic about new opportunities thanks to technology.

Billy A. Ferguson and Paul Milgrom, "Market Design for Surface Water"

Billy A. Ferguson and Paul Milgrom examine how market design could help solve humanity's mounting water crisis, using California's parched landscape as their laboratory. California's traditional response to water shortages—damming rivers and desalinating oceans—may be increasingly antiquated. However, water markets, which could allocate this precious resource more efficiently, remain stubbornly underdeveloped. The reasons are as complex as California's water rights system itself. One is the "return flow" conundrum: irrigation water that seeps back into streams affects downstream users, creating externalities. The water rights system is also Byzantine, where rights are often held by irrigation districts rather than individual farmers, and measurement poses challenges. Drawing inspiration from America's spectrum auctions, Ferguson and Milgrom analyze a novel approach: procurement auctions that would let farmers voluntarily swap their existing rights for more flexible ones. These new rights would permit water storage and borrowing—making them more attractive to trade than their predecessors. Technology could grease the wheels. Satellite-based evapotranspiration monitoring promises greater transparency, while standardized hydrological models could prevent courtroom battles over water rights. A stricter definition of "beneficial use" might curtail water-intensive crops like alfalfa, which contribute little economic value. Australia's Murray-Darling Basin offers a glimpse of what's possible. There, water markets help farmers weather dry spells through efficient trading. Ferguson and Milgrom argue that by applying market design principles to water management—through voluntary rights conversion, better measurement, and robust legal frameworks—efficient, sustainable, and legally sound water markets can be created to address global water scarcity issues.

William Arnesen and Rachel Glennerster, "Market Shaping to Combat Climate Change"

While carbon pricing garners headlines, William Arnesen and Rachel Glennerster argue that the thornier challenge lies in designing markets that drive the technological breakthroughs needed to decarbonize everything from concrete mixers to cargo ships. Arnesen and Glennerster think that traditional market design, with its focus on optimizing existing systems, falls short when confronting climate change. The reason is that the task requires reinventing how humanity heats buildings, moves goods, and produces food. Innovation languishes, hobbled by market failures that carbon prices alone cannot fix. Inefficiencies and knowledge spillovers mean inventors capture only a fraction of their innovations' value. Arnesen and Glennerster divide the policy toolkit into "push" and "pull" mechanisms. The former, like research grants, subsidize inputs. The latter reward outputs through prizes or advance market commitments (AMCs). Past experiences suggest the promise of such tools: a $1.5 billion AMC helped deliver pneumococcal vaccines to developing countries. Replicating such experiences for carbon removal is trickier, given the diversity of potential technologies and their uncertain costs. Arnesten and Glennerster discuss concrete production, which accounts for 8 percent of global emissions. The challenge in this case extends beyond energy use to the chemistry itself. Similarly, hydrogen fuel development stalls as complementary innovations from production to storage. Long-term government commitments could break such deadlocks. America's government purchases half the country's concrete—market power that could accelerate adoption of green alternatives. The challenge lies in providing the certainty that innovation requires. Arnesen and Glennerster argue that if the goal is to accelerate decarbonization, it may be necessary to develop an expanded view of market design focused on stimulating innovations and by addressing challenges such as complementary innovations, long-term commitments, and government procurement policies.

Mete Şeref Ahunbay, Martin Bichler, and Johannes Knörr, "Challenges in Designing Electricity Spot Markets"

Electricity markets are not simple affairs of supply meeting demand. Mete Şeref Ahunbay, Martin Bichler, and Johannes Knörr reveal that today's power markets are vast computational beasts, with their complexity multiplied by the fickle nature of wind and solar generation. Europe's day-ahead market alone, processing most of the continent's electricity consumption, resembles a giant mathematical optimization problem more than a traditional marketplace. America embraces nodal pricing, setting rates for each point in the grid, which is precise but computationally demanding. Europe opts for zonal pricing, with single prices per country or region, which is simpler but potentially less efficient. Institutional considerations are first-order. Power plants cannot switch on and off. Their start-up and shutdown costs create non-convexities. The AC optimal power flow problem is complex and requires approximations, sometimes triggering price spikes. American markets emphasize efficiency, using "make-whole payments" to keep generators solvent. Europeans, via their PCR Euphemia algorithm, prefer avoiding such side payments, even at the cost of some efficiency. As markets shift from hourly to 15-minute settlements, the computational challenges intensify. Ahunbay, Bichler, and Knörr argue that multi-objective optimization could better balance efficiency against other goals. Further innovations in optimization and market design could also address the challenges posed by the increasing integration of renewable energy sources.

Kevin Leyton-Brown, Paul Milgrom, Neil Newman, and Ilya Segal, "Artificial Intelligence and Market Design: Lessons Learned from Radio Spectrum Reallocation"

In their chapter, Kevin Leyton-Brown, Paul Milgrom, Neil Newman, and Ilya Segal argue that AI is transforming how markets function. The authors describe America's Federal Communications Commission's spectrum auction. The challenge involved persuading television broadcasters to surrender valuable airwaves for mobile networks while solving an NP-complete graph coloring puzzle to prevent signal interference. Traditional economic theory alone proved insufficient. A cocktail of AI techniques—from satisfiability solvers to algorithm configuration—helped crack the computational conundrum. The resulting system balanced economic efficiency with computational feasibility, saving billions in auction costs. The authors see this as the prologue. AI promises to revolutionize everything from behavioral game theory to preference elicitation. More intriguingly, markets themselves must evolve to accommodate AI's peculiarities. How should AI services be priced? How can strategic manipulation of AI systems be prevented? As algorithms increasingly mediate economic activity, a host of interesting questions arise.

Tayfun Sönmez and M. Utku Ünver, "Influencing Policy and Transforming Institutions: Lessons from Kidney/Liver Exchange"

Tayfun Sönmez and M. Utku Ünver argue that market designers could learn much from surgeons. By adopting "minimally invasive" techniques to repair failing allocation systems—nowhere more critically than in organ donation—Sönmez and Ünver believe that successful market design often requires delicate, targeted interventions rather than wholesale system overhauls. In kidney exchange programs, economists did not create new organ markets—they simply enhanced existing donation processes, working hand-in-glove with transplant surgeons and policymakers. Sönmez and Ünver recount how this surgical approach to market design has proved remarkably effective. By respecting institutional frameworks and stakeholder objectives, economists have helped save lives without triggering ethical controversies or political backlash. There are similar experiences in other settings: from school choice to military assignments, minimal intervention has yielded maximal results. Yet challenges remain, particularly in expanding kidney exchanges globally. The transplant community's mixed reactions and fears about organ trafficking highlight the importance of careful stakeholder management. As liver exchange programs develop, similar sensitivities must be navigated. Sönmez and Ünver's lesson is that in market design, as in clinical medicine, a gentle touch rather than radical reform may be most effective.

Fanyin Zheng, "Matching Hospital Resources with Patients in Need"

Americans spend $1.3 trillion annually on hospital care—a third of all health care expenditure. Fanyin Zheng addresses ways to improve the allocation of hospital resources, such as ICU beds and operating rooms, to enhance efficiency and patient outcomes. Intensive care units and operating theatres—hospitals' most precious resources—often sit idle or overflow unpredictably. Physicians, focused on their immediate patients, display short-term thinking. Zheng argues the consequences are severe. Patients endure longer hospital stays and higher post-surgical complications, and costs spiral. The problem lies in systemic design flaws. Multiple decision-makers—doctors, administrators, policymakers—pursue different objectives with imperfect information. Real-time data and demand forecasting tools could help doctors make better decisions. Incentive structures could be redesigned to align physician behavior with hospital-wide efficiency goals. Artificial intelligence might smooth out the behavioral quirks that lead some doctors to hoard resources while others practice just-in-time medicine. But implementing such reforms requires delicate handling since physicians bristle at administrative oversight, administrators fear liability, and patients demand immediate care. Zheng describes how the challenge lies in designing markets that respect medical autonomy while promoting system-wide efficiency.

Derek Neal and Joseph Root, "The Provision of Information and Incentives in School Assignment Mechanisms"

The elegant algorithms underlying school choice mechanisms may be solving the wrong problem. Derek Neal and Joseph Root emphasize that the challenge may not be simply preventing strategic manipulation of preferences but helping parents develop informed preferences in the first place. Parents face a dizzying array of options, each with its own teaching philosophy, academic results, and extracurricular offerings. Simple theory assumes they can rank these choices with complete knowledge of options. Reality proves messier. Many parents lack basic information about available schools, let alone the nuanced understanding needed to make optimal choices. The costs of gathering comprehensive school data—visiting campuses, interviewing teachers, analyzing test scores—often exceed the benefits for any individual family. As a result, parents make decisions based on incomplete information, rendering even perfectly designed assignment mechanisms suboptimal. Neal and Root argue simple interventions—standardized school quality reports, parent mentoring programs, school fairs—could yield great improvements within existing choice systems and call upon market designers to consider the design of information that participants bring to choice to be front-and-center in the design problem.

1 Market Design and Maintenance

Alvin E. Roth

1.1 Introduction

Market design is an ancient human activity, but only in the last three decades or so have economists begun to apply insights from game theory to the practical design of marketplaces. Market design has brought into focus some of the things that successful marketplaces accomplish (Roth 2008). They must help the market become *thick*, so that enough transactions are available to attract participants to the marketplace. They must avoid *congestion* arising from the time it takes to identify, evaluate, and complete transactions when there are many potential transactions available, and limited time. They must make the marketplace itself *safe* and (relatively) simple for participants, and sometimes they must also be acceptable to nonparticipants (Roth 2007).

Notice that I speak not only of markets but also of market*places*. Practical market designers are typically designing a marketplace situated in a larger economic environment. Potential marketplace participants have large strategy sets that may include actions before or after transacting in

Alvin E. Roth is the Craig and Susan McCaw Professor of Economics at Stanford University, the Gund Professor of Economics and Business Administration Emeritus at Harvard University, and a research associate of the National Bureau of Economic Research.

This paper began as a presentation at the NBER conference on New Directions in Market Design, in the Spring of 2023. My work on this paper was partially supported by the National Science Foundation under Grant DMS-1928930 and by the Alfred P. Sloan Foundation under grant G-2021-16778, while I was from time to time at the Simons Laufer Mathematical Sciences Institute (formerly MSRI) in Berkeley, California, during the Fall of 2023. For acknowledgments, sources of research support, and disclosure of the author's material financial relationships, if any, please see https://www.nber.org/books-and-chapters/new-directions-market-design/market-design-and-maintenance.

the marketplace, and even strategies that may involve transacting entirely outside the marketplace. So the designer needs to make the marketplace more attractive than alternative venues, in addition to being concerned with equilibrium (and other) behavior in the game induced by the mechanism inside the marketplace.

This means that market design is different from theoretical mechanism design. Loosely speaking, the theoretical mechanism design literature conceives of marketplaces as if they were the entire market. The mechanism designer in this theoretical literature thus designs the entire universe that participants will inhabit, the entire strategy set of every participant, and how their choices interact to produce the market outcome.

But not only must actual marketplaces operate within a larger economic environment, this larger environment is likely to change over time, which may change the relationship of the marketplace to the larger market. By analogy, when you build a new house, a lot of construction is required. Decades later, some features of the house are no longer as well adapted to the inhabitants as they used to be, while other things need to be updated because of developments outside the house—for instance, you need to upgrade the electrical system after buying an electric car. So maintenance and renovation may supplement or even supplant some of the original construction.

In this spirit, I'll discuss several venerable market design projects in which I have been privileged to play a role over a period of years. I'll describe design changes in response to changing environments, as well as some current issues those markets are facing that may call for continuing redesign. Each of these markets had long intervals in which participants adjusted their behavior to the incentives created by the existing marketplace rules, followed by focused periods of market design, and then again by periods of behavioral response, and technological and social change in the larger market. My goal in this paper is to focus on how the design of marketplaces has interacted with developments in the larger market, rather than with the technical details of design (about which I'll simply cite references).[1]

In section 1.2 I'll discuss the American market for new doctors, and the marketplace called the match. That market, initially quite decentralized, began with the development of medical licensure around 1900, when it became important for new medical school graduates to obtain "postgraduate" medical education as interns/residents in hospitals, where they gained experience under the supervision of more senior (and already licensed/board certified) physicians. It went through a long period of adjustments in how

1. Other veteran market designers could give you a different perspective, but by focusing on markets I have lived with for a long time I can draw on information that may not have made it into published reports. It also allows me to indicate how market design can offer the satisfactions (and frustrations) of intimate involvement with particular markets over enough time to observe their evolution and to be able to diagnose and occasionally help address some of their problems.

market participants behaved. From year to year, offers were made earlier and at more diffuse times in medical students' careers, for positions that would be filled only upon graduation after four years of medical school. This made the market less thick: students were often faced with a single offer, which would expire before any other offers might be made. By 1944, these offers eventually came as early as students' second year in medical school. When uniform times were established before which offers shouldn't be made, congestion in the process of making and accepting/rejecting offers of employment also occurred, with verbal acceptances sometimes demanded immediately, in the same phone call in which the offer was made. This eventually led, with some trial and error, to the construction of a centralized clearinghouse in the early 1950s, which solved that congestion problem and survived with relatively minor changes until the mid-1990s, when accumulated changes required a redesign. That in turn led to a long period of orderly operation, which is presently troubled by congestion, not in making and responding to offers but before that, in processing the many applications (and subsequent interviews) that have developed with the introduction of computerized application services.

In section 1.3 I'll describe the decentralized process(es) by which new PhD economists get their first positions. Being decentralized, that market offers many paths for economists to find employment, among a wide set of employers (not just economics departments at universities). A publication of the American Economic Association (AEA) advertising Job Openings for Economists (JOE) helped make the market thick in the 1970s, and a widely attended January conference run by the AEA helped coordinate the timing of the market, since a very large percentage of job market interviews was conducted there. The interviewing process became congested, and a signaling mechanism was introduced to help coordinate interviews without causing other major changes in the marketplace. Then came the COVID-19 pandemic, and in-person interviews were replaced by Zoom interviews, which proved very popular. Today we are seeing more early interviews, and also a limited number of early offers (with short times during which offers remain open), and the AEA has offered guidance in the hope of constructing a new equilibrium that will keep the market thick.

In section 1.4 I'll discuss a very different kind of matching market, involving *kidney exchange* to increase the availability of living donor kidney transplants, in the face of almost universal laws forbidding the compensation of donors. To work well, kidney exchange needs coordination among hospitals, which demanded from the outset that transplant centers would make substantial changes in their previously customary procedures. And unlike the labor markets for new physicians or economics PhDs, it operates continually rather than once a year. Consequently, it has experienced changes frequently rather than annually, and its ongoing design still requires substantial innovation.

1.2 Matching New Doctors to Positions[2]

Today, and since the 1950s, almost all graduates of American medical schools participate in the National Resident Matching Program (NRMP), also called the Match®, the centralized clearinghouse that matches applicants to their first clinical jobs as medical residents (upon completion of which they can become licensed physicians).[3] In the course of their senior year in medical school they will apply to many residency programs and be invited by some of them to participate in an interview, after which both the applicants and residency programs will fill out rank order lists of whom they would like to be matched to, in order of their preferences. Then a centralized matching mechanism, powered by an algorithm that is in large part a deferred acceptance algorithm,[4] will produce a match that will determine who fills which positions, and almost all positions will be filled in this way.

The use of a centralized clearinghouse began in the 1950s to solve a series of marketplace failures in the prior decentralized market for new doctors, which played out in the first half of the 20th century.

Internships and residencies became a standard part of medical school graduates' careers around 1900, and, in the early days, job searches were conducted around the end of a student's last year of medical school. But competition among hospitals for good students, and among students for desirable jobs, first gradually and then quickly made the dates of appointment earlier, and more diffuse in time. Around the 1930s positions had come to be mostly filled around the beginning of the calendar year, i.e., halfway through students' fourth year of medical school, and by the 1940s the hiring date had moved to the summer after their second year. Because the timing of job offers had substantial variance, students often had to respond to an offer with a decision before knowing what other jobs might be offered to

2. This section draws on some of the market history recounted in Roth (1984, 2003). To engage with some of the current issues facing the match that I will describe, I joined the Board of Directors of the NRMP for a term from June 2020–2024.

3. In 2023, about 5,500 residency programs offered approximately 40,000 postgraduate positions to about 48,000 registered applicants, of whom nearly 20,000 were new MD graduates and over 7,000 were new DO (Doctor of osteopathic medicine) graduates of American medical schools, with most of the other applicants being graduates of foreign medical schools (NRMP 2023).

4. The deferred acceptance algorithm came to wide attention through the work of Gale and Shapley (1962), who proposed and analyzed it from the point of view of stable matching. Their paper launched the market design literature concerned with matching. Roth (1984) discovered that the algorithm used by the resident match in the 1950s was different from but equivalent to deferred acceptance (with hospitals proposing). The algorithm presently used by the match was designed by Roth and Peranson (1999). It is roughly a hybrid of deferred acceptance combined with an algorithm for fixing instabilities (Roth and Vande Vate 1990) that arise from the need to address a number of features of the medical labor market that were not standard in the theoretical study of matching, including the presence of couples looking for two positions, and reversions of unfilled positions from one residency program to another at the same hospital (about which see Niederle 2007).

them later if they rejected the present offer and knowing that many desirable positions would indeed be filled two years in advance.

Lots of information needed for a good match is missing two years in advance, and this was a widely recognized problem that was addressed when the medical schools agreed not to release information about students before fixed dates. This succeeded, in the sense that the hiring date for medical graduates was moved later, first to the third year of medical school, and in subsequent years back to the second half of the fourth and final year of school. But a new difficulty emerged, as hospitals came to demand immediate responses to their offers. So, once again, students had to respond to offers without knowing what other jobs might be offered to them if they could wait even a little longer.

In the period when offers were early and diffuse in time, the market lacked thickness, and applicants and employers weren't able to consider many possible matches at the same time. And multiple offers also couldn't be considered in parallel in the period of exploding offers, when too many offers had to be made and considered in too little time, i.e., when the process of offers and responses was congested.

The introduction of a centralized clearinghouse in the early 1950s (after a little trial and error) solved these timing problems for offers and acceptances. Because both applicants and residency programs submitted rank order preference lists of one another, the clearinghouse could consider all the preferences simultaneously; applicants could indicate their preferences for all the positions for which they had applied and were interviewed, and offers from programs could be processed, sequentially if necessary, without fear that some applicants would be "captured" early by competitor programs that moved first.

As mentioned earlier, the algorithm by which the early clearinghouse produced matches was equivalent to the deferred acceptance algorithm. In particular, Roth (1984) showed that the algorithm produced a matching that was "pairwise stable" in the sense defined by Gale and Shapley (1962): no doctor and residency program not matched to one another would prefer to be matched together. And empirically, there was good reason to think that this kind of stability was important for the success of the match, since similarly organized clearinghouses that didn't produce stable matchings tended to fail.[5]

This worked well when the medical labor market looked like a simple many-to-one matching problem between residency programs and applicants, but changes in the demographics of the labor force, and in the organization of postgraduate education, created some features that were difficult to

5. For example, unstable matches tended to fail in the UK's National Health Service (Roth 1990, 91), with some exceptions (Ünver 2001, 05) related to details of some markets there that involved a single hospital and medical school.

incorporate into a stable matching mechanism. Among these changes were changes in the larger economic environment, such as increased enrollment of women in medical schools, with the consequence that some graduates went on the market as part of a married couple looking for two positions.[6]

Amidst this and other stresses on the market, I was asked to direct the redesign of the match algorithm. I count this as the moment I became committed to practical market design, which changed the way I think about economic theory. For example, in Roth (1984) I showed that when couples were present, the set of stable matchings might be empty, so the presence of couples presented a hard problem for market design. But when I agreed to help redesign the match, I adopted that problem as one that I would have to address in a practical way, despite the fact that the available theory didn't yet shed much light on stable matchings involving couples. So theory would have to be supplemented with computation and experimentation to make progress. Roth and Peranson (1999) were able to show computationally that we could expect to find stable matchings reliably given the relatively small proportion of couples in the market. But it wasn't until much later that we began to gain theoretical insight into this in Kojima et al. (2013) and Ashlagi, Braverman, and Hassidim (2014).[7]

One issue for which the available theory was a considerable help involved the distribution of new doctors to rural hospitals. These are generally not the most preferred places at which to do a residency, and they often did not fill all the positions they offer. In addition, rural hospitals are often matched to graduates of foreign medical schools. One thing that I sometimes heard from medical administrators was that if a new algorithm was to be designed, it would be useful if it could help rural hospitals hire more residents, and more graduates of American medical schools. However, given the importance of achieving a stable match, I could confidently answer that this was not something that we could do, because the Rural Hospital theorem (Roth 1986) shows that the set of positions filled doesn't vary from one stable matching to another, and employers who fail to fill all of their positions are matched with exactly the same employees at every stable matching.

Since going live in the late 1990s, the Roth-Peranson algorithm has powered the match, without incident.[8] However, in the intervening quarter cen-

6. In 2023, 2,748 individuals participated in the match as part of 1,239 couples (NRMP 2023).

7. Another computational demonstration in Roth and Peranson (1999) was that the size of the set of stable matchings for new doctors and residency programs is very small. We began to gain a good theoretical understanding of that only with the theoretical work of Immorlica and Mahdian (2005), Kojima and Pathak (2009), and Ashlagi, Kanoria and Leshno (2013, 2017). (In 2023 Immorlica and Mahdian [2005], and Ashlagi, Kanoria, and Leshno [2013] were awarded the Test of Time award by the Association for Computing Machinery's Special Interest Group on Economics and Computation, see award information and past winners at https://www.sigecom.org/award-tot.html.)

8. See, e.g., Agarwal (2015).

tury the process of *preparing* for the match has become time consuming for both applicants and residency programs.

Growing congestion in applications and interviews before the opening of the match has caused difficulties for both residency programs and applicants. Electronic application systems make it easy for applicants to apply to many programs but don't make it quicker or cheaper to fully evaluate each application. And many applications by others cause applicants to want to submit more applications themselves, and cause programs to want to interview more applicants (so that they can rank them in the match), as the growth in applications and interviews (by others) reduces the probability that any single application or interview will lead to a match.

Before the COVID-19 pandemic, interviews were in person, and applicants were primarily responsible for paying their own travel expenses. Thus participating in many interviews was not only time consuming but could also add thousands of dollars to medical student debt. The scheduling of interviews started to exhibit some of the pathologies that unraveling of offers once exhibited. For example, some programs allocated a fixed number of interviews on a first come, first served basis after inviting a larger number of applicants to be interviewed, so that available slots were filled by those who could reply most quickly.

During the pandemic, interviews were primarily conducted by Zoom, and as COVID-19 concerns have receded, it appears that remote interviews will persist. So the out-of-pocket costs of interviews were substantially reduced, but the time requirements of many interviews remained a burden to both sides of the market.

Another concern about many applications and interviews was that programs were paying too much attention to easy-to-compare applicant attributes, such as their score on the first US Medical Licensing Exam (USMLE-Step 1). In reaction, the USMLE-Step 1 stopped reporting numerical grades, and (since 2022) now reports only pass/fail results. This of course doesn't make it easier to quickly (although perhaps inappropriately) eliminate some applicants from further consideration; indeed its goal was to promote more "holistic" evaluation of all applicants. It is too soon to know how this will influence concentration on other easy-to-observe attributes such as the school each applicant has attended, and how this will influence the mix of residents at different programs.

Not all proposals considered seriously by the medical community had much potential upside. One that gathered early support was to match 50 percent of OBGYN positions early in a single-specialty match, with the other 50 percent being in the regular NRMP match later. It's easy to see that this would produce unstable matches. (Consider a program with two positions, and two applicants it ranks highly and who rank it first. At any stable match those applicants would be matched to that program, but in an early match at which only one of the two positions is available, one of those applicants can be matched early only to another program that he or she likes less.)

This proved to be a difficult argument to convey, particularly since the American Medical Association had funded and promoted this proposal. But a simulation with preference data from previous years showed that such a two-stage match limited to a subset of the available positions in the first stage would not only produce instabilities but would also harm many more applicants than it would help (Ashlagi et al. 2023). This demonstration seems to have eliminated this proposal from further consideration. Playing defense is sometimes a part of market maintenance.

Motivated by the practice of signaling in the job market for new economics PhDs, many medical specialties have begun offering to transmit signals of interest from applicants to residency programs, in an effort to convey some of the information that used to be conveyed by applying for a position, before applicants began applying to so many. (In economics, the American Economic Association offers each applicant the ability to submit up to two such signals to potential employers, which are meant to aid in employers' decisions about which applicants to invite to interviews, and thus to help deal with the congestion involved in matching applicants to interviews, Coles et al. 2010). Each medical specialty has acted independently in choosing the number of signals, and so there is a disorganized natural experiment of sorts presently playing out, with some very preliminary indications from the first years of signaling. Many medical specialties adopted essentially the economics approach of having relatively few signals (I'm taking single-digit numbers to be few). The first two years of results seem to indicate that residency directors in these specialties are paying attention to signals, but that not receiving a signal from an otherwise interesting applicant does not make him or her less interesting. A notable exception is orthopedic surgery, which invites applicants to send 30 signals. It appears that this acts like a soft cap on the number of applications that a candidate can effectively submit, since residency directors report that they would not interview even a highly attractive applicant who didn't send them a signal. But these observations are still largely anecdotal.[9] It remains to collect and analyze data in coming years on how signals are used and how this influences which interviews are conducted, and which applicants are ultimately matched to which positions.

Thus, even in a market that operates largely on an annual basis, and which has a smoothly running labor market clearinghouse, it seems likely that as the larger economic environment in which physicians work continues to change, there will continue to be new design challenges for various parts of the marketplace for new physicians.

9. These (anecdotal) observations come in part from the session "Advising residency applicants in the era of program signaling," from the Transition to Residency conference held in Boston, MA, October 5–7, 2023. See the conference agenda at the National Resident Matching Program website, http://nrmpconference.org/agenda.html.

1.3 Navigating the Job Market for New PhD Economists[10]

Another set of labor markets that operate largely on an annual basis are the markets for newly graduating PhDs. Different disciplines organize (or fail to organize) themselves differently. Prior to 1970, the market for new economists was almost entirely decentralized, with academic departments announcing searches largely by word of mouth, and information passing through networks of colleagues and academic advisors, and in response to letters of inquiry. Starting around 1974, the American Economic Association (AEA) has helped make the market thicker by publishing *Job Openings for Economists* (JOE), which has been successful in gathering most US academic job openings for new PhDs, and many other (industrial, government, and foreign) job openings as well.

An annual conference, the Allied Social Science Associations (ASSA) meetings, organized each year by the AEA in early January, served as a venue for most interviews for academic positions for new PhDs. The conference took place in cities whose convention centers offered enough hotel and meeting space for thousands of economists (around 13,000 attended the year that I organized the conference). Recruiting committees invited candidates to interview, often in rooms in one of the conference hotels, during one of the two and a half days of the conference. So interviews were congested, both to attend (as perhaps a thousand well-dressed young economists queued for the hotel elevators to arrive at interviews that began on the hour or half hour), and to schedule. A busy recruiting committee might have time to interview no more than two dozen candidates in the time available but had to select these from possibly several hundred applications. The limited number of interviews that a committee could conduct in the time available became an increasingly salient constraint as the number of applications grew, aided by the advent of electronic applications over the internet.[11]

Following the interviews, departments invited some candidates to visit their campus for day-long "flyouts," after which departments began to make offers to selected candidates. These offers had varying durations, some long enough so that candidates could collect and consider offers from January to March, but some requiring answers within two weeks (or sometimes less). So candidates at times faced difficult decisions, and often asked for and were frequently (but not always) granted deadline extensions so that they could hear at least from employers with whom they had already interviewed and who were almost ready to make offers. And every year, around the end of March, there were departments that had not filled their positions,

10. The market history in this section draws on Coles et al. (2010), which reports on the work of the AEA's ad hoc committee on the job market.

11. Coles et al. (2010) reported that the survey the AEA conducted on behalf of our committee showed an average of 80 applications per candidate in 2006–8. My sense is that number has grown further since then.

and candidates who had not received offers, but this part of the market was decentralized and thin, with little help outside of personal networks in connecting people still in need of jobs with departments that might still be seeking to fill openings.

In 2005 I began to chair the new AEA committee on the job market, tasked with investigating and perhaps designing ways to ameliorate the congestion in interviewing, and the lack of thickness and coordination in the late part of the market. In 2006 we rolled out the signaling mechanism discussed above in connection with how years later it influenced the market for new physicians. And we also initiated a late-stage "scramble" for economists, modeled on the aftermarket that had long existed for new physicians.[12] Our scramble was simply a website maintained by the AEA, on which applicants and departments could indicate their continued availability after many positions had already been filled, and then contact one another directly.

Both of these interventions operated as part of the existing market procedures, which themselves continued to organize the market up until the COVID-19 pandemic. However one concern that surfaced before COVID-19, and has become more salient since, is that there was increasing objection to interviews being conducted in hotel rooms. While some departments could afford to reserve suites with separate space for interviews, many departments conducted interviews in a hotel room in which some faculty member was staying while attending the conference. This led to crowded interviews, with some committee members sometimes seated on a bed, and the objection was that this created an unprofessional atmosphere that could be hostile to women candidates. The AEA issued statements suggesting that interviews in hotel rooms were undesirable and should be moved to more public parts of the conference venue.

But before this guidance could have much effect, in-person interviews had to be abandoned during the pandemic. Instead, interviews, and often flyouts as well, were conducted remotely, by Zoom (or similar software). Zoom interviews were effective and popular, and by the time in-person meetings could resume, it no longer seemed obvious that interviews should return to being in-person. In addition, the 2023 meetings were held in New Orleans and the 2024 meetings in San Antonio, and following the 2022 US Supreme Court decision in *Dobbs v. Jackson Women's Health Organization* overturning prior US law on abortion, many AEA members felt it would be unfair and possibly unsafe to require women candidates to attend meetings in states like Louisiana and Texas that restricted reproductive care. These concerns and the earlier concerns about hotel room interviews led the AEA to suggest

12. The aftermarket for new physicians has since undergone substantial change, but that is a story for another time.

that interviews be conducted remotely, and prior to the meetings so as not to conflict with them.[13]

Following three years of Zoom meetings it became apparent that allowing interviews to be conducted earlier than usual had sometimes facilitated earlier flyouts, followed by earlier offers, more often with deadlines that compelled applicants to make difficult decisions before they could receive offers or even flyouts from other departments at which they had interviewed. So immediately after the 2023 meetings, the AEA's job market committee (now chaired by John Cawley) formed a subcommittee on job market design to consider the possibility that the market for new economists might substantially unravel in the coming years.[14]

In the absence of comprehensive data yet to become available about the timing of events in the previous years' job markets, we conducted focus group interviews of recruiting committees from a variety of academic and nonacademic employers. These revealed that many employers felt compelled to act earlier than in previous years and would be unreceptive to guidelines from the AEA if they were to try to prohibit early actions. Some employers, such as small liberal arts colleges, felt competitive pressure to act early, from other early actors, such as federal agencies, or from early moving overlapping markets like those for agricultural economists.

The AEA guidelines for the 2023–24 job market simply suggested dates and time intervals: interview invitations shouldn't be issued before the AEA transmitted applicant signals around December 1, and offers should remain open until January 31, and for at least two weeks, at least in the early part of the market (Rousseau 2023).

Earlier, the American Finance Association (AFA) had published guidelines for the 2022–23 job market, with a much stronger suggestion. Their guidelines (AFA, 2022) say in part: "*[T]he AFA promotes the following professional norm: If a job candidate receives and accepts a coercive exploding offer (i.e., one that expires before February 20), the AFA does not consider such an acceptance to be binding.*"

The AFA is hoping to promote an equilibrium in which early exploding offers will not be made because they will neither effectively bind applicants (who can later change their mind) nor bind (other) employers, who can continue to woo applicants who have accepted early offers. Establishing norms like this has been successful in the market for PhD admissions, in which very many universities subscribe to the Council of Graduate Schools' "April 15

13. The location of AEA meetings is arranged several years in advance, as it traditionally involved negotiation with convention centers in cities big enough to host the conference in hotels located closely enough together to allow applicants to move from one interview to another.

14. See Committee on the Job Market, American Economic Association, https://www.aeaweb.org/about-aea/committees/job-market.

resolution," which empowers applicants who have accepted an offer earlier to change their minds before that date and accept a different offer.[15]

The experience of other markets suggests that establishing this kind of norm as an equilibrium is sensitive to details of market culture. For example, this kind of policy has been successfully implemented in the medical labor market for gastroenterology Fellows, but proved impractical in the apparently similar market for orthopedic surgery Fellows, in which it was felt that applicants couldn't effectively be empowered to change their minds after accepting an early offer.[16] It is still too early to tell how the markets for finance and economics PhDs are going to play out in this respect. Market culture is at issue here, as it is in many markets with potentially multiple equilibria.

I anticipate that the economics job market may see more early offers before we reach a new equilibrium.[17]

1.4 Kidney Exchange[18]

Kidney failure is one of the top causes of death around the world, and the best treatment is a kidney transplant. A person with failed kidneys can receive a new one from a deceased donor, or from a living donor, because healthy people have two kidneys and can remain healthy with one. But most people with kidney failure will die without receiving a transplant.

In the United States, for example, there are approximately 800,000 people with kidney failure,[19] among whom not quite 90,000 are on a nationally maintained waiting list to receive a deceased donor kidney. But in 2022 only 19,636 kidneys from deceased donors were transplanted. So the wait is long and hazardous: 4,423 potential recipients died while on the waiting

15. The latest version of which (CGS 2019) states, "Students are under no obligation to respond to offers of financial support prior to April 15; earlier deadlines for acceptance of such offers violate the intent of this Resolution. If a student accepts an offer before April 15 and subsequently desires to withdraw that acceptance, the student may submit a written resignation of the appointment at any time through April 15. Applicants are not required to obtain a formal release from the program whose offer they accepted, either before or after the April 15 deadline. Once applicants have informed the program that they are withdrawing their acceptance of the offer, they then can accept any other offers."

16. On gastroenterologists, see Niederle et al. (2006), and on orthopedic surgeons see Harner et al. (2008), but note that both of those design efforts involved discouraging exploding offers in the decentralized market that preceded a new centralized matching marketplace, rather than (as is the case for economists) to coordinate timing in a decentralized labor market. See Niederle and Roth (2009) for a laboratory experiment designed to clarify the role of different market cultures regarding exploding offers.

17. A new equilibrium may also involve communication via social media. For a field experiment about the effect of Twitter (X) on the job market for new PhD economists, see Qiu et al. (2024).

18. For a technical account see Ashlagi and Roth (2021).

19. US Renal Data Service (USRDS) 2023 Annual Data Report, Figure 1.5. About 500,000 of them receive hemodialysis at a dialysis center, while substantially smaller numbers receive home dialysis or receive transplants.

list, and 4,396 were removed from the waiting list when they became too sick to transplant in 2022.[20] To be clear, the opportunity to receive a transplant slips away each year from about 10 percent of even those formally enrolled on the deceased donor waiting list. Kidneys from living donors are also in short supply; in 2022 there were 5,864 kidney transplants from living donors in the United States.

When economists see long queues of people waiting for a scarce, rationed good, we suspect that the price mechanism must not be working to increase supply. And indeed, it is against the law almost everywhere in the world to compensate a living donor or the family of a deceased donor, largely out of concern that allowing compensation could lead to the exploitation of the vulnerable. In the United States, the National Organ Transplant Act (1984) forbids payments to donors, and similar laws are widespread.[21] There are black markets, and vigorous enforcement of laws against compensating donors have in many countries driven those black markets out of hospitals and into venues that offer dangerous, substandard medical care to both paid donors and recipients.[22] The only country with a recognized legal monetary market for kidneys is the Islamic Republic of Iran. That market is controversial both inside and outside Iran, but the resulting nephrectomies and transplants and postsurgical care are apparently delivered in established medical institutions meeting international standards of care.[23]

I think economists need to understand better how and when repugnance to certain kinds of transactions leads to legal bans, how bans lead to black markets, and how we might better conduct and regulate controversial markets with an eye to both equity and efficiency.[24]

Kidney exchange is a way to increase the supply of living donor kidney transplants while (largely) avoiding the repugnance with which financial transactions for organs are widely viewed. Not everyone who is healthy enough to donate one of their kidneys can actually donate to their intended recipient, since kidneys need to be medically compatible. Until recently, a patient with an incompatible living donor had no choice but to remain on the waiting list in the hope that a compatible deceased donor kidney would

20. See National Data from the Organ Procurement and Transplantation Network, https://optn.transplant.hrsa.gov/data/view-data-reports/national-data/.

21. The US National Transplant Act of 1984 contains the following: "TITLE III—PROHIBITION OF ORGAN PURCHASES SEC. 301. (a) It shall be unlawful for any person to knowingly acquire, receive, or otherwise transfer any human organ for valuable consideration for use in human transplantation if the transfer affects interstate commerce." (A later paragraph refers to the broad interpretation of interstate commerce.)

22. See, e.g., Columb (2020).

23. See, e.g., Roth et al. (2022) and the references there. A related discussion in the European Union has to do with other Substances of Human Origin (SoHO), such as blood plasma (Elias et al. 2024).

24. It appears from survey experiments that there isn't a simple connection between legal bans and repugnance among the general population. See, e.g., Leider and Roth (2010), Elias et al. (2019), Roth and Wang (2020).

become available, while their incompatible donor was sent home. But kidney exchange allows incompatible patient-donor pairs to exchange kidneys with one another, so that each patient receives a compatible kidney from another patient's donor.

Kidney exchange was proposed conceptually by Rapaport (1986), but the first exchange in the United States, between two patient-donor pairs, wasn't carried out until 2001 in the Rhode Island Hospital.[25] Roth et al. "Kidney Exchange" (2003, 2004) proposed how kidney exchange could scale beyond two-pair exchange in a single hospital.[26] We sent the 2003 working paper to a number of transplant surgeons, but the only one who replied was my Harvard colleague Frank Delmonico, and we helped him and his transplant colleagues start the New England Program for Kidney Exchange (Delmonico et al. 2004; Roth et al. 2005a). But our surgical colleagues weren't yet prepared to consider exchanges involving more than two patient-donor pairs, and so we proposed a simpler system for pairwise exchanges (Roth et al. 2005b), with which NEPKE began operations. Each exchange was to be done simultaneously, to make sure that no pair gave a kidney and subsequently didn't receive one in return.

Actually implementing inter-hospital kidney exchange involved addressing many issues related to the larger environment of hospital workflows and health care payments.[27]

An immediate and formidable obstacle was the need for coordination between hospitals. Before kidney exchange, transplant centers seldom had to coordinate with one another: each center transplanted its own patients. But efficient exchange, which requires a large pool of eligible patient-donor pairs, often involved patients at different hospitals. In New England alone, there were 14 transplant centers. Because they were relatively close to each other, inter-hospital exchange in New England between two patient-donor pairs was arranged by having each patient remain at the hospital where he or she was being treated, and admitting the relevant donor to that hospital for the nephrectomy. But operating rooms in a hospital are a scarce resource that needs to be scheduled, and a living donor kidney transplant is an elective surgery, which can be scheduled in advance. So, at each hospital, there was a customary day when living donor kidney transplants were done. Although

25. For early kidney exchange history, see Wallis et al. (2011); for an account of the first US exchange, see Zarsadias (2010).

26. Roth et al. "Kidney Exchange" (2004) was based largely on the top trading cycles algorithm described in Shapley and Scarf (1974) and studied in Roth and Postlewaite (1977) and Roth (1982) and extended in Abdulkadiroğlu and Sönmez (1999). For a survey on top trading cycles (in connection with its 50th anniversary), see Morrill and Roth (2024).

27. There was some early opposition to kidney exchange phrased in terms of the "valuable consideration" wording in the NOTA, but in 2007 both houses of Congress unanimously passed Public Law 110 - 144 - the Charlie W. Norwood Living Organ Donation Act, "to amend the National Organ Transplant Act to provide that criminal penalties do not apply to human organ paired donation . . ." (The phrase "paired donation" avoids use of the word "exchange" that made some people think of organ sales.)

these were mostly Tuesdays, Wednesdays, or Thursdays, it nevertheless often meant that if two hospitals wished to engage in a simultaneous exchange, one of them had to operate on a day that was irregular for them. This involved not just a negotiation between the two kidney transplant programs (each of which would prefer their customary day) but also with colleagues doing other kinds of surgeries at the same hospital, whose operations might also have to be rescheduled.[28]

This was one reason our surgical colleagues initially felt that they could perform only exchanges between two patient-donor pairs. Exchanges involving three or more pairs could require coordination among three or more hospitals (while a three-way simultaneous exchange at a single hospital would involve six operating rooms and surgical teams, which would strain the resources of all but the biggest transplant centers). As experience was gained, three-way exchanges became feasible, and short chains initiated by nondirected donors and also involving three transplants and nephrectomies could be scheduled simultaneously.

A nondirected donor (NDD) donates without having a particular recipient in mind. A short, simultaneous chain of transplants involves the NDD donating a kidney to a patient in a patient-donor pair, whose donor donates to another pair, whose donor passes it forward again, to someone who does not have a willing living donor and would otherwise languish on the deceased donor waiting list (Saidman et al. 2006).

However, unlike an exchange involving only patient-donor pairs, a chain could be conducted nonsimultaneously, with every patient-donor pair receiving a kidney before donating their own, which would lessen the cost should a link be broken, since no pair would be at risk of donating a kidney without receiving one (Roth et al. 2006). The first long, nonsimultaneous NDD chain was reported in Rees et al. (2009), and today (after overcoming considerable controversy),[29] such chains account for the majority of American kidney exchange transplants, which recently number well over a thousand a year.[30] Because NDD chains can be conducted nonsimultaneously they can be long, since fewer resources need to be simultaneously available. And

28. Since deceased-donor transplants are emergency surgeries, there was some customary flexibility that allowed more coordination than otherwise might have been achievable.

29. Nonsimultaneous nondirected donor chains didn't become standard practice until after the publication of Ashlagi et al. (2011a, 2011b). NEPKE never adopted nonsimultaneous chains, and ceased organizing kidney exchange in July, 2011, having completed only 83 exchange transplants. Its operations were folded into a pilot program operated by the United Network for Organ Sharing (UNOS), which joined national kidney exchange networks already operated by the Alliance for Paired Kidney Donation (APKD) and the National Kidney Registry (NKR), as well as exchanges operated within single hospitals and hospital chains.

30. In 2020 there was a pandemic-related drop to 835 kidney exchange transplants. I don't think that the numbers reported for kidney exchange ("paired donation") take account of the nondirected donors ("Non-Biol,unrel: Anonymous Donation") in the OPTN data (see National Data from the Organ Procurement and Transplantation Network, https://optn.transplant.hrsa.gov/data/view-data-reports/national-data/), who now number in the hundreds.

because they ease the coordination problems between hospitals, they open up kidney exchange to a larger pool of patients and donors, including hard to match patient-donor pairs who are unlikely to match when exchanges are restricted to be among small numbers of pairs.

As kidney exchange has grown, and exchange chains extend across the country, donors travel less often and kidneys are shipped, so coordination of inter-hospital kidney exchange has become complex in different ways. Now surgeries sometimes are arranged to take account of airline schedules.[31] And hospitals in different Medicare regions levy different charges, so that hospitals needed to be reimbursed for nephrectomies that may have been charged at vastly different amounts. (This obstacle has now been largely overcome by the introduction of standard acquisition charges, see Rees et al. [2012].).[32] Reflecting these difficulties in inter-hospital coordination, Agarwal et al. (2019) report that as of 2014 more than 60 percent of all exchange transplants in the United States were (still) internal exchanges made within a single hospital.[33] That is, the demands of inter-hospital coordination, which was such a large obstacle to kidney exchange when it began, has taken years to overcome in the United States, although we have slowly made considerable progress.

However much more progress is needed. One innovation that has yet to be widely accepted in the United States is to start chains with a nondirected deceased donor. (Almost all deceased donors are nondirected, but current practice is to use each deceased donor kidney for a single transplant to someone on the deceased donor waiting list.) However, a proposal for deceased donor originated chains in Melcher et al. (2016) has been productively implemented in Italy (in a collaboration between physicians and economists there; see Furian et al. 2020).[34]

Big gains could still be made by organizing kidney exchange across national borders, which today happens only seldom, in exceptional circumstances. All the coordination difficulties that had to be overcome before kidney exchange could become a significant source of transplants in the United States are magnified when borders must be crossed. Some of these difficulties are financial, but these should be manageable because transplantation is much cheaper than dialysis, so transplants generate savings for national

31. Direct airline flights also facilitate sharing of deceased donor organs, see Wang et al. (2022).

32. Melcher et al. (2013) report the results of a "consensus conference" aimed at solving other coordination problems.

33. See also Agarwal et al. (2018).

34. In the United States, deceased donation is regulated by a large national bureaucracy, while living donor transplants are much less regulated. Merging these two systems so that a deceased donor kidney could start a chain of transplants that began within the kidney exchange pool and ended with a transplant to someone on the deceased donor waiting list will involve changes in regulations that have now been under consideration for several years. (Early ideas about integrating deceased donors into exchange pools can already be found in Delmonico et al. 2004 and Roth, Sönmez, and Ünver 2004).

health systems when a patient who would otherwise languish on dialysis is transplanted (Rees et al. 2017). To date, only handfuls of foreign patients have been included in American kidney exchange chains, or involved in cross-border exchange in Europe (Biró et al. 2019). This is partly because cross-border exchange, particularly when funded by savings from forgone dialysis, was initially characterized by some opponents as being similar to illegal organ trafficking (but fortunately this is changing).[35]

But there remain countries (such as Germany and Brazil) where even domestic kidney exchange faces legal bans, and other countries where it is practiced not at all (such as China), or only with difficulty (such as India). So there are big gains yet to be made domestically in these large countries as well.[36]

Small countries, however, may not be able to operate kidney exchange at efficient scale domestically, and so may especially benefit from cross-border cooperation. For example, Israel and the UAE each have populations of around ten million, which isn't big enough to reliably find matches for hard to match pairs. In 2021 I had the privilege of visiting the UAE in connection with the first kidney exchange between those two nations, which gives an indication that all sorts of obstacles—medical, logistical, social, and political—can be overcome to save lives.[37] If Israel and the UAE can do it, it may eventually even be possible for the United States and Canada. . . .

Kidney exchange thus remains a work in progress.

1.5 Conclusions

Effective market design often requires attention both to how participants interact with one another within a marketplace, and to how the marketplace interacts with a larger market and a still larger economy.

This dual mandate has contributed to a changed view of game theory. When I studied game theory in the 1970s, the received wisdom, largely following von Neumann and Morgenstern (1944), was that there were two kinds of game theory—cooperative and noncooperative—for two kinds of games. But market design has called for combining those approaches.

35. See, e.g., Minerva et al. (2019), Ambagtsheer et al. (2020) for recent assessments.

36. China and India, while they are not internationally competitive in the number of transplants per million population, nevertheless do more *total* kidney transplants than any country other than the United States. (And Brazil, where kidney exchange isn't yet legal, is fourth in the world in total kidney transplants.) So the potential for increased transplantation in these large countries is enormous. In India, there is a thriving kidney exchange program in the state of Gujarat, despite the fact that nondirected donation is not allowed (amidst many other restrictions). Novel ways to organize kidney transplants in the face of these difficulties have been pioneered there; see, e.g., Kute et al. (2021). As I write this in 2024, steps are being taken in Germany and Brazil that may allow kidney exchange there also.

37. See, e.g., "More on the UAE-Israel kidney exchange," October 4, 2021, on the *Market Design* website, https://marketdesigner.blogspot.com/2021/10/more-on-uae-israel-kidney-exchange.html, and della Cava (2021).

Dominant strategies and equilibrium (tools of noncooperative game theory) are helpful for thinking about behavior in rule-based interactions within a marketplace, within which participants' strategies can be modeled well. Outside of the marketplace, strategy sets can be large and largely unobservable, and the tools of cooperative game theory (like coalitional models, stable matchings and the core) are helpful in modeling the incentives that may exist for transacting in the larger world (Roth and Wilson 2019).[38]

And because no marketplace operates in isolation from the larger world, marketplace designs may need to adapt to changes in the larger environments.

In labor markets such as those in medicine and economics, these changes in the environment have included the growing number of two-career households, the rise in electronic applications, and lately social media and the easy availability of remote interviewing. Market designs also need to take account of societal constraints, including reservations framed in moral or ethical terms, concerning for example interviews in hotel rooms or in states with gaps in reproductive health care, or payments to kidney donors, or kidney exchange across borders between countries with different medical systems and situations.

But while practical market design presents a host of challenges, it also offers many rewards. Among the rewards to market designers themselves is the opportunity to become intimately familiar with markets that shape the lives and careers of their participants.

References

Abdulkadiroğlu, Atila, and Tayfun Sönmez. 1999. "House Allocation with Existing Tenants." *Journal of Economic Theory* 88(2): 233–60.

Agarwal, Nikhil. 2015. "An Empirical Model of the Medical Match." *American Economic Review* 105(7): 1939–1978.

Agarwal, Nikhil, Itai Ashlagi, Eduardo Azevedo, Clayton Featherstone, and Ömer Karaduman. 2018. "What Matters for the Productivity of Kidney Exchange?" *AEA Papers and Proceedings* 108: 334–40.

Agarwal, Nikhil, Itai Ashlagi, Eduardo Azevedo, Clayton R. Featherstone, and Ömer Karaduman. 2019. "Market Failure in Kidney Exchange." *American Economic Review* 109(11): 4026–4070.

Ambagtsheer, Frederike, Bernadette Haase-Kromwijk, Frank JMF Dor, Greg Moorlock, Franco Citterio, Thierry Berney, and Emma K. Massey. 2020. "Global Kidney Exchange: Opportunity or Exploitation? An ELPAT/ESOT Appraisal." *Transplant International* 33(9): 989–98.

38. The interaction between centralized marketplaces and the decentralized market opportunities that may precede them are worth special attention, see, e.g., Benjamin Roth and Shorrer (2021).

American Finance Association (AFA). 2022. "Guidelines for the AFA Rookie Recruiting Cycle." https://afajof.org/news/guidelines-for-the-afa-rookie-recruiting-cycle/.
Ashlagi, Itai, Mark Braverman, and Avinatan Hassidim. 2014. "Stability in Large Matching Markets with Complementarities." *Operations Research* 62(4): 713–32.
Ashlagi, Itai, Duncan S. Gilchrist, Alvin E. Roth, and Michael A. Rees. 2011a. "Nonsimultaneous Chains and Dominos in Kidney Paired Donation—Revisited." *American Journal of Transplantation* 11(5): 984–94. http://www.stanford.edu/~alroth/papers/Nonsimultaneous%20Chains%20AJT%202011.pdf.
Ashlagi, Itai, Duncan S. Gilchrist, Alvin E. Roth, and Michael A. Rees. 2011b. "NEAD Chains in Transplantation." *American Journal of Transplantation* 11: 2780–2781. http://web.stanford.edu/~iashlagi/papers/NeadChains2.pdf.
Ashlagi, Itai, Yashodhan Kanoria, and Jacob D. Leshno. 2013. "Unbalanced Random Matching Markets." *EC* 13: 27–28.
Ashlagi, Itai, Yash Kanoria, and Jacob D. Leshno. 2017. "Unbalanced Random Matching Markets: The Stark Effect of Competition." *Journal of Political Economy* 125(1): 69–98.
Ashlagi, Itai, Ephy Love, Jason I Reminick, and Alvin E. Roth. 2023. "Early vs. Single Match in the Transition to Residency: Analysis Using NRMP Data from 2014–21." *Journal of Graduate Medical Education*, April.
Ashlagi, Itai, and Alvin E. Roth. 2021. "Kidney Exchange: An Operations Perspective." *Management Science* 67(9): 5455–5478. https://pubsonline.informs.org/doi/abs/10.1287/mnsc.2020.3954.
Biró, P., B. Haase-Kromwijk, T. Andersson, E. I. Ásgeirsson, T. Baltesová, I. Boletis, C. Bolotinha, G. Bond, G. Böhmig, L. Burnapp, and K. Cechlárová. 2019. "Building Kidney Exchange Programmes in Europe—An Overview of Exchange Practice and Activities." *Transplantation* 103(7): 1514.
Coles, Peter, John H. Cawley, Phillip B. Levine, Muriel Niederle, Alvin E. Roth, and John J. Siegfried. 2010. "The Job Market for New Economists: A Market Design Perspective." *Journal of Economic Perspectives* 24(4): 187–206. https://www.aeaweb.org/articles?id=10.1257/jep.24.4.187.
Columb, Seán. 2020. *Trading life: Organ Trafficking, Illicit Networks, and Exploitation.* Stanford University Press.
Council of Graduate Schools (CGS). 2019. "April 15 Resolution." https://cgsnet.org/resources/for-current-prospective-graduate-students/april-15-resolution.
della Cava, Marco. 2021. "How Three Jewish and Arab families Swapped Kidneys, Saved Their Mothers and Made History." *USA Today*, October 8.
Delmonico, Francis L., Paul E. Morrissey, George S. Lipkowitz, Jeffrey S. Stoff, Jonathan Himmelfarb, William Harmon, Martha Pavlakis, et al. 2004. "Donor Kidney Exchanges." *American Journal of Transplantation* 4(10): 1628–1634.
Elias, Julio J., Nicola Lacetera, and Mario Macis. 2019. "Paying for Kidneys? A Randomized Survey and Choice Experiment." *American Economic Review* 109(8): 2855–2888.
Elias, Julio J., Nicola Lacetera, Mario Macis, Axel Ockenfels, and Alvin E. Roth. 2024. "Quality and Safety for Substances of Human Origins: Scientific Evidence and the New EU Regulations." *BMJ Global Health* 9(4). April 21.
Furian, Lucrezia, Antonio Nicolò, Caterina Di Bella, Massimo Cardillo, Emanuele Cozzi, and Paolo Rigotti. 2020. "Kidney Exchange Strategies: New Aspects and Applications with a Focus on Deceased Donor-Initiated Chains." *Transplant International* 33(10): 1177–184.
Gale, David, and Lloyd S. Shapley. 1962. "College Admissions and the Stability of Marriage." *The American Mathematical Monthly* 69(1): 9–15.
Harner, Christopher D., Anil S. Ranawat, Muriel Niederle, Alvin E. Roth, Peter J.

Stern, Shepard R. Hurwitz, William Levine, G. Paul DeRosa, and Serena S. Hu. 2008. "Current State of Fellowship Hiring: Is a Universal Match Necessary? Is It Possible?" *Journal of Bone and Joint Surgery* 90: 1375–1384.

Immorlica, Nicole, and Mohammad Mahdian. 2005. *Proceedings of the 16th Annual ACM-SIAM Symposium on Discrete Algorithms (SODA)*, 53–62.

Kojima, Fuhito, and Parag A. Pathak. 2009. "Incentives and Stability in Large Two-Sided Matching Markets." *American Economic Review* 99(3): 608–27.

Kojima, Fuhito, Parag A. Pathak, and Alvin E. Roth. 2013. "Matching with Couples: Stability and Incentives in Large Markets." *Quarterly Journal of Economics* 128(4): 1585–1632.

Kute, Vivek B., Himanshu V. Patel, Pranjal R. Modi, Sayyad J. Rizvi, Pankaj R. Shah, Divyesh P. Engineer, Subho Banerjee, Hari Shankar Meshram, Bina P. Butala, Manisha P. Modi, Shruti Gandhi, Ansy H. Patel, Vineet V. Mishra, Alvin E. Roth, Jonathan E. Kopke, and Michael A. Rees. 2021. "Non-Simultaneous Kidney Exchange Cycles in Resource-Restricted Countries without Non-directed Donation." *Transplant International* 34(4): 669–80.

Leider, Stephen, and Alvin E. Roth. 2010. "Kidneys for Sale: Who Disapproves, and Why?" *American Journal of Transplantation* 10: 1221–1227.

Melcher, M. L., C. D. Blosser, L. A. Baxter-Lowe, F. L. Delmonico, S. E. Gentry, R. Leishman, . . . and S. Feng. 2013. "Dynamic Challenges Inhibiting Optimal Adoption of Kidney Paired Donation: Findings of a Consensus Conference." *American Journal of Transplantation* 13(4): 851–60.

Melcher, Marc L., John P. Roberts, Alan B. Leichtman, Alvin E. Roth, and Michael A. Rees. 2016. "Utilization of Deceased Donor Kidneys to Initiate Living Donor Chains." *American Journal of Transplantation* 16(5): 1367–1370.

Minerva, F., J. Savulescu, and P. Singer. 2019. "The Ethics of the Global Kidney Exchange Programme." *Lancet* 394: 1775–8.

Morrill, Thayer, and Alvin E. Roth. 2024. "Top Trading Cycles." *Journal of Mathematical Economics* 112.

National Organ Transplant Act, STAT. 2339 Public Law 98–507 98th Congress. https://www.govinfo.gov/content/pkg/STATUTE-98/pdf/STATUTE-98-Pg2339.pdf.

National Resident Matching Program (NRMP). 2023. Results and Data 2023 Main Residency Match®. https://www.nrmp.org/wp-content/uploads/2023/05/2023-Main-Match-Results-and-Data-Book-FINAL.pdf.

Niederle, Muriel. 2007. "Competitive Wages in a Match with Ordered Contracts." *American Economic Review* 97(5): 1957–1969.

Niederle, Muriel, Deborah D. Proctor, and Alvin E. Roth. 2006. "What Will Be Needed for the New GI Fellowship Match to Succeed?" *Gastroenterology* 130: 218–24.

Niederle, Muriel, and Alvin E. Roth. 2009. "Market Culture: How Rules Governing Exploding Offers Affect Market Performance." *American Economic Journal: Microeconomics* 1(2): 199–219.

Public Law 110 - 144 - Charlie W. Norwood Living Organ Donation Act, 2007. https://www.govinfo.gov/app/details/PLAW-110publ144.

Qiu, Jingyi, Yan Chen, Alain Cohn, and Alvin E. Roth. "Social Media and Job Market Success: A Field Experiment on Twitter." May 20, 2024. Available at SSRN: https://ssrn.com/abstract=4778120 or http://dx.doi.org/10.2139/ssrn.4778120.

Rapaport, Felix T. 1986. "The Case for a Living Emotionally Related International Kidney Donor Exchange Registry." *Transplantation Proceedings* 18(3) Suppl. 2: 5–9.

Rees, Michael A., Jonathan E. Kopke, Ronald P. Pelletier, Dorry L. Segev, Matthew E. Rutter, Alfredo J. Fabrega, Jeffrey Rogers, Oleh G. Pankewycz, Janet Hiller, Alvin E. Roth, Tuomas Sandholm, Utku Ünver, and Robert A. Montgomery. 2009. "A Non-Simultaneous Extended Altruistic Donor Chain." *New England Journal of Medicine* 360(11): 1096–1101. https://www.nejm.org/doi/full/10.1056/NEJMoa0803645.

Rees, Michael A., Mark A. Schnitzler, E. Y. Zavala, James A. Cutler, Alvin E. Roth, Frank D. Irwin, Stephen W. Crawford, and Alan B. Leichtman. 2012. "Call to Develop a Standard Acquisition Charge Model for Kidney Paired Donation." *American Journal of Transplantation* 12(6): 1392–97.

Rees, Michael A., Ty B. Dunn, Christian S. Kuhr, Christopher L. Marsh, Jeffrey Rogers, Susan E. Rees, Alejandra Cicero, Laurie J. Reece, Alvin E. Roth, Obi Ekwenna, David E. Fumo, Kimberly D. Krawiec, Jonathan E. Kopke, Samay Jain, Miguel Tan, and Siegfredo R. Paloyo. 2017. "Kidney Exchange to Overcome Financial Barriers to Kidney Transplantation." *American Journal of Transplantation* 17(3): 782–90.

Roth, Alvin E. 1982. "Incentive Compatibility in a Market with Indivisible Goods." *Economics Letters* 9(2): 127–32.

Roth, Alvin E. 1984. "The Evolution of the Labor Market for Medical Interns and Residents: A Case Study in Game Theory." *Journal of Political Economy* 92: 991–1016. http://web.stanford.edu/~alroth/papers/evolut.pdf.

Roth, Alvin E. 1986. "On the Allocation of Residents to Rural Hospitals: A General Property of Two-Sided Matching Markets." *Econometrica* 54: 425–27.

Roth, Alvin E. 1990. "New Physicians: A Natural Experiment in Market Organization." *Science* 250: 1524–28.

Roth, Alvin E. 1991. "A Natural Experiment in the Organization of Entry Level Labor Markets: Regional Markets for New Physicians and Surgeons in the United Kingdom." *American Economic Review* 81: 415–40.

Roth, Alvin E. 2003. "The Origins, History, and Design of the Resident Match." *JAMA. Journal of the American Medical Association* 289(7): 909–12.

Roth, Alvin E. 2007. "Repugnance as a Constraint on Markets." *Journal of Economic Perspectives* 21(3): 37–58. https://www.aeaweb.org/articles?id=10.1257/jep.21.3.37.

Roth, Alvin E. 2008. "What Have We Learned from Market Design?" *Economic Journal* 118: 285–310. https://academic.oup.com/ej/article/118/527/285/5089495.

Roth, Alvin E., Ignazio R. Marino, Kimberly D. Krawiec, and Michael A. Rees. 2022. "Criminal, Legal, and Ethical Kidney Donation and Transplantation: A Conceptual Framework to Enable Innovation." *Transplant International* 35. doi: 10.3389/ti.2022.10551. https://www.frontierspartnerships.org/articles/10.3389/ti.2022.10551/full.

Roth, Alvin E., and Elliott Peranson. 1999. "The Redesign of the Matching Market for American Physicians: Some Engineering Aspects of Economic Design." *American Economic Review* 89(4): 748–80. https://www.aeaweb.org/articles?id=10.1257/aer.89.4.748.

Roth, Alvin E., and Andrew Postlewaite. 1977. "Weak versus Strong Domination in a Market with Indivisible Goods." *Journal of Mathematical Economics* 4(2): 131–37.

Roth, Alvin E., Tayfun Sönmez, and M. Utku Ünver. 2003. "Kidney Exchange." NBER Working Paper No. 10002. Cambridge, MA: National Bureau of Economic Research.

Roth, Alvin E., Tayfun Sönmez, and M. Utku Ünver. 2004. "Kidney Exchange." *Quarterly Journal of Economics* 119(2): 457–88. https://academic.oup.com/qje/article-abstract/119/2/457/1894508.

Roth, Alvin E., Tayfun Sönmez, and M. Utku Ünver. 2005a. "A Kidney Exchange

Clearinghouse in New England." *American Economic Review: Papers and Proceedings* 95(2): 376–80.

Roth, Alvin E., Tayfun Sönmez, and M. Utku Ünver. 2005b. "Pairwise Kidney Exchange." *Journal of Economic Theory* 125(2): 151–88.

Roth, Alvin E., Tayfun Sönmez, M. Utku Ünver, Francis L. Delmonico, and Susan L. Saidman. 2006. "Utilizing List Exchange and Undirected Good Samaritan Donation through 'Chain' Paired Kidney Donations." *American Journal of Transplantation* 6(11): 2694–2705.

Roth, Alvin E., and John H. Vande Vate. 1990. "Random Paths to Stability in Two-Sided Matching." *Econometrica* 58: 1475–80.

Roth, Alvin E., and Stephanie W. Wang. 2020. "Popular Repugnance Contrasts with Legal Bans on Controversial Markets." *Proceedings of the National Academy of Sciences (PNAS)* 117(33): 19792–98.

Roth, Alvin E., and Robert B. Wilson. 2019. "How Market Design Emerged from Game Theory: A Mutual Interview." *Journal of Economic Perspectives* 33(3): 118–43. https://www.aeaweb.org/articles?id=10.1257/jep.33.3.118.

Roth, Benjamin N., and Ran I. Shorrer. 2021. "Making Marketplaces Safe: Dominant Individual Rationality and Applications to Market Design." *Management Science* 67(6): 3694–13.

Rousseau, Peter. 2023. "AEA Guidance on the 2023–24 Economics Job Market Cycle." Member announcement, American Economic Association, July 27. https://www.aeaweb.org/news/member-announcements-2023-july-27.

Saidman, Susan L., Alvin E. Roth, Tayfun Sönmez, M. Utku Ünver, and Francis L. Delmonico. 2006. "Increasing the Opportunity of Live Kidney Donation by Matching for Two and Three Way Exchanges." *Transplantation* 81(5): 773–82.

Shapley, Lloyd, and Herbert Scarf. 1974. "On Cores and Indivisibility." *Journal of Mathematical Economics* 1(1): 23–37.

Ünver, M. Utku. 2001. "Backward Unraveling Over Time: The Evolution of Strategic Behavior in the Entry Level British Medical Labor Markets." *Journal of Economic Dynamics and Control* 25(6–7): 1039–80.

Ünver, M. Utku. 2005. "On the Survival of Some Unstable Two-Sided Matching Mechanisms." *International Journal of Game Theory* 33: 239–54.

US Renal Data Service (USRDS). 2023. 2023 Annual Data Report, Figure 1.5. https://usrds-adr.niddk.nih.gov/2023/end-stage-renal-disease/1-incidence-prevalence-patient-characteristics-and-treatment-modalities.

von Neumann, John, and Oskar Morgenstern. 1944. *Theory of Games and Economic Behavior.* Princeton University Press.

Wallis, C. Bradley, Kannan P. Samy, Alvin E. Roth, and Michael A. Rees. 2011. "Kidney Paired Donation." *Nephrology Dialysis Transplantation* 26(7): 2091–99. https://academic.oup.com/ndt/article/26/7/2091/1896342/Kidney-paired-donation.

Wang, Guihua, Ronghuo Zheng, and Tinglong Dai. 2022. "Does Transportation Mean Transplantation? Impact of New Airline Routes on Sharing of Cadaveric Kidneys." *Management Science* 68(5): 3660–79.

Zarsadias, Prizzi. 2010. "Anthony P. Monaco and Paul E. Morrissey: A Pioneering Paired Kidney Exchange." *BMJ* 340.

2 Market Design for the Environment

Estelle Cantillon and Aurélie Slechten

2.1 Introduction

Nature provides a number of essential goods and services that support our lives and economies (Costanza et al. 1997). These include seafood and timber, life-supporting processes (such as water purification and photosynthesis), regulation of ecosystems (for example, through carbon storage and erosion control), and cultural and recreational services. These goods and services are all subject to externalities, leading to overexploitation, degradation, and underprovision. Climate change, biodiversity collapse, eutrophication of oceans and lakes, soil and groundwater pollution are some of the symptoms of our collective inability to manage natural capital sustainably.

Property rights organize our relationship with nature and determine the types of governance that can be established to conserve and manage this natural capital. When it comes to natural resources and ecosystems, Schlager and Ostrom (1992) distinguish between, on the one hand, the right to access and to use (e.g., obtain the product of a natural resource or release toxic effluents) and, on the other hand, management and control rights (deciding who has access, how usage rights are transferred . . .). Clearly, these rights

Estelle Cantillon is a Fonds de la Recherche Scientifique (FNRS) Research Director and a professor of economics at the Université Libre de Bruxelles, and a research fellow at the Centre for Economic Policy Research.

Aurélie Slechten is a senior lecturer at Lancaster University Management School.

We are grateful to Parag Pathak, Simon Quemin, Leo Stimpfle and participants at the NBER Advances in Market Design conference and the CEPR Paris Symposium for comments and suggestions. Financial support from FNRS (CDR grant J.0029.22) and the British Academy (MCFSS22\220044 grant) is gratefully acknowledged. For acknowledgments, sources of research support, and disclosure of the authors' material financial relationships, if any, please see https://www.nber.org/books-and-chapters/new-directions-market-design/market-design-environment.

affect the incentives that individuals face to conserve and develop the natural capital to which these rights apply. Sterner and Coria (2013) describe how these rights differ across countries and contexts and how they have evolved over time as a result of societal demands. To the extent that these property rights can be traded, we have a market.

Environmental markets are not new. In fact, communities and governments have used markets to allocate fishing rights, water withdrawal rights, and pollution rights for decades. But improvements in monitoring technology and increasing pressures to address environmental degradation and resource scarcity have expanded their scope of application over time.

This chapter reviews existing and developing uses of markets for natural capital from a market design perspective. We first provide a typology of environmental problems for which markets can provide a solution. This leads us to distinguish between overexploitation, degradation, and underprovision problems. Overexploitation and degradation problems happen when the goods and services provided by nature are not excludable and property rights are shared or nonexistent. Underprovision problems arise when the natural resource, over which well-established access and usage rights exist, creates positive externalities for agents who do not benefit from any property rights to the resource. We argue that each natural resource is characterized by its specific biophysical process which constrains the definition of what can be traded and the choice of design to support the goals of the market.

We illustrate these considerations in the context of climate change mitigation, where compliance markets for emissions reduction and voluntary carbon markets are playing an increasingly important role. The history of the EU emissions trading scheme over the past 20 years illustrates how apparently small design decisions can impact the performance of a market and the challenges of generating an informative and stable price signal, an important desideratum to foster cost efficiency. The current discussions around the integrity of voluntary carbon markets show the importance of the definition of what is traded, and how technology and nature constrain it.

An important remark at the outset is that markets may not be the only way, let alone the best way, to address environmental overexploitation, degradation, and underprovision. Ostrom (1990) has powerfully argued that communities can successfully overcome the so-called tragedy of the commons, where natural resources are overexploited, without the recourse to markets or even price mechanisms. Others have raised the concern that markets, and the price tag that they bring to the goods and services produced by nature, are incapable of capturing the complexity of human societies' interactions with nature (Kosoy and Corbera 2010) and can even change the way individuals and firms view and interact with it (Bowles 2016; Sandel 2012).

In this chapter, we leave these discussions aside and take as starting point the observation that the reach of markets for environmental goods and services is expanding on the ground and that there is, therefore, need for scholarship and expertise to design these markets so that they meet their goals.

2.2 Typology of Environmental Problems

It is useful to distinguish three types of environmental problems for which markets can and often already do provide solutions. These problems are defined by the nature of the environmental good or service at hand and existing property rights arrangements.

2.2.1 Overexploitation of Renewable Resources

The first category of environmental problems consists of environmental goods and services that are not excludable, or at least difficult to exclude, but rival in use, and for which property rights are shared or nonexistent. This is the classic case of what has been called common pool resources.

Fish stocks in oceans or lakes, game in forests, and water in rivers are all examples of common pool resources. These resources are additionally renewable. Fish, game, and other animal species reproduce. Their natural reproduction rate depends on environmental conditions and is often modeled as a bell-shaped relationship between species density and population growth rate. At low levels of species density, mating probabilities are low, and so are reproduction rates. Likewise, at high species density levels, the ecosystem's carrying capacity is stretched, and competition for food limits population growth. Maximum sustainable yields are obtained at intermediate density levels when fish or game harvest is equal to the natural growth rate of the population. Harvest in excess of the natural reproduction rate drives species density down. Water withdrawal (from a river or basin) is similar, except that water stock dynamics are determined by hydrological and weather conditions, and users upstream impact users downstream but not those upstream to them.

The prime concern for sustainability in these situations is to ensure that harvest levels and withdrawals (a flow) are set such that the stock of the underlying resource is stable at a desirable level. The challenge is that this condition is unlikely to be met in the presence of multiple users and shared or nonexistent property rights. Each user individually does not account for the externality they exert on other users, potentially leading to the collapse of the natural resource in what has been coined the "tragedy of the commons" by Hardin (1968).

Quotas have long been used around the world to address the risk of overexploitation of renewable natural resources (Costello et al. 2008). Fishermen, hunters, and farmers receive quotas that determine how much they can fish, hunt, or withdraw water. These quotas specify the quantity of the renewable resource holders can harvest or withdraw over a specific period in a particular area. They are coupled with monitoring and enforcement systems. Once a holder has reached their quota, they must cease all harvest and withdrawal activities. The number of quotas can be adjusted over time based on the stock of the natural resource. Effectively, quotas create property rights on the use of the natural resource and address the sustainability issue (making sure catch levels and withdrawals are not too high).

Not all quota systems integrate a market mechanism in their design, either for the initial allocation of these quotas or for participants to exchange quotas among themselves. For example, since 1983, the European Union has allocated fishing quotas to its Member States but leaves it to them to decide how they allocate these to their fishermen. In some countries, quotas are not transferable (van Hoof 2013).

The main motivation for using markets and market-based mechanisms in these contexts is to enhance the efficiency of the allocation and encourage the sustainable use of scarce natural resources (productive efficiency). Given the increasing pressures on natural resources, we can expect that these efficiency concerns will drive further adoption of markets.[1]

Markets can be useful at three levels. One approach is to allow quota holders to trade them. These are often referred to as Individual Transferable Quotas (ITQs). Users with the highest value for the natural resource will buy quotas from those with a lower value, enhancing efficiency. Another approach, feasible when no preexisting property rights exist, is to auction these quotas. Again, this will ensure that the quotas end up in the hands of those who value them the most. The price tag will also incentivize users to save the natural resource. Finally, markets can also be used to induce preexisting property rights holders to relinquish their rights to promote superior allocations (see Ferguson and Milgrom 2026).

Depending on preexisting rights, these markets can be organized by a regulatory authority (public governance) or by the users themselves (private governance). Private governance is more common when the natural resource is geographically circumvented, and users are well identified and not too numerous. For example, private governance by local fishermen is observed for lobsters, a sedentary species, off the coast of Maine.

2.2.2 Pollution and Environmental Degradation

Environmental degradation problems are mirror problems to overexploitation problems. Environmental quality is a (local) public good, and ownership of the environmental resource is either shared or nonexistent. Because pollution is typically a by-product of an otherwise profitable activ-

1. See Wheeler et al. (2023) for a similar point in the context of water markets. For good starting points to this literature, see Tietenberg (2002), Newell et al. (2005) for fish markets, and Wheeler (2021) for water markets.

ity, economic agents will tend to generate too much pollution because they do not bear the full consequences.

Governments use different approaches to regulate pollution, starting from command-and-control approaches, such as imposing a technology standard or forbidding the use of some toxic substances as inputs, to more market-based solutions. Among these, cap-and-trade markets have gained prominence as a cost-effective approach to pollution. This has especially been the case in contexts where polluters are numerous and heterogeneous, the source of pollution is well defined, measurement and monitoring of pollution is relatively easy, and the pollution's geographical impact is sufficiently large that concerns for pollution hot spots, whereby trading results in pollution being geographically concentrated, are low.

The idea originates with Dales (1968), who imagined a cap-and-trade market for water discharge rights as a cost-effective solution to regulating water quality in lakes. In his solution, public authorities would partition space into regions and cap the yearly volume of waste discharge in each area. They would issue a commensurate amount of "pollution permits" and impose the obligation on polluters to surrender as many permits as their volume of pollution over the year. Permits could be bought and sold. Montgomery (1972) provided a formal proof of Dales's conjecture in a static competitive equilibrium framework, essentially proving cost efficiency as a corollary of the First Welfare Theorem. In the competitive equilibrium, marginal costs of abatement are equalized across firms. Firms with high abatement costs abate less and buy surplus allowances from firms with low abatement costs.

Early applications of cap-and-trade markets for pollution took place in the 1980s in the United States, but the first grand-scale experiment was the nationwide 1990 Clean Air Act that imposed a cap on sulfur dioxide emissions from electricity production. The market launch was preceded by extensive testing and fine-tuning of different aspects of the design (see Joskow et al. 1998 and Ellerman et al. 2000 for accounts of the design phase and early performance).

The Clean Air Act provided a template for the introduction of emissions trading as part of the Kyoto Protocol, which, in turn, paved the way for the introduction of the EU carbon emissions trading scheme in Europe in 2005. Carbon emissions are particularly well suited for a market approach because sources of carbon emissions are heterogeneous and face different abatement costs, and carbon's impact on climate is the same independently of where it was emitted. Hence, the cost-efficiency gains from trading are likely to be large and concerns for pollution hot spots limited.

Today, "pollution markets" are used for pollutants as diverse as CO_2 (a global, long-lived point-source pollutant mostly connected to the combustion of fossil fuels); other greenhouse gases (all global and point-source pollutants but with different lifetimes in the atmosphere); sulfur dioxide (a regional, short-lived point-source pollutant, produced by the combustion of coal); nitrogen oxides (a local, short-lived point-source pollutant that is a precursor to ground-level ozone); nitrogen and phosphorous effluents from farms (a local, non-point source pollutant responsible for eutrophication and groundwater pollution); waste water discharges (a local, point-source pollutant). In each case, careful consideration must be given, when designing the property rights and the market, to the underlying biophysical process, the geographical reach of the pollutant, and how to measure it.[2]

Market mechanisms for pollution reduction are not limited to trading of allowances between polluters. Auctions can be used to set the initial allocation of allowances. Auctions are also used to decide which polluting firms should exit the market and the compensation they are eligible for to exit.[3]

2.2.3 Underprovision of Natural Capital

Unlike the other two environmental problems reviewed so far, ownership rights on the natural resource are well established for the third category of environmental problems. Think about a forest, a lake, or a nature reserve under private ownership. The issue now is that the benefits that this natural resource generates are not entirely captured by its owner. As a result, the owner may not invest in or conserve its natural resource at a sufficiently high level. The challenge, therefore, is to find a way to provide this incentive.

Payment for ecosystem services (PES) is defined as a voluntary transaction where a well-defined environmental service (or a land use likely to secure that service) is bought by one or several buyers from one or several providers on the condition that they secure this service provision (Wunder 2005; Engel et al. 2008). Put simply, the idea is that the beneficiaries of the environmental service pay the owner of the natural resource for the difference in value and costs borne by this owner from adapting their practice or use, to conserve or develop the natural resource.

The origins of payments for ecosystem services can be traced back to the 1930s when the US government paid farmers for soil conservation (Claassen et al. 2008). The practice further developed as intensive agricultural practices increasingly competed with other uses of natural resources. Perrot-Maître (2006), Depres et al. (2008), and Defrance (2015) provide detailed descriptions of the contractual arrangements between, respectively, Vittel and Evian, and the local farmers whose lands run off into the aquifers used to

2. The original article of Dales provides an early illustration of the kind of design questions wannabe market designers need to ask themselves. See also Kerr et al. (2007), Cox et al. (2013), and McDonald and Kerr (2011) for a discussion of design considerations in the context of nutrients trading; Fisher-Vanden and Olmstead (2013) in the context of water quality trading; Teytelboym (2019) for settings with complementarities; and Tietenberg (2010) for a general introduction to markets for pollution.

3. See, for example, the coal exit auctions used in Germany to select which coal power plants to close as part of the country's coal phase-out plan (Srivastav and Zaehringer 2024).

Table 2.1 The use of markets for solving environmental problems

	Overexploitation	Degradation	Underprovision
Typical legacy ownership	Shared or nonexistent property rights	Shared or nonexistent property rights	Private property rights
Policy objective	Ensure sustainable exploitation	Limit pollution	Encourage provision
Role for markets	Efficiency	Cost-effectiveness	Efficiency
Market governance	Public or private	Public	Public or private
Applications	Fishing quotas, water rights, hunting permits	Pollutants at different scales (SO_2, CO_2, NOx, pollution discharge)	Carbon sequestration, biodiversity, other ecosystemic services

extract these mineral waters. One lesson from these cases is that the financial component of the arrangement is only a small part of the overall negotiation and that these PESs can be quite complex and long to negotiate. This effectively rules them out when beneficiaries are numerous and diverse, as in the case of a global public good like climate change mitigation.

An important step forward in terms of scaling up market mechanisms for conservation was the introduction of project-based credits in the Kyoto Protocol, whereby investors in signatory countries could claim carbon credits, eligible for compliance, from emission reduction or removal projects in third countries.[4]

The creation of carbon credits was a major breakthrough because it transformed a non-excludable environmental benefit (climate mitigation) into a private good, used for compliance. While Clean Development Mechanisms and Joint Implementation projects have had their teething problems (see Schneider 2009)—essentially around additionality, measurement, and verification—the logic underlying their creation has remained. In 2008, the United Nations launched the Reducing Emissions from Deforestation and Forest Degradation (REDD) program to support conservation projects in the Global South and help channel funding to them through the issuance of credits. Since then, increasing demand for carbon credits from the private sector to support their climate commitments has spurred the development of a sizable voluntary carbon market, a subject to which we return in section 2.4.

4. Specifically, Clean Development Mechanisms (CDM) covered carbon reduction or removal projects in developing countries, and Joint Implementation (JI) mechanisms covered carbon reduction or removal projects in developed countries.

The potential is enormous: Griscom et al. (2017) evaluate that nature-based climate solutions could contribute 37 percent of cost-effective emissions reductions through 2030, and Grassi et al. (2017) document that land use and forests contribute a quarter of the emissions reductions planned by countries in their nationally determined contributions (NDCs) submitted in fulfillment of their obligations under the Paris Agreement. And, of course, the scope for markets to address underprovision is not limited to climate. The recent Kunming-Montreal Global Biodiversity Framework agreed in December 2022 has, for example, increased interest in biodiversity credits and markets. Table 2.1 summarizes the discussion of this section.

2.3 Compliance Carbon Markets

Today, carbon markets play a central role in countries' efforts to mitigate their greenhouse gas (GHG) emissions. According to the World Bank's Carbon Pricing Dashboard, 36 carbon markets were in operation in 2024, covering approximately 19 percent of global GHG emissions. Twenty-five emissions trading schemes were also scheduled or under consideration. In comparison, only 6 percent of global GHG emissions were covered by a carbon tax in 2024.

As argued in the previous section, the economic case in favor of carbon trading is strong. However, emissions markets' ability to lower total abatement costs hinges upon their ability to generate an accurate price signal that reflects the distribution of firms' opportunity costs and can guide companies' abatement investments. In turn, this depends on their design.

2.3.1 Market Design Parameters

There is a wide range of market design parameters that must be decided when setting up a carbon market. While cost efficiency remains the primary objective, other considerations are also relevant. In this section, we review the main design parameters for compliance carbon markets, underlining the arbitrages that they involve.

Market scope. A first important design choice is the scope of the market in terms of sectors, geography, pollutants and time. In terms of geography and sectors, theory suggests that the larger the market, the better, given the global nature of the pollutant and the heterogeneity in abatement opportunities across countries and sectors. There are nevertheless some caveats. At the sector level, the availability of a consistent, affordable, and accurate monitoring, verification, and reporting system is key to the integrity and environmental efficiency of the emissions trading scheme. The efficiency gains from expanded coverage must be balanced with the increased monitoring and verification costs across ever smaller or less precisely measured emitting sources.

Another caveat is that the unilateral introduction of an emissions trading scheme in one jurisdiction might lead regulated companies to shift their activities (and therefore their carbon emissions) to countries with less stringent environmental policies. This is the well-known pollution haven hypothesis, also referred to as *carbon leakage* in the context of climate change (see Dechezleprêtre and Sato 2017 for a review). Here as well, there is a trade-off between the gains from expanding sectoral coverage and the environmental and economic losses of including sectors with a high risk of leakage.

Expanding the geographical scope by linking carbon markets constitutes a possible solution to carbon leakage. However, when discussing the possibility of linking carbon markets, it is important to take into account the level of design alignment, including the similarities in policy objectives, between the two systems, and the increased transmission of political or economic shocks across jurisdictions in case of linking (Flachsland et al. 2009; Fankhauser and Hepburn 2010; Doda et al. 2019).[5]

While CO_2 is the most common greenhouse gas, other gases contribute to global warming (e.g., methane and nitrous oxide). Including other GHGs can bring additional cost efficiency gains but requires reliable conversion factors and a consensus on which ones to use.[6]

Finally, allowing regulated companies to trade allowances across compliance periods (i.e., to save carbon allowances for future use or to borrow allowances from future compliance periods) provides further cost efficiency gains, as it allows firms to exploit intertemporal arbitrage opportunities (Rubin 1996; Schennach 2000; Newell et al., "Managing Permit Markets," 2005). Depending on the nature of the pollutant, unrestricted banking and borrowing of allowances may not be socially desirable, however. For example, CO_2 is a stock pollutant and therefore, the time path of emissions matters. Allowing firms to delay their investments in abatement (through massive allowances borrowing) may increase total social damages.[7] Allowing for unrestricted banking and borrowing can also affect companies' trading and compliance behavior. Banking and borrowing reduce the incentives for firms to participate early in the market, slowing down the price discovery process. Borrowing, combined with the ability of the regulating authority to adjust the stringency of the climate policy in the future, might also result in the so-called *ratchet effect* and *hold-up problem* (Hepburn 2006). First, borrowing allowances from future compliance periods might result in a scarcity

5. See also Ranson and Stavins (2016) for a policy discussion.

6. To aggregate different greenhouse gases, the Paris Agreement relies on the *Global Warming Potential* (GWP) produced by the IPCC. The GWP is a conversion factor from physical units of greenhouse gases to CO_2 equivalent, accounting for how long these greenhouse gases remain in the atmosphere. The current GWP conversion factors are those calculated for 100 years (CO_2 has a normalized value of 1, and every other gas has a value that corresponds to their warming power relative to CO_2 during that time frame) (Denison et al. 2019).

7. In the scenarios assessed in the last IPCC report (2023), limiting global warming to 1.5°C requires immediate action and global GHG to peak before 2025 at the latest.

situation later on and be used to signal to the regulator that the environmental policy is too costly. This could lead to the negotiation of a more lenient target for the next compliance phase (ratchet effect). Second, the payoffs from long-term investments in clean technologies depend on the stringency of future climate policies. As regulators have the discretion to adjust (relax) the cap after the investments have been made (hold-up problem), borrowing might be used to delay these investments.

Market cap. The economically efficient market cap reflects the level of pollution that equates the marginal social and economic benefits of the polluting activity with its marginal environmental costs. In practice, uncertainty and measurement challenges on both sides of this trade-off imply that the market cap is a political decision. Still, it does make sense for the cap to adjust to economic conditions and new information. When abatement costs are lower than expected, the efficient level of the cap decreases. Likewise, if the economy is booming, it may make sense to raise the cap.

Hybrid mechanisms, which combine price- and quantity-based instruments, have been proposed to regulate pollution in the presence of uncertainty (Roberts and Spence 1976). In the context of cap-and-trade markets, hybrid mechanisms take the form of price collars (Pizer 2002; Burtraw et al. 2010). Practically, such hybrid mechanisms work as a regular cap-and-trade market so long as the allowance price is between the floor and ceiling prices. When either the floor price or the ceiling price is reached, the scheme behaves like a tax and regulators inject or remove allowances as needed to support the price.[8] Alternatively, one can condition the injection or removal of extra allowances on the quantity of allowances in circulation, rather than on the observed price (quantity collars). If placement in the reserve is temporary and allowances can be canceled, the total cap on emissions is affected (Kollenberg and Taschini 2016, 2019).

These hybrid mechanisms adjust the cap in the intended direction: they tighten the cap if abatement costs are lower than expected, as evidenced by low prices or excess allowances in circulation, and, reversely, they increase the cap if abatement costs are higher than expected.

However, these adjustments, with thresholds of intervention set ex ante, may not be efficient ex post. The literature has explored more sophisticated cap adjustment mechanisms that account for the information revealed by the operation of the market. Pizer and Prest (2020) and Burtraw et al. (2022) make the point that dynamic adjustments of the cap, based on price realizations, are welfare-improving. Karp and Traeger (2025) propose the use of

8. Regulators' intervention can be capped too. This is the case when the price collar is implemented through an allowance reserve and a pre-set maximum number of allowances that can be added to the market when the price ceiling is reached (Murray et al. 2009; Fell et al. 2012). In that case, the price can rise above the ceiling price, unless there is some rationing when the reserve is empty.

a price-responsive conversion factor between allowances to emissions to account for new information.

Allowances allocation. Regulators are faced with three alternatives to allocate allowances to regulated firms. They can allocate them for free, auction them, or sell them for a fixed fee. Auctioning allowances forces all market participants to actively participate, whereas free allocation makes it possible, when banking is allowed, for firms with surplus allowances not to interact with the market. This, in turn, can hamper price discovery. Consignment auctions, where firms receiving an initial allocation of free allowances are required to submit some of them to an auction, have the price discovery advantage of auctions while reducing the overall costs to market participants (see Burtraw and McCormack 2017 and Khezr and MacKenzie 2018). Such auctions have been used at the launch of the sulfur dioxide market in the United States, and Joskow et al. (1998) argue that they contributed to price discovery.

Free allocation of allowances, and in particular grandfathering under which allocations are based on past emissions or output, may also lead to a perverse ratchet effect where companies have an incentive to emit more in the short-term to increase their future allocation (Böhringer and Lange 2005; Harstad and Eskeland 2010).

Nevertheless, free allocation of allowances is common in the early stages of carbon markets. It alleviates concerns about international competitiveness and contributes to early acceptance by market participants. This choice is further supported by the idea that the initial allocation of allowances has no impact on the performance of the market, a property known as the independence property and initially shown by Montgomery (1972). However, the independence property relies on the absence of market frictions and fails in the presence of market power (Hahn 1984) and transaction costs (Stavins 1995). Zaklan (2023) has empirically tested the independence property in the context of the EU ETS and found it to hold for large emitters in the power sector, but not for small ones.

Compliance. Existing compliance markets have adopted different rules regarding compliance. Some, like the EU ETS, have annual compliance cycles, but others have longer cycles. Holland and Moore (2013) show that compliance timing does not impact expected compliance costs as long as there is intertemporal price arbitrage for allowances. This is the case if market participants are not subject to borrowing constraints, for example, and if there is no price cap. If not, compliance timing matters and impacts abatement costs.

The nature and level of the non-compliance penalty can also have very different implications. If the payment of the penalty is an alternative to surrendering missing allowances, this penalty effectively acts as a price ceiling.

This is not the case if non-compliant firms have to pay the penalty but are still obliged to surrender the allowances corresponding to their past emissions (see Stranlund 2017 for a review of the literature on enforcement in emissions markets).

Market organization and legal status of allowances. As illustrated in table 2.2, market organization and the legal status of emissions allowances vary considerably across jurisdictions. Allowances can be considered as a physical asset, as an administrative authorization to emit CO_2, or as a financial instrument. This has important consequences. Commodities and financial assets are treated differently from an accounting and tax perspective. In Europe, for example, commodities are subject to a value-added tax (VAT), but financial assets are not. Markets for commodities and for financial assets are also regulated differently.

The way the market is organized (i.e., who is allowed to trade, where, and what type of assets) also affects its ability to aggregate information about the distribution of abatement opportunities and generate a stable price signal. There is a long and rich literature in finance on the impact of market design on information aggregation and the price discovery process (see O'Hara 1998 for a review).

2.3.2 A Market Design Perspective on the History of the EU ETS

We illustrate these design considerations in the context of the EU ETS, the oldest and, to this day, largest carbon market in value in the world. The market was launched in 2005 as a trial phase before the 2008–12 Kyoto compliance period. The market covered the carbon emissions from around 11,000 installations from the power and energy-intensive industrial sectors, representing about 45 percent of the greenhouse gas emissions of the European Union.[9] Since then, the market has continued to be organized in phases, each with clear rules (sectors covered, initial allocations, total cap, etc.) announced a few years before (see table 2.3 for an overview). The market is currently in its fourth phase (2021–2030).

The history of the EU ETS is a vivid illustration of the importance of design and the continuous need to adjust it as circumstances change (on this, see Roth 2026). This was not anticipated by the early architects of the EU ETS who envisaged a limited role for market design:

> The legal framework of the ETS does not lay down how and where trading in allowances should take place. Companies and other participants in the market may trade directly with each other or buy and sell via a broker, exchange or any other type of market intermediary that may spring up to take advantage of a new market of significant size. The price of allow-

9. For an early account of the EU ETS, see Ellerman et al. (2010).

Table 2.2 **Carbon market design choices around the world**

	EU ETS (2005)	California ETS (2012)	Korea ETS (2015)	China ETS (2021)
Market Scope				
Sectoral Coverage	Domestic Aviation, Industry, Power	Industry, Power, Transport, Buildings	Domestic Aviation, Industry, Power, Waste, Transport, Buildings	Power
Number of entities	9,000+ entities	400+ entities	680+ entities	2,100+ entities
Pollutants covered	CO_2, N_2O, PFCs	CO_2, CH4, N_2O, SF6,	CO_2, CH_4, N_2O, PFCs, HFCs, SF6, HFCs, PFCs, NF3, and other fluorinated GHGs	CO_2
% of GHG covered	38% of GHG	75% of GHG	74% of GHG	44% of GHG
Allowances Allocation	Daily auctions	Quarterly auctions	Free allocations + some auctions	Free allocations
Status of allowances	Financial instrument	Limited tradable authorizations	Not defined	Physical asset
Market organization				
Secondary market	OTC + EEX, ICE, and Nasdaq	OTC + ICE + CME	OTC + KRX	Shanghai EEE
Derivatives market	EEX, ICE, and Nasdaq	ICE and CME	—	—
Who can trade?	Compliance traders + others (investors, brokers, other service providers)	Compliance traders, holders of offsets, firms offering clearing services	Compliance traders, authorized market makers, brokers (position limit)	Compliance traders
Average Price	83.10 USD/tCO2e	28.08 USD/tCO2e	17.99 USD/tCO2e	8.20 USD/tCO2e

Note: This table was created based on information from the International Carbon Action Partnership (2023). The average price for the EU ETS, California ETS, and Korea ETS are the average auction prices in 2022. The average price for the China ETS is the average secondary market price in 2022.

Table 2.3 **A brief History of the EU ETS**

	Phase I (2005–07)	Phase II (2008–12)	Phase III (2013–20)	Phase IV (2021–30)
SCOPE	EU, 5 industrial sectors	Norway, Iceland and Liechtenstein	Integration of aviation, and new gases added (N_2O and PFCs)	Phase-in of maritime transport (2024), separate ETS for buildings & road transport (2027)
FUNGIBILITY	Bankability and limited borrowability within phase	Allowances can be banked for the future		
LINKAGES		International credits from CDM and JI	International credits phased out (no new project), Linkage to Swiss ETS (2020)	
MARKET CAP	EC guidelines, national choice		Top-down cap setting Backloading of allowances Market stability reserve (2019)	Accelerated decrease in cap
ALLOCATION	Grandfathering		Auctions as default allocation Free allocation for some sectors based on benchmarking	Phase-out of free allowances (phase-in of CBAM starting in 2026)
INFRASTRUCTURE	National Registries		Single EU Registry	
OTHER EVENTS		Hacking events, VAT fraud, Economic crisis creates a market glut	Market regulated under MiFID	Fit-for-55 reforms (2023)

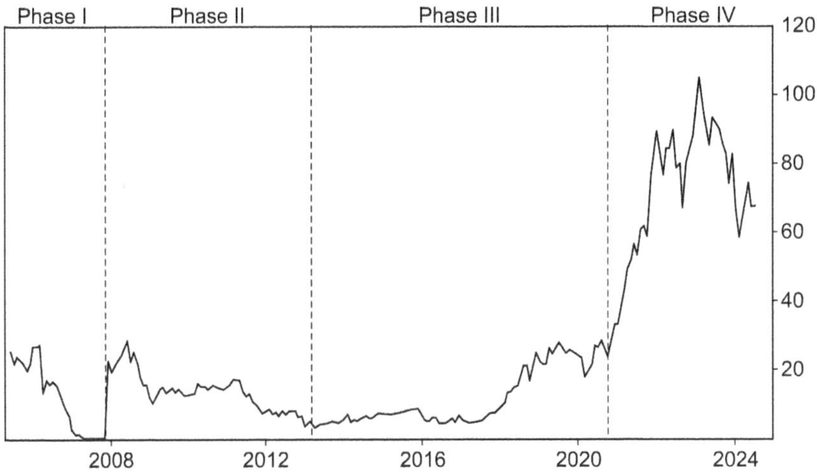

Fig. 2.1 Evolution of the EUA spot price (April 2005–July 2024)
Source: Trading Economics website, https://tradingeconomics.com/.

ances will be determined by supply and demand as in any other market. (European Commission 2005)

As a result, and unlike the US sulfur dioxide market, the EU ETS benefited from very little support, beyond the creation of allowances and the registries to record ownership and transfers of allowances. This hands-off approach changed over time as new problems arose and changes in rules were required. Today, thorough discussions take place several years before the beginning of a phase to evaluate the performance of the market and potential reforms.

As a background to the discussion in this section, figure 2.1 plots the observed allowance prices between April 2005 and July 2024. These prices have been extensively commented upon in the specialized press and the academic literature.[10] During the first phase, the price increased from around 10 euros in March 2005 to nearly 30 euros in April 2006. The price then dropped to around 10 euros within three days, upon the release of verified emissions in several countries that showed them to be significantly below allocations. The allowance price then slowly converged to zero as it became increasingly clear that there were excess allowances in the market, which could not be banked for the second phase. The allowance price shortly rose again afterwards but remained relatively low until 2018. Since 2018, the price has been steadily increasing. It exceeded 100 euros per ton in February 2023 and was around 70 euros per ton by mid-2024.

10. See, e.g., Ellerman et al. 2010; Quemin and Trotignon 2021; Carbon Pulse website, https://carbon-pulse.com/, for industry coverage.

Market scope. Experience, improved data, and advances in monitoring have enabled the gradual extension of the EU ETS to more countries, more greenhouse gases, and more sectors.[11] In the second phase of the EU ETS, credits generated by Clean Development Mechanisms and Joint Implementation projects under the Kyoto Protocol could be used for compliance, with restrictions on the quantity. These credits were phased out in phase III following concerns about their reliability (Schneider 2009).

In 2023, as part of the Fit-for-55 package, the EU decided to create a new ETS to cover emissions from fuel combustion in buildings and road transport (ETS2). The new market will come into force in 2027.[12] Instead of simply expanding the scope of the existing ETS, the EU opted for a separate market to balance the efficiency gains from carbon trading with distributional and political considerations. Indeed, abatement costs in the buildings and road transport sectors are expected to be higher than those in the sectors covered by the current ETS. Integrating both markets, therefore, would result in higher prices and lower (proportionally) emissions reductions in these new sectors. This would delay the long-term investments needed in these sectors to reach the EU climate ambitions and run the risk of exacerbating carbon leakage in the existing ETS sectors. The two markets approach that the EU has adopted has the additional benefit of providing time for all stakeholders to ramp up their market readiness and avoid disruptions for the existing ETS (see European Commission 2021, and Edenhofer et al. 2021, for a discussion of this and other considerations).

Market cap. An evolution of the EU ETS that has been driven by lessons learned from past performance is the approach to cap setting. Initially, the allocation of allowances was decided at the national level, under guidelines from the European Commission. This decentralized process determined the EU-wide cap, as the sum of the national caps. It contributed, at least partially, to the over-allocation of allowances: each Member State in isolation was tempted to be more lenient with its domestic firms. Since phase III, the cap is set at the European level. An annual linear reduction rate applies (initially set up at 1.74 percent of 2008–2012 baseline emissions). Allowances are no longer allocated on a national basis but, instead, through auctions or to individual installations.

11. During the discussions over the ETS market reform for phase III, the availability of accurate monitoring and reporting system was explicitly mentioned as one of the reasons why shipping could be included in the EU ETS, while other sectors (such as agriculture) were not considered. CO_2 emissions from aviation have been included in the EU ETS since 2012, but international aviation was exempted due to concerns regarding competitiveness and carbon leakage. The exemption was established to allow time for the adoption of a global deal at the UN level, the Carbon Offsetting and Reduction Scheme for International Aviation (CORSIA).

12. Compared to the existing ETS that regulates direct emitters (point sources), the ETS2 will regulate precursor activities to emission sources (i.e., fuel suppliers rather than households or car drivers).

However, setting the cap at the EU level was insufficient to avoid excess allocations. Following the 2008 financial crisis, industrial activity and carbon emissions slumped. At the same time, Member States and the EU enacted other climate policies that reduced baseline emissions. Annual carbon allowances issued began to exceed actual annual emissions. A large surplus of allowances built up through banking. Prices went down.

At that time, there was no mechanism to adjust the cap to changes in economic conditions. In 2015, the EU decided to backload the issuance of some of the allowances to the end of the phase to support prices, and to introduce a market stability reserve (MSR), starting from 2019. Under the MSR, allowances are temporarily removed from the market (and set aside in a reserve) when the number of allowances in circulation is above a threshold, while allowances are injected (from the reserve) when the number of allowances in circulation is below a threshold.[13] The long-term cap neutrality (as allowances are only temporarily removed from the market) of the MSR raised concerns that it would not help increase the price of allowances and might instead increase its volatility (Perino and Willner 2016; Kollenberg and Taschini 2019). In 2018, the MSR was complemented by a cancellation mechanism (implemented in 2023), fixing the maximum volume in the MSR to 400 MtCO2e.

Recent research suggests that these market interventions contributed to the increase in carbon prices observed since 2018 (Bruninx et al. 2020; Quemin and Trotignon 2021). However, these articles also emphasize that the MSR can trigger feedback loops that disrupt the normal operations of the market in the presence of a tightening cap (see also Perino et al. 2022). Specifically, when firms expect a stricter cap in the future, it is rational for them to start abating more today and bank allowances to equalize marginal abatement costs across periods as much as possible. But banking increases the number of allowances in circulation and triggers removals given the existing rules of the MSR, further tightening the cap (for a detailed discussion of the MSR and its properties, see Borghesi et al. 2023).

Allowances allocation. Allowances were initially allocated freely to regulated entities based on past CO_2 emissions. This discouraged participation by small compliance traders who faced high transaction costs and could save unused allowances or borrow the equivalent of one year of allowances instead of interacting with the market (Jaraitė-Kažukauskė and Kažukauskas 2015; Baudry et al. 2021).

In their review of the EU ETS in preparation for phase III, the European

13. Formally, the total number of allowances in circulation (TNAC) is defined as the supply of allowances (Demand + MSR). The supply of allowances consists of the allowances banked from the previous phase, allowances issued for the current phase, and the allowances in the New Entrants Reserve. The demand is determined by the number of allowances that have already been surrendered for compliance or canceled.

Commission recognized the limitations of free allocations and the efficiency benefits of auctioning (European Commission 2008). But they remained concerned about carbon leakage and competitiveness. For this reason, the European Commission opted for a hybrid allocation scheme. Auctions became the default allocation mechanism, but sectors at risk of carbon leakage continued to receive some of their allowances for free. The allocation rule was adapted, however. Instead of allocating allowances based on past emissions, allowances were allocated based on a benchmark made of the top 10 percent best performers (in terms of carbon intensity).[14] As a result, firms in sectors at risk of carbon leakage whose carbon intensity was higher than the benchmark received fewer allowances than they needed and had to buy the difference in the market.

While a combination of free allocation based on benchmarking and auctioning is an improvement compared to the initial allocation methods chosen in the EU ETS, Martin et al. (2014) argue that this is still inefficient. The new rules protect firms with the highest probability of relocating their activities, i.e. carbon-intensive and trade-exposed industries. Efficiency, instead, requires taking the expected aggregate damages from relocation into account. They show that the efficient compensations (in the form of free allowances) equalize the marginal propensities to relocate, weighted by the damages caused by their relocation, across firms.

The latest development in the free allocation-carbon leakage debate is the introduction of a Carbon Border Adjustment Mechanism (CBAM), taking effect in 2026. Instead of granting free allowances to sectors exposed to international competition, as a way to ensure that domestic and foreign firms face a common level-playing field in the EU, the CBAM charges imports from select sectors for their carbon content, unless they have been subject to an equivalent carbon price in their home country. Free allowances will be phased out accordingly. In essence, the CBAM puts domestic and foreign firms on an equal footing in the EU, but this time they both face a carbon price.[15]

Market organization and legal status of allowances. As was the case for the decisions regarding the cap on emissions, the original infrastructure of the EU ETS was decentralized. National registries recorded ownership and transfers of allowances. These national registries were linked together through the Community Independent Transaction Log. The decision

14. A benchmark is defined for each product sold by sectors covered by the EU ETS. Performance is measured in terms of emissions intensity (tons of CO_2 equivalent per unit of output) in 2007–2008. The product benchmark is the average GHG emission performance of the 10 percent best-performing installations that produce this product. See Stenqvist and Åhman (2016) for details.

15. See "Carbon Border Adjustment Mechanism," March 28, 2025, on the European Commission website, https://taxation-customs.ec.europa.eu/carbon-border-adjustment-mechanism_en for a description; also Ambec (2022) and Cosbey et al. (2019) for analyses.

regarding the legal status of allowances was also left to Member States. Some countries viewed them as commodities, subject to VAT, while others considered them as financial assets.

During the second phase, several national registries were hacked and allowances were stolen. Additionally, some traders took advantage of the difference in legal treatment of emissions allowances across countries, resulting in a massive VAT carousel between EU countries (Interpol 2013; Robert 2012). Fraudsters bought tax-free allowances in one country, sold them in another Member State where they were subject to VAT, pocketed the VAT, and then disappeared without ever paying it back to fiscal authorities. According to some estimates, these fraudulent activities led to a loss of tax revenues of around 5 billion euros (Berrittella and Cimino 2017). In response, operations were centralized in 2012 into a single EU registry managed by the European Commission. Furthermore, allowances are considered financial instruments and have been regulated under the Markets in Financial Instruments Directive (MiFiD II) since 2018.

2.3.3 The Challenge of Producing Stable Informative Signals

The cost-efficiency argument in favor of cap-and-trade schemes rests on their ability to produce prices that are informative of economic conditions and of firms' current and future abatement opportunities. Cronshaw and Kruse (1996) and Rubin (1996) have extended the efficiency result in Montgomery (1972) to a dynamic setting with no uncertainty. They show that arbitrage across periods leads to prices being equated across time periods, up to a discount factor. In practice, however, there is some uncertainty about the state of the economy and future emissions. In that case, prices are updated following the arrival of new information. Schennach (2000) shows that, in the full information equilibrium, prices follow a martingale: current prices are equal to expected future prices, up to discounting. New information arrival does lead to price changes, but these are typically muted because shocks are spread over all future compliance periods (Cantillon and Slechten 2018). In other words, we do not expect the kind of price movements seen in figure 2.1.[16] Volatility is surprisingly high in the EU ETS, given the absence of storage costs and the high intertemporal fungibility of EU allowances. For example, in 2018–19, the coefficient of variation of EU allowance prices was between 0.3–0.4. This is much higher than for other major commodities for which storage costs are typically larger, including oil (0.23), gas (0.16), and base metal (0.12).

This level of volatility is a concern for the cost-effectiveness of the market, given that price uncertainty reduces investment incentives (Dixit and

16. In the presence of constraints on borrowing, prices can rise suddenly following an increase in emissions. However, given the timing of issuance of allowances in the EU ETS, borrowing constraints are unlikely to bind for most firms as compliance firms can effectively borrow the equivalent of one year of allowances.

Pindyck 1994; Bloom et al. 2007). There is a need to understand and address price volatility in the EU ETS.

A number of explanations have been proposed. Quemin and Trotignon (2021) have hypothesized that regulated companies do not fully exploit arbitrage opportunities over time due to shortsightedness. Long-term hedging markets could help mitigate the impact of shortsightedness, but they are underdeveloped for this purpose. For example, in 2024, the Intercontinental Exchange (ICE), the dominant platform for European allowances trading, did not list any futures contracts beyond 2030. This is considerably shorter than the typical horizon for investments in abatement technologies (e.g., installing a new blast furnace in a steel mill). Moreover, liquidity decreases rapidly along the maturity curve.

A second explanation is that overlapping policies lead to large shocks in business-as-usual emissions that even intertemporal arbitrage cannot smooth (Borenstein et al. 2019). This raises questions about the ability of cap adjustment mechanisms, and the reformed MSR in particular, to account for these overlapping policies (Perino et al. 2019).

Market participation and rules regarding who is allowed to trade are another explanation that has been proposed for the high level of volatility observed in the EU ETS. Non-compliance entities (e.g., financial intermediaries, speculators, or hedgers) now make up a large share of allowances trading on the European carbon market. Participation by non-compliance traders brings liquidity and can help small emitters access the market (Cludius and Betz 2020). Financial intermediaries also provide hedging services to compliance traders. However, Quemin and Pahle (2023) argue that the non-regulated entities that have recently entered the EU ETS are very different from the financial intermediaries and market makers present so far. The new traders are mostly investment funds, that trade for other reasons not directly linked to compliance (e.g., hedging against inflation, greening their portfolio, or diversifying the risk of their portfolio . . .). Their presence may induce excess volatility relative to market fundamentals due to spillover effects from shocks in other markets, an argument made by Sockin and Xiong (2015) in the context of commodity markets.

Concerns regarding the financialization of carbon markets and its effect on price volatility have also been raised recently by the European Commission.[17] The choice made by the EU regarding who has access to the EU ETS is very different from the choices made in other jurisdictions (see table 2.2).

17. The Commission asked the European Securities and Markets Authority (ESMA) to analyze the trading of emission allowances. The final report concluded that "*the emergence of new participants (and instruments) with buy and-hold strategies warrants future monitoring to the extent that they may lead to a reduction in the supply of physical emission allowances available for trading, even though the available evidence suggests that their impact is only limited so far.*" (European Securities and Markets Authorities [ESMA] 2022).

In the Korean emissions trading scheme, only designated market makers are allowed to trade allowances to ensure a level playing field for all traders. In the Chinese market, non-compliance firms are excluded. It is an open question to what extent these different rules on participation facilitate price discovery by compliance traders.

A fourth explanation relates to the microstructure of the EU ETS. The EU ETS has historically been and is still today a highly fragmented market, weaving together centralized exchanges, dealers, brokers, and other financial intermediaries (Borghesi and Flori 2018; Karpf et al. 2018). While fragmentation does not necessarily result in inferior price discovery or higher price volatility (Jensen 2007; Chen and Duffie 2021), Cantillon and Slechten (2024) find that in the EU ETS, it hampered the ability of market participants to get a full picture of the prevailing balance between supply and demand in the market, and failed to ensure an equal level playing field among traders. In turn, incomplete information aggregation is likely to lead to overreaction to new information. This raises several design questions regarding the way those markets are organized: Should we have a centralized exchange? Should we have market makers?

Relatedly, carbon markets, typically characterized by annual compliance cycles, tend to be thin, which contributes to price volatility. There have been suggestions to lower the frequency of the market to pool liquidity or implement staggered compliance cycles to ensure that there is sufficient liquidity throughout the year.

Finally, in ongoing work, we explore the impact of risk management practices as a potential driver of price volatility. Interviews and descriptive analysis of trading behavior suggest that compliance and non-compliance traders are subject to risk management constraints, accumulating spot allowances close to futures maturities. These risk management constraints introduce an endogenous borrowing constraint on the market and lead the price to deviate from market fundamentals and overreact to shocks on the availability of allowances.

2.4 Voluntary Carbon Markets

Voluntary carbon markets bring together projects that reduce carbon emissions or remove carbon from the atmosphere, and individuals, companies, or public entities eager to offset their emissions, typically on a voluntary basis.[18] Projects are diverse: some are based on nature (our focus here), some are based on technology. Some reduce emissions relative to a business-as-usual situation (emissions avoidance), others *physically remove*

18. An exception is the aviation sector which can use some of these credits to meet their obligations under the Carbon Offsetting and Reduction Scheme (CORSIA).

carbon from the atmosphere (carbon removal). For example, low-carbon cookstoves qualify as a technology-based carbon avoidance project. Planting trees is a nature-based carbon removal project.[19]

Projects generate carbon credits, which are then traded on the market. Buyers can hold them for resale later on or "retire" them, i.e., redeem them against their own emissions. In that case, the credit can no longer be traded.

In 2023, 261 million carbon credits were issued and around 170 million were retired in the voluntary carbon market globally (one carbon credit represents one ton of carbon) (World Bank 2024). To put this in perspective, the yearly cap on emissions from stationary installations in the EU ETS was 1,485 million tons the same year.[20] Many observers remain bullish about the voluntary carbon market, however, with new participants and intermediaries joining the market *en masse.* First, the number of companies taking voluntary action to reduce their emissions is increasing. These companies typically need to complement their internal mitigation efforts by carbon offsets. Second, ongoing negotiations around Article 6 of the Paris Agreement will expand the possibilities for countries and companies to use carbon credits to meet their climate mitigation commitments.[21]

2.4.1 Project Qualification and Market Governance

A number of conditions are imposed on projects before issuing credits. These conditions seek to ensure that the project and the emissions reductions that go with it would not have happened without funding (additionality condition), that the claimed emissions reductions are properly measured (baseline accuracy and absence of leakage conditions) and permanent (permanence condition).[22] Credits are recorded in a registry for traceability and to avoid any risk of double counting. Projects meeting these conditions can reassure buyers that the credit they buy corresponds indeed to one ton of carbon avoided or removed.

The market is supported by an ecosystem of standard setters, certifiers, registries, and trading platforms. Standard setters play a major role. They define what projects can generate credits and set the methodologies to assess the amount of carbon avoided or removed. Independent standard-setting

19. While both types of projects reduce net emissions, carbon removal projects tend to be viewed more positively, among others, because their additionality claims are considered more reliable. See Tanzer and Ramírez (2019) for details.

20. EU ETS emissions cap, European Commission, https://climate.ec.europa.eu/eu-action/eu-emissions-trading-system-eu-ets/emissions-cap-and-allowances_en (accessed July 30, 2024).

21. Article 6 of the Paris Agreement describes ways in which countries can "pursue voluntary cooperation" to reach their climate targets. Article 6.2 deals with bilateral and multilateral exchanges between countries. Article 6.4 lays the basis for a global carbon market supervised by the United Nations. It will eventually replace the Clean Development Mechanism.

22. Leakage refers to the increase in emissions outside of the accounting boundary of a project, as a result of the project. For example, if forest protection in one area leads to a shift of logging to another area.

organizations, such as Verra and Gold Standard, are responsible for the majority of credits issued. They coexist with public international, national, and regional crediting mechanisms, such as the Clean Development Mechanism (CDM), established by the Kyoto Protocol, and the California Compliance Offset Program.

The main categories of projects eligible for crediting are forestry and land use, renewable energy, energy efficiency/fuel switching, waste disposal, and household devices. Each category is itself divided into subcategories of projects, each with its own methodologies. Credits remain uniquely identified by their projects and their vintage. Buyers know, when they buy a credit, the identity of the project that generated this credit.

Standard setters work with a network of independent certifiers that apply the standard's methodology to evaluate projects and propose the number of credits to be issued. Registries document credited projects and retirements and ensure that projects are not credited twice. They contribute to market transparency.[23]

In 2022, the market was dominated by bilateral deals between project developers and end buyers, but intermediaries, exchanges, and funds had recently entered and were offering their services to this growing market (World Bank 2022, 2023).

2.4.2 Challenges

As of today, the voluntary carbon market is best characterized as immature: liquidity and transparency are low, and prices are dispersed and volatile. Credits from carbon removals such as afforestation, for example, trade at a premium relative to nature-based avoidance projects (preventing deforestation) or renewable energy projects. Even within these categories, price differences prevail. The nature of credits traded and buyers' preferences for direct contact with credit-issuing projects are part of the explanation. Attempts by exchanges to bundle credits meeting specific requirements have met with resistance from market participants eager to avoid adverse selection (World Bank 2023).

More damaging for the market, a number of scientific articles have raised concerns about the tangibility of the climate benefits provided by certified projects. Researchers have documented large and systematic over-crediting (Haya et al. 2020; West et al. 2020; Badgley et al. 2022; Gill-Wiehl et al. 2023); absence of additionality (Schneider 2009; Calel et al. 2021); and leakage (Heilmayr et al. 2020). These concerns were further publicized when a syndicate of investigative journalists reported in January 2023 that more than 90 percent of rainforest carbon offsets certified by Verra, one of the

23. Typically, these registries are paired with certification bodies, but a database, developed by the Berkeley Carbon Trading Project at UC Berkeley, aggregates the projects from the largest four registries, essentially covering most of the voluntary carbon credit market.

largest standard setters, were worthless.[24] These, and subsequent developments such as increasingly frequent large-scale forest fires, have led to large drops in prices for nature-based credits, from around 16 USD per ton at the end of 2021 to 1 USD per ton in July 2024.[25]

2.4.3 Market Design Options

The tribulations of the voluntary carbon market illustrate the complexity of designing markets for environmental goods and services. Scale—the main benefit that markets bring—requires some form of standardization and legal certainty about the asset traded. For technical and economic reasons, these have until now eluded the voluntary carbon market: project-based emission reductions are measured with uncertainty and subject to revisions, exposing buyers to reputational and legal risks.

The pragmatic route of certification *cum* market segmentation taken so far has only partially addressed these concerns, as evidenced by the continued dominance of bilateral trades between project developers and buyers and the underdevelopment of the secondary market.

Researchers have proposed different solutions to address the credibility issues with which the voluntary carbon market is confronted. Proposed solutions cover project design and qualification, credit use, and measurement. For example, Mason and Plantinga (2013) propose to use contract menus, into which project developers self-select, to address exaggerated additionality claims (see also Li et al. 2023, and Aspelund and Russo 2023). Streck (2021) proposes to address leakage with a combination of project design, intended to minimize leakage, and standards imposed on users of credits. Filewod and McCarney (2023) recommend that upper-bound estimates of leakage be systematically used (unlike today) to derate the estimated carbon saved or avoided. In addition, they argue that such credits should not be used for compliance. In non-compliance settings, these credits should only be used to offset emissions that are themselves quite poorly estimated, such as beyond-value chain emissions.

Balmford et al. (2023) suggest replacing the usual buffer approach to the risk of impermanence of nature-based credits, whereby a buffer is added to the issued carbon credits in case the carbon savings do not materialize (e.g., because of a forest fire), with a dynamic accounting approach tracing changes in carbon stocks over time and issuing or canceling credits accordingly. Their approach, which capitalizes on recent advances in near-time granular satellite imagery and data processing, has the added benefit of encouraging project developers to preserve and conserve the project's benefits.

24. "Revealed: More Than 90 percent of Rainforest Carbon Offsets by Biggest Certifier Are Worthless, Analysis Shows," Patrick Greenfield, *The Guardian*, January 18, 2023, https://www.theguardian.com/environment/2023/jan/18/revealed-forest-carbon-offsets-biggest-provider-worthless-verra-aoe.

25. Source: S&P Global Platts.

Developments on the ground point to the direction of stricter standards on credits and standard harmonization, on the one hand, and stricter conditions on disclosure and use by buyers to prevent green-washing, on the other hand.[26]

While these developments are likely to improve the integrity of current voluntary carbon markets, they will, in effect, restrict market size, focusing it on the high-quality segment. Moreover, these developments do not address more conceptual questions about the nature of carbon credits and the contractual arrangements supporting them. One such concern is the intrinsic intellectual difficulty of having different prices for carbon credits that have the same face value (one ton), and the continued market fragmentation that results. Another concern is to what extent carbon reduction and carbon removal projects are best served by production-based financing, such as the one provided by voluntary carbon markets, which reward a flow of emissions reductions, rather than project finance that funds the investment upfront.

2.5 An Agenda for Market Design Research

Nature is essential for our lives and economies. Yet, our ways of living have gradually encroached on nature to the point that several tipping points have been reached (Richardson et al. 2023). In this chapter, we have reviewed areas where markets are used or being considered to address environmental overexploitation, degradation, and underprovision.

The starting point of any such scheme is a sound understanding of the biophysical process underlying the environmental problem at hand. This biophysical process determines what can be traded and the arbitrages which any market designer must make. For example, the fact that carbon dioxide is a stock pollutant means that the trajectory of emissions over time, and not only their level at any point in time, is what matters. This implies that constraints on borrowing are a good idea, despite preventing some intertemporal cost optimization. Likewise, the fact that carbon dioxide is also a global pollutant means that boundary issues and leakage should be first-order considerations. When it comes to nature-based provisions of carbon emissions reduction, their non-permanence requires that crediting be adapted over time. More generally, defining the object of trade can prove very difficult for nature-based solutions because natural capital typically comes as a bundle of services and attributes that may be space and context-dependent (Griscom et al. 2017; von Jeetze et al. 2023). As our discussion has illustrated, this complexity is a challenge for building thick and liquid nature-based markets. Progress in measurement and technology will help, but more sophisticated asset designs and tailored market designs are also needed.

26. See World Bank (2024) for an overview, and European Commission (2022) and European Commission (2023) for recent legislative initiatives in the EU.

2.5.1 Asset Design, Maturity Alignment, and Risk Sharing

When it comes to limiting environmental overexploitation and degradation or increasing the provision of environmental services, it is natural to focus on flows (emissions of a pollutant, removal of carbon, catch of fish). Therefore, unsurprisingly, most environmental markets reward or penalize these flows.

The issue, however, is that reducing environmental overexploitation and degradation, or increasing the provision of natural capital, sometimes requires heavy upfront investments. This is, for example, the case for decarbonizing industry. The difference in the timing of the investment and the timing of its benefits may limit investment if investors are credit-constrained or risk-averse.

Appropriate asset designs can play a role. In compliance markets, investment subsidies, possibly awarded through auctions, are an alternative mechanism to foster investment in abatement technologies.[27] In voluntary carbon markets, project finance could play this role. Project finance funds the owner to invest in conserving or developing their natural capital, rather than paying them for the service flow from their investment; this reduces investment risk and alleviates credit constraints. In the same spirit, Aldy and Halem (2024) argue that treating carbon offsets as bonds, which will generate a coupon only if the benefits materialize, can shift some risks to the buyer. Flammer et al. (2023) discuss the role of blended finance—where private investment capital is blended with public or philanthropic capital—in biodiversity conservation.

The right level of risk sharing walks a fine line between risk insurance and incentives. Keeping some risk with investors is desirable if the flow benefits depend on their care in maintaining the natural capital they invested in. For example, guaranteeing a purchase price for carbon credits, much like contracts-for-differences or feed-in-tariffs do in electricity markets, protects investors from market risk, over which they have little control, but not from production risks, over which they have agency.

2.5.2 Accounting for Policy Overlap

A challenge that all environmental markets will increasingly face as governments ramp up action on climate and biodiversity is their interactions with overlapping policies. As discussed in section 2.3.3, interactions with other policies can generate large uncertainty about future prices in pollution markets, reducing incentives for investment. In provision markets, evolving

27. An independent and separate argument for considering subsidies for R&D or research procurement is that R&D is subject to a knowledge externality (see, e.g., Acemoglu et al. 2012 and Arnesen and Glennerster 2026).

policies may impact the counterfactual against which a project is assessed to evaluate its environmental benefit, generating risk for project developers (Aldy and Halem 2024). Market designs need to account for these interactions and hedge market participants from unnecessary risks.

2.5.3 Should Voluntary and Compliance Markets Be Integrated?

Integration between voluntary and compliance carbon markets is an area of intense policy interest. Ongoing negotiations on Art. 6 of the Paris Agreement and pending legislative proposals in the EU and the UK pave the way for the eventual use of carbon credits for compliance. Proponents argue that pooling sources of emissions mitigation and carbon removals will encourage investment in carbon removals and mitigation and contribute to greater cost-effectiveness of climate action.

The question is what conditions to put on these credits and on their use so that integration does not harm the integrity of compliance markets. Past experience with CDM and JI projects provides a cautionary tale about the risks and benefits of such integration. Clearly, raising standards and improving measurement and monitoring to increase accuracy, ensure additionality, and limit leakage can be part of the solution.

Still, the most exacting standard for nature-based carbon removals will never be able to guarantee permanence. For these nature-based carbon credits, Balmford et al. (2023) suggest using a dynamic accounting system to correct dynamically for the changes in carbon stocks over time. Alternatively, Edenhofer et al. (2023) suggest derating these carbon credits for the non-permanence of the carbon removals associated with them, and creating a European Carbon Central Bank to cover any remaining liabilities.

Distinguishing pollution markets from provision markets provides a complementary perspective and cautions against integrating nature-based credit removals into emissions reduction compliance markets. The reason is that these markets pursue different goals: the former aim to encourage the provision of nature-based carbon removals, the latter aim to reduce emissions from human activities. This matters because existing Paris-aligned emissions trajectories treat these two goals *separately* and require both to be met simultaneously. Making nature-based carbon removals also count toward emissions reduction in the other sectors, as implied by market integration, would amount to double-counting. Interestingly, the discussion at the EU level about market integration only concerns industrial carbon removals at this stage and thus avoids this double-counting trap (European Commission 2024). The UK proposal does not.[28]

28. "UK ETS consults on integrating carbon removal," Carbon Pulse, May 23, 2024, https://carbon-pulse.com/289140/.

References

Acemoglu, D., P. Aghion, L. Bursztyn, and D. Hemous. 2012. "The Environment and Directed Technical Change." *American Economic Review* 102(1): 131–66.

Aldy, J. E., and Z. M. Halem. 2024. "The Evolving Role of Greenhouse Gas Emission Offsets in Combating Climate Change." *Review of Environmental Economics and Policy* 18(2).

Ambec, S. 2022. "The European Union's Carbon Border Adjustment Mechanism: Challenges and Perspectives." TSE Working Paper.

Arnesen, W., and Rachel Glennerster. 2026. "Market Shaping to Combat Climate Change." In *New Directions in Market Design*, edited by Irene Lo, Michael Ostrovsky, and Parag A. Pathak. National Bureau of Economic Research Conference Report. This volume, ch. 4. Chicago: University of Chicago Press.

Aspelund, K., and A. Russo. 2023. "Additionality and Asymmetric Information in Environmental Markets: Evidence from Conservation Auctions." Technical Report, Working Paper.

Badgley, G., J. Freeman, J. J. Hamman, B. Haya, A. T. Trugman, W. R. Anderegg, and D. Cullenward. 2022. "Systematic Over-Crediting in California's Forest Carbon Offsets Program." *Global Change Biology* 28(4): 1433–1445.

Balmford, A., S. Keshav, F. Venmans, D. Coomes, B. Groom, A. Madhavapeddy, and T. Swinfield. 2023. "Realizing the Social Value of Impermanent Carbon Credits." *Nature Climate Change* 13(5478): 1172–178.

Baudry, M., A. Faure, and S. Quemin. 2021. "Emissions Trading with Transaction Costs." *Journal of Environmental Economics and Management* 108: 102468.

Berrittella, M., and F. A. Cimino. 2017. "An Assessment of Carousel Value-Added Tax Fraud in the European Carbon Market." *Review of Law & Economics* 13(2): 20140023.

Bloom, N., S. Bond, and J. Van Reenen. 2007. "Uncertainty and Investment Dynamics." *Review of Economic Studies* 74(2): 391–415.

Böhringer, C., and A. Lange. 2005. "On the Design of Optimal Grandfathering Schemes for Emission Allowances." *European Economic Review* 49(8): 2041–2055.

Borenstein, S., J. Bushnell, F. A. Wolak, and M. Zaragoza-Watkins. 2019. "Expecting the Unexpected: Emissions Uncertainty and Environmental Market Design." *American Economic Review* 109(11): 3953–3977.

Borghesi, S., and A. Flori. 2018. "EU ETS Facets in the Net: Structure and Evolution of the EU ETS Network." *Energy Economics* 75: 602–35.

Borghesi, S., M. Pahle, G. Perino, S. Quemin, and M. Willner. 2023. "The Market Stability Reserve in the EU Emissions Trading System: A Critical Review." *Annual Review of Resource Economics* 15: 131–52.

Bowles, S. 2016. *The Moral Economy: Why Good Incentives Are No Substitute for Good Citizens.* Yale University Press.

Bruninx, K., M. Ovaere, and E. Delarue. 2020. "The Long-Term Impact of the Market Stability Reserve on the EU Emission Trading System." *Energy Economics* 89: 104746.

Burtraw, D., C. Holt, K. Palmer, and W. Shobe. 2022. "Price-Responsive Allowance Supply in Emissions Markets." *Journal of the Association of Environmental and Resource Economists* 9(5): 851–84.

Burtraw, D., and K. McCormack. 2017. "Consignment Auctions of Free Emissions Allowances." *Energy Policy* 107: 337–44.

Burtraw, D., K. Palmer, and D. Kahn. 2010. "A Symmetric Safety Valve." *Energy Policy* 38(9): 4921–4932.

Calel, R., J. Colmer, A. Dechezleprêtre, and M. Glachant. 2021. "Do Carbon Offsets Offset Carbon?" CESifo Working Paper.
Cantillon, E., and A. Slechten. 2018. "Information Aggregation in Emissions Markets with Abatement." *Annals of Economics and Statistics* (132): 53–79.
Cantillon, E., and A. Slechten. 2024. "Who Gains from Market Fragmentation? Evidence from the Early Stages of the EU Carbon Market." Centre for Economic Policy Research Working Paper 18118.
Chen, D., and D. Duffie. 2021. "Market Fragmentation." *American Economic Review* 111(7): 2247–274.
Claassen, R., A. Cattaneo, and R. Johansson. 2008. "Cost-Effective Design of Agri-Environmental Payment Programs: US Experience in Theory and Practice." *Ecological Economics* 65(4): 737–52.
Cludius, J., and R. Betz. 2020. "The Role of Banks in EU Emissions Trading." *The Energy Journal* 41(2).
Cosbey, A., S. Droege, C. Fischer, and C. Munnings. 2019. "Developing Guidance for Implementing Border Carbon Adjustments: Lessons, Cautions, and Research Needs from the Literature." *Review of Environmental Economics and Policy* 13(1).
Costanza, R., R. d'Arge, R. De Groot, S. Farber, M. Grasso, B. Hannon, K. Limburg, S. Naeem, R. V. O'Neill, J. Paruelo, et al. 1997. "The Value of the World's Ecosystem Services and Natural Capital." *Nature* 387(6630): 253–60.
Costello, C., S. D. Gaines, and J. Lynham. 2008. "Can Catch Shares Prevent Fisheries Collapse?" *Science* 321(5896): 1678–1681.
Cox, T., J. Rutherford, S. C. Kerr, D. Smeaton, and C. Palliser. 2013. "An Integrated Model for Simulating Nitrogen Trading in an Agricultural Catchment with Complex Hydrogeology." *Journal of Environmental Management* 127: 268–77.
Cronshaw, M. B., and J. B. Kruse. 1996. "Regulated Firms in Pollution Permit Markets with Banking." *Journal of Regulatory Economics* 9: 179–89.
Dales, J. H. 1968. "Land, Water, and Ownership." *Canadian Journal of Economics* 1(4): 791–804.
Dechezleprêtre, A., and M. Sato. 2017. "The Impacts of Environmental Regulations on Competitiveness." *Review of Environmental Economics and Policy* 11(2).
Defrance, P. 2015. "Financial Compensation for Environmental Services: The Case of the Evian Natural Mineral Water (France)." In *Use of Economic Instruments in Water Policy. Global Issues in Water Policy*, vol. 14, edited by M. Lago, J. Mysiak, C. Gómez, G. Delacámara, and A. Maziotis. Springer, Cham. https://doi.org/10.1007/978-3-319-18287-2_24.
Denison, S., P. M. Forster, and C. J. Smith. 2019. "Guidance on Emissions Metrics for Nationally Determined Contributions Under the Paris Agreement." *Environmental Research Letters* 14(12): 124002.
Depres, C., G. Grolleau, and N. Mzoughi. 2008. "Contracting for Environmental Property Rights: The Case of Vittel." *Economica* 75(299): 412–34.
Dixit, A. K., and R. S. Pindyck. 1994. *Investment Under Uncertainty*. Princeton University Press.
Doda, B., S. Quemin, and L. Taschini. 2019. "Linking Permit Markets Multilaterally." *Journal of Environmental Economics and Management* 98: 102259.
Edenhofer, O., M. Franks, M. Kalkuhl, and A. Runge-Metzger. 2023. "On the Governance of Carbon Dioxide Removal—A Public Economics Perspective." CESifo Working Paper.
Edenhofer, O., M. Kosch, M. Pahle, and G. Zachmann. 2021. "A Whole-Economy Carbon Price for Europe and How to Get There." *Bruegel Policy Contribution 06/2021*.

Ellerman, A. D., F. J. Convery, and C. De Perthuis. 2010. *Pricing Carbon: The European Union Emissions Trading Scheme*. Cambridge University Press.
Ellerman, A. D., P. L. Joskow, R. Schmalensee, J.-P. Montero, and E. Bailey. 2000. *Markets for Clean Air: The US Acid Rain Program*. Cambridge University Press.
Engel, S., S. Pagiola, and S. Wunder. 2008. "Designing Payments for Environmental Services in Theory and Practice: An Overview of the Issues." *Ecological Economics* 65(4): 663–74.
European Commission. 2005. *EU Emissions Trading: An Open Scheme Promoting Global Innovation to Combat Climate Change*. Directorate-General for Environment.
European Commission. 2008. *Annex to the impact assessment: Document accompanying the proposal for a directive of the European Parliament and of the Council amending Directive 2003/87/EC* (SEC [2008] 85 final). Brussels.
European Commission. 2021. Proposal for a Directive Amending Directive 2003/87/EC Establishing a System for Greenhouse Gas Emissions Allowance Trading Within the Union. COM(2021) 551 final.
European Commission. 2022. Proposal for a Regulation Establishing a Union Certification Framework for Carbon Removals. COM(2022) 672 final.
European Commission. 2023. Proposal for a Green Claims Directive. COM(2023) 166 final.
European Commission. 2024. Towards an Ambitious Industrial Carbon Management for the EU. COM(2024) 62 final.
European Securities and Markets Authorities (ESMA). 2022. "Emission Allowances and Associated Derivatives." Final Report ESMA70–445–38.
Fankhauser, S., and C. Hepburn. 2010. "Designing Carbon Markets, Part II: Carbon Markets in Space." *Energy Policy* 38(8): 4381–4387.
Fell, H., D. Burtraw, R. D. Morgenstern, and K. L. Palmer. 2012. "Soft and Hard Price Collars in a Cap-and-Trade System: A Comparative Analysis." *Journal of Environmental Economics and Management* 64(2): 183–98.
Ferguson, B. A., and Paul Milgrom. 2026. "Market Design for Surface Water." In *New Directions in Market Design*, edited by Irene Lo, Michael Ostrovsky, and Parag A. Pathak. National Bureau of Economic Research Conference Report. This volume, ch. 3. Chicago: University of Chicago Press.
Filewod, B., and G. McCarney. 2023. "Avoiding Carbon Leakage from Nature-Based Offsets by Design." *One Earth* 6(7): 790–802.
Fisher-Vanden, K., and S. Olmstead. 2013. "Moving Pollution Trading from Air to Water: Potential, Problems, and Prognosis." *Journal of Economic Perspectives* 27(1): 147–72.
Flachsland, C., R. Marschinski, and O. Edenhofer. 2009. "To Link or Not to Link: Benefits and Disadvantages of Linking Cap-and-Trade Systems." *Climate Policy* 9(4): 358–72.
Flammer, C., T. Giroux, and G. Heal. 2023. "Biodiversity Finance." Technical Report, National Bureau of Economic Research.
Gill-Wiehl, A., D. Kammen, and B. Haya. 2023. "Cooking the Books: Pervasive Over-Crediting from Cookstoves Offset Methodologies." Mimeo.
Grassi, G., J. House, F. Dentener, S. Federici, M. den Elzen, and J. Penman. 2017. "The Key Role of Forests in Meeting Climate Targets Requires Science for Credible Mitigation." *Nature Climate Change* 7(3): 220–26.
Griscom, B. W., J. Adams, P. W. Ellis, R. A. Houghton, G. Lomax, D. A. Miteva, W. H. Schlesinger, D. Shoch, J. V. Siikamäki, P. Smith, et al. 2017. "Natural Climate Solutions." *Proceedings of the National Academy of Sciences* 114(44): 11645–11650.

Hahn, R. W. 1984. "Market Power and Transferable Property Rights." *Quarterly Journal of Economics* 99(4): 753–65.
Hardin, G. 1968. "The Tragedy of the Commons: The Population Problem Has No Technical Solution; It Requires a Fundamental Extension in Morality." *Science* 162(3859): 1243–1248.
Harstad, B., and G. S. Eskeland. 2010. "Trading for the Future: Signaling in Permit Markets." *Journal of Public Economics* 94(9–10): 749–60.
Haya, B., D. Cullenward, A. L. Strong, E. Grubert, R. Heilmayr, D. A. Sivas, and M. Wara. 2020. "Managing Uncertainty in Carbon Offsets: Insights from California's Standardized Approach." *Climate Policy* 20(9): 1112–126.
Heilmayr, R., K. M. Carlson, and J. J. Benedict. 2020. "Deforestation Spillovers from Oil Palm Sustainability Certification." *Environmental Research Letters* 15(7): 075002.
Hepburn, C. 2006. "Regulation by Prices, Quantities, or Both: A Review of Instrument Choice." *Oxford Review of Economic Policy* 22(2): 226–47.
Holland, S. P., and M. R. Moore. 2013. "Market Design in Cap and Trade Programs: Permit Validity and Compliance Timing." *Journal of Environmental Economics and Management* 66(3): 671–87.
Interpol. 2013. *Guide to Carbon Trading Crime*. Environmental Crime Programme. Interpol.
Jaraitė-Kažukauskė, J., and A. Kažukauskas. 2015. "Do Transaction Costs Influence Firm Trading Behaviour in the European Emissions Trading System?" *Environmental and Resource Economics* 62: 583–613.
Jensen, R. 2007. "The Digital Provide: Information (Technology), Market Performance, and Welfare in the South Indian Fisheries Sector." *Quarterly Journal of Economics* 122(3): 879–924.
Joskow, P. L., R. Schmalensee, and E. M. Bailey. 1998. "The Market for Sulfur Dioxide Emissions." *American Economic Review* 88(4): 669–85.
Karp, L., and C. Traeger. 2025. "Smart Cap." *Journal of the European Economic Association* 23(2): 554–593. https://doi.org/10.1093/jeea/jvae030.
Karpf, A., A. Mandel, and S. Battiston. 2018. "Price and Network Dynamics in the European Carbon Market." *Journal of Economic Behavior & Organization* 153: 103–22.
Kerr, S., K. Lock, and K. Rutherford. 2007. "Nutrient Trading in Lake Rotorua: Goals and Trading Caps." Available at SSRN 1003321.
Khezr, P., and I. A. MacKenzie. 2018. "Consignment Auctions." *Journal of Environmental Economics and Management* 87: 42–51.
Kollenberg, S., and L. Taschini. 2016. "Emissions Trading Systems with Cap Adjustments." *Journal of Environmental Economics and Management* 80: 20–36.
Kollenberg, S., and L. Taschini. 2019. "Dynamic Supply Adjustment and Banking Under Uncertainty in an Emission Trading Scheme: The Market Stability Reserve." *European Economic Review* 118: 213–26.
Kosoy, N., and E. Corbera. 2010. "Payments for Ecosystem Services as Commodity Fetishism." *Ecological Economics* 69(6): 1228–1236.
Li, W. D., I. Ashlagi, and I. Lo. 2023. "Simple and Approximately Optimal Contracts for Payment for Ecosystem Services." *Management Science* 69(12): 7821–7837.
Martin, R., M. Muûls, L. B. De Preux, and U. J. Wagner. 2014. "Industry Compensation Under Relocation Risk: A Firm-Level Analysis of the EU Emissions Trading Scheme." *American Economic Review* 104(8): 2482–2508.
Mason, C. F., and A. J. Plantinga. 2013. "The Additionality Problem with Offsets: Optimal Contracts for Carbon Sequestration in Forests." *Journal of Environmental Economics and Management* 66(1): 1–14.

McDonald, H., and S. Kerr. 2011. "Trading Efficiency in Water Quality Trading Markets: An Assessment of Trade-offs." Available at SSRN 1975598.
Montgomery, W. D. 1972. "Markets in Licenses and Efficient Pollution Control Programs." *Journal of Economic Theory* 5(3): 395–418.
Murray, B. C., R. G. Newell, and W. A. Pizer. 2009. "Balancing Cost and Emissions Certainty: An Allowance Reserve for Cap-and-Trade." *Review of Environmental Economics and Policy* 3(1).
Newell, R., W. Pizer, and J. Zhang. 2005. "Managing Permit Markets to Stabilize Prices." *Environmental and Resource Economics* 31: 133–57.
Newell, R. G., J. N. Sanchirico, and S. Kerr. 2005. "Fishing Quota Markets." *Journal of Environmental Economics and Management* 49(3): 437–62.
O'Hara, M. 1998. *Market Microstructure Theory*. John Wiley & Sons.
Ostrom, E. 1990. *Governing the Commons: The Evolution of Institutions for Collective Action*. Cambridge University Press.
Perino, G., R. A. Ritz, and A. Van Benthem. 2019. "Overlapping Climate Policies." Technical Report, National Bureau of Economic Research.
Perino, G., and M. Willner. 2016. "Procrastinating Reform: The Impact of the Market Stability Reserve on the EU ETS." *Journal of Environmental Economics and Management* 80: 37–52.
Perino, G., M. Willner, S. Quemin, and M. Pahle. 2022. "The European Union Emissions Trading System Market Stability Reserve: Does It Stabilize or Destabilize the Market?" *Review of Environmental Economics and Policy* 16(2): 338–45.
Perrot-Maître, D. 2006. "The Vittel Payments for Ecosystem Services: A Perfect PES Case?" London: International Institute for Environment and Development (IIED).
Pizer, W. A. 2002. "Combining Price and Quantity Controls to Mitigate Global Climate Change." *Journal of Public Economics* 85(3): 409–34.
Pizer, W. A., and B. C. Prest. 2020. "Prices Versus Quantities with Policy Updating." *Journal of the Association of Environmental and Resource Economists* 7(3): 483–518.
Quemin, S., and M. Pahle. 2023. "Financials Threaten to Undermine the Functioning of Emissions Markets." *Nature Climate Change* 13(1): 22–31.
Quemin, S., and R. Trotignon. 2021. "Emissions Trading with Rolling Horizons." *Journal of Economic Dynamics and Control* 125: 104099.
Ranson, M., and R. N. Stavins. 2016. "Linkage of Greenhouse Gas Emissions Trading Systems: Learning from Experience." *Climate Policy* 16(3): 284–300.
Richardson, K., W. Steffen, W. Lucht, J. Bendtsen, S. E. Cornell, J. F. Donges, M. Drüke, I. Fetzer, G. Bala, W. von Bloh, et al. 2023. "Earth Beyond Six of Nine Planetary Boundaries." *Science Advances* 9(37): eadh2458.
Robert, A. 2012. *Carbone connexion: Le casse du siècle-Essais-documents*. Max Milo.
Roberts, M. J., and M. Spence. 1976. "Effluent Charges and Licenses Under Uncertainty." *Journal of Public Economics* 5(3–4): 193–208.
Roth, A. E. 2026. "Market Design and Maintenance." In *New Directions in Market Design*, edited by Irene Lo, Michael Ostrovsky, and Parag A. Pathak. National Bureau of Economic Research Conference Report. This volume, ch. 1. Chicago: University of Chicago Press.
Rubin, J. D. 1996. "A Model of Intertemporal Emission Trading, Banking, and Borrowing." *Journal of Environmental Economics and Management* 31(3): 269–86.
Sandel, M. J. 2012. *What Money Can't Buy: The Moral Limits of Markets*. Macmillan.
Schennach, S. M. 2000. "The Economics of Pollution Permit Banking in the Context

of Title IV of the 1990 Clean Air Act Amendments." *Journal of Environmental Economics and Management* 40(3): 189–210.
Schlager, E., and E. Ostrom. 1992. "Property-Rights Regimes and Natural Resources: A Conceptual Analysis." *Land Economics* 68(3): 249–62.
Schneider, L. 2009. "Assessing the Additionality of CDM Projects: Practical Experiences and Lessons Learned." *Climate Policy* 9(3): 242–54.
Sockin, M., and W. Xiong. 2015. "Informational Frictions and Commodity Markets." *Journal of Finance* 70(5): 2063–2098.
Srivastav, S., and M. Zaehringer. 2024. "The economics of coal phaseouts: auctions as a novel policy instrument for the energy transition." *Climate Policy* 24(6): 754–765.
Stavins, R. N. 1995. "Transaction Costs and Tradeable Permits." *Journal of Environmental Economics and Management* 29(2): 133–48.
Stenqvist, C., and M. Åhman. 2016. "Free Allocation in the 3rd EU ETS Period: Assessing Two Manufacturing Sectors." *Climate Policy* 16(2): 125–44.
Sterner, T., and J. Coria. 2013. *Policy Instruments for Environmental and Natural Resource Management*. Routledge.
Stranlund, J. K. 2017. "The Economics of Enforcing Emissions Markets." *Review of Environmental Economics and Policy* 11(2): 227–46.
Streck, C. 2021. "REDD+ and Leakage: Debunking Myths and Promoting Integrated Solutions." *Climate Policy* 21(6): 843–52.
Tanzer, S. E., and A. Ramírez. 2019. "When Are Negative Emissions Negative Emissions?" *Energy & Environmental Science* 12(4): 1210–1218.
Teytelboym, A. 2019. "Natural Capital Market Design." *Oxford Review of Economic Policy* 35(1): 138–61.
Tietenberg, T. 2002. "The Tradable Permits Approach to Protecting the Commons: What Have We Learned?" Available at SSRN 315500.
Tietenberg, T. 2010. *Emissions Trading: Principles and Practice*. Routledge.
van Hoof, L. 2013. "Design or Pragmatic Evolution: Applying ITQs in EU Fisheries Management." *ICES Journal of Marine Science* 70(2): 462–70.
von Jeetze, P. J., I. Weindl, J. A. Johnson, P. Borrelli, P. Panagos, E. J. Molina Bacca, K. Karstens, F. Humpenöder, J. P. Dietrich, S. Minoli, et al. 2023. "Projected Landscape-Scale Repercussions of Global Action for Climate and Biodiversity Protection." *Nature Communications* 14(1): 2515.
West, T. A., J. Börner, E. O. Sills, and A. Kontoleon. 2020. "Overstated Carbon Emission Reductions from Voluntary REDD+ Projects in the Brazilian Amazon." *Proceedings of the National Academy of Sciences* 117(39): 24188–24194.
Wheeler, S. A. 2021. *Water Markets: A Global Assessment*. Edward Elgar Publishing.
Wheeler, S. A., C. Nauges, and R. Q. Grafton. 2023. "Water Pricing, Costs and Markets." Technical Report, Global Commission on the Economics of Water, Paris.
World Bank. 2022. *State and Trends of Carbon Pricing 2022*. World Bank Publications.
World Bank. 2023. *State and Trends of Carbon Pricing 2023*. World Bank Publications.
World Bank. 2024. *State and Trends of Carbon Pricing 2024*. World Bank Publications.
Wunder, S. 2005. "Payments for Environmental Services: Some Nuts and Bolts." CIFOR Occasional Paper No. 42, Center for International Forestry Research, Bogor, Indonesia.
Zaklan, A. 2023. "Coase and Cap-and-Trade: Evidence on the Independence Property from the European Carbon Market." *American Economic Journal: Economic Policy* 15(2): 526–58.

3

Market Design for Surface Water

Billy A. Ferguson and Paul Milgrom

3.1 Introduction

The new field of market design is changing the way economists think about markets. Traditionally, most economists conceived markets in terms of bilateral exchange, often illustrating their ideas with examples in which one supplier of a good sells to one buyer, or two parties enter into some contract involving future deliveries or actions. Inspired by the work of Coase (1959, 1960), any persistently inefficient allocations were attributed to transaction costs that disrupt or impair bilateral trade, which would otherwise correct the inefficiency. These costs were conceived broadly to include frictions due to limited or asymmetric information, imperfect enforcement of agreements, or insecure property rights. While externalities can lead to inefficient allocations, Coase emphasized that with no transaction costs, parties would not need the help of the government to resolve those externalities: they could agree for themselves on mutually profitable, efficiency-enhancing deals. Often, the lesson taken from Coasian analyses is that government

Billy A. Ferguson is a PhD candidate in Economics at the Stanford Graduate School of Business.

Paul Milgrom is the Shirley R. and Leonard W. Ely, Jr. Professor in Humanities and Sciences in the Department of Economics at Stanford University.

Milgrom's research was supported by NSF grant SES1947514. This report is also based in part upon work supported by the National Science Foundation under Grant No. DMS-1928930 and by the Alfred P. Sloan Foundation under grant G-2021-16778, while the author was in residence at the Simons Laufer Mathematical Sciences Institute (formerly MSRI) in Berkeley, California, during the Fall 2023 semester. We thank Bilen Essayas and Barton Thompson for helpful suggestions. The views expressed herein are those of the authors and do not necessarily reflect the views of the National Bureau of Economic Research. For acknowledgments, sources of research support, and disclosure of the authors' material financial relationships, if any, please see https://www.nber.org/books-and-chapters/new-directions-market-design/market-design-surface-water.

policy can best promote efficiency by establishing clear, tradeable property rights, avoiding regulations, and mitigating frictions that impair bilateral trade, while leaving the remaining details to free market participants to work out for themselves.

Early contributions to market design went beyond the conception of markets as bilateral exchange between parties that had already been identified. Market design researchers and practitioners often focused on multiple, heterogeneous buyers or sellers and the possible need for multilateral coordination or long periods of time for bilateral trades to match the right buyers and sellers. Examples were highlighted in which combinatorial issues led to the possibility of inefficiency even when no profitable bilateral trades remained or in which processing issues led to markets taking too long to find efficient allocations. Because older economic analyses assumed away these problems, the scholars studying matching markets and radio spectrum auctions needed to rethink how markets could be designed to overcome these challenges (Milgrom 2007; Roth and Xing 1994).

This paper returns to the analysis of property rights, externalities and transaction costs, but takes a different view compared to both Coase and past market designers, emphasizing that the design of rights can alter the balance between externalities and transaction costs.[1] In a modern example, rights to residential land may include the right for landowning coalitions—or in some cases individual owners—to veto the construction of nearby wind farms. Such rights provide strong protections against negative externalities on residents, like the noise and ugliness of wind farms, but they also increase transaction costs, so that even if a wind farm is very valuable, it can be hard to negotiate an efficiency-enhancing deal that builds one—an effect known as the "tragedy of the anticommons" (Kashner 2023; Heller 1998).

Some examples used to discuss externalities in the earlier property rights literature have a structure similar to the wind farm example. In one, Coase writes about how the right of a factory to spew smoke may harm a nearby laundry business, but the same smoke may reach and harm many local households. In another, the right of a railroad to operate its trains without spark-arresters may threaten not just a single farmer along the track but all the other farms and businesses along its route. The specification of a property right determines whose agreement is needed to cancel or transfer it, and that specification affects both the potential externalities and the difficulty of negotiating a rights transfer.

In many historical cases, early rights were created and assigned to be suitable for their original uses. For example, in the United States, radio and television broadcasters received licenses granting them rights to broadcast

1. In a very recent related paper, Dworczak and Muir (2023) adopt a related view. They take a mechanism design approach to optimal property rights, emphasizing that the structure of rights affects the balance between an owner's investment incentives and related trading frictions.

in a specified geographic area using particular sets of frequencies with protection from interference. Although that solved an interference problem in the early radio industry, those areas, rights, and protections are all different from what is needed today to use the same frequencies for efficient broadband communications networks. Similarly, water rights to divert surface flows specify a location, a season, a point of diversion, and a particular use. Specifying details like those limits externalities from changing uses, but also makes beneficial changes harder and interferes with the trading of rights (Colby 1990). In both of these examples, the externalities—radio interference or return flows—associated with different actions can be technically challenging to measure. The specification of property rights that best balances externalities and transaction costs thus depends on factors like optimal uses and measurement technologies that are changing over time, posing the twin challenges of how to redefine rights and how to design and promote a transition from the old rights to the new ones.

We examine these market design challenges in the context of *surface water*, which is the water that comes to a region annually from precipitation and flows in streams and rivers. This water can feed farms, ranches, cities, and the environment, or restore aquifers and reservoirs. Long ago, soon after our early human ancestors turned to farming, they began to use and compete for surface water for irrigation, and developed a system of rights to coordinate and limit those uses. Often, *riparian* rights were attached to lands adjacent to a stream, allowing landowners to use the stream for irrigation but not to sell the water. In other places, first users gained *appropriative* rights giving them priority to continue their historical uses before latecomers got any water allocation.[2]

Fast-forward to California today. The crops that are farmed in the state are quite heterogeneous, with very different requirements. Tree crops need a reliable annual supply, or the trees might die. Annual crops can sometimes be left unplanted to save water in a low-water year. Cities, which grew most in population after early farms were established, now have millions of people with relatively modest individual water needs. There is huge heterogeneity not only in uses but also in the prices that water users pay. In San Diego, the urban water supply costs $2,855 per acre-foot, while alfalfa growers in the nearby Imperial Irrigation District pay just $20 (Hagerty 2024). With these differences, water trading would seem to be an obvious way to make allocations more efficient, especially in drought years when supplies are tight, but the volume of trading remains limited (Hagerty 2024).

Why is there so little water trading in California despite the heterogeneous uses and huge price differences? The consensus among many economists studying water is that much of the problem lies in an archaic system of

2. In other countries, the terms may be different, but adjacency rights and priority-based rights are still common forms.

property rights, which was perhaps simple and clear enough to function well when California was first settled, but which is dysfunctional today. We will argue below that trading in traditional water rights creates externalities, so efficiency-enhancing changes in water allocations cannot be achieved by exhausting profitable bilateral trades. Rather, it requires a coordinated, multilateral effort. The next section on the institutional background provides a description of water rights and the externalities that can result from trade or from certain other decisions about uses. What is most novel in this paper comes after that: we analyze a mechanism that enacts a change in water rights that could lead to much more efficient trade.

Our analysis draws on lessons learned from the US Broadcast Incentive Auction in 2016–17, in which some rights to use radio spectrum for television broadcast were combined, converted, and subdivided into more flexible rights that were better suited for wireless broadband communications. This was accomplished using an auction procedure designed to provide an "incentive" for broadcasters to participate. As in that auction, participation in an analogous Water Rights Incentive Auction could be entirely voluntary, with current water users incentivized to participate because they could trade their existing rights for new, more flexible rights and possibly additional payments as determined by an auction. Just as the Broadcast Incentive Auction achieved its goals described in the National Broadband Plan even though many broadcasters chose not to sell their rights, a Water Incentive Auction could provide the substantial benefits of more flexible water rights even if many water users decline to participate. We describe some details of a possible Water Incentive Auctions in a later section of this paper.

3.2 Institutional Background on Water Property Rights

Traditional Coasian analysis suggests that efficient water allocations are best promoted by clear, tradeable property rights and few regulations, but that analysis holds the rights themselves fixed. It omits analysis of how the content of water rights and the costs of exchanging them are intricately interdependent and cannot be neatly separated, because the allocation of water diversion rights between two uses can affect the availability of water to third parties. The location, timing, purpose, and method of water use can affect both the quantity and quality of water available elsewhere in the system and local economic opportunity (Young 1986). Clear surface water property rights designed to handle these complexities are necessary for efficient, trustworthy, and responsible water management. But pervasive interdependencies among water uses can make surface water reallocation either impossible to achieve or riddled with externalities (Colby 1990; Womble and Hanemann 2020). In this section, we first explain some of the ways in which surface water resources are physically interdependent. We show how cities, farmers, and the environment are affected by these interdependencies and can be harmed by irresponsible/naive transfers. Lastly, we discuss the economic dependence on water resources and how existing regulatory regimes try to protect local agricultural economies.

The physical processes by which surface water flows through and is used along hydrological systems distinguish it from other scarce resources like land. While land can be easily partitioned into discrete units of property to allocate, surface water is always in flux. A key structural property of surface water supply and use is that a single molecule of water may be used many times in a system before being lost to evaporation or transpiration (Young 1986, Hanemann 2005).[3] When a farmer diverts water from a stream to irrigate his crop, any water not consumed by the crop becomes *return flow* that enters a watercourse downstream either through runoff or groundwater percolation (Chong and Sunding 2006, 241). A farmer downstream may then again divert and reuse the same water that was already diverted by a farmer upstream. The surface water system is a complex and interdependent network of diversions, uses, and return flows that is subject to highly variable climatic conditions (Livingston 1995).

> Most diversionary uses of water return up to 50 percent of the original offtake to aquifer or stream. Users who are downstream and/or interconnected through an aquifer are greatly affected (for good or ill) by the quantity, quality, and timing of releases, return flows, or leaks by upstream users. (Young 1986)

Unfortunately, accurately measuring these interdependencies is not at all easy. Uncertain hydrology, interactions among sources, and time lags between application of water and the availability of return flow combine to complicate the measurement process (Leonard et al. 2019, 46). Only recently have advances in hardware and modeling made useful approximations possible. When California was beginning to allocate formal property rights to surface water, measurement was nearly nonexistent.[4] Because regulators could not estimate flows under counterfactual water uses, they were mostly limited to eliciting information about current uses and then fixing and protecting those. California allocated *appropriative water rights*[5] by asking all water users to report their season of diversion, total quantity and rate of diversion, point of diversion, location of use, type of use, and when they began diverting water (Hanemann et al. 2015, 53). If all water users contin-

3. At a larger scale, even water lost to evaporation/transpiration is not truly lost; it just reenters the global water cycle at another point (Rockström et al. 2023).

4. This was true for much of the American West, but we focus on California here.

5. The State Water Commission began regulating appropriative water rights in 1914. Users who claimed water before the state assumed legal control in 1914 are said to have *pre-1914* rights. These rights are senior to those rights allocated after 1914. During periods of drought, pre-1914 senior rights holders are entitled to divert their full quantity, while the remaining junior users face curtailments (Hanemann et al. 2015). Pre-1914 appropriative rights are also not subject to the same regulatory scrutiny.

ued the same patterns in how they were diverting and using water, then the viability of the system could be assured even with their limited understanding of the hydrological details. In drought years, the appropriative system adopted a simple allocation rule: the "first in time, first in right" principle that allocated water property rights in full, in order of seniority—the year in which diversions began (Hanemann et al. 2015, 53). While such a system makes it easier to monitor and enforce rights, it limits shifting water in drought years to more valuable uses and limits users' abilities to share risk.

To illustrate interdependencies from return flows, consider the following example motivated by the competing uses of surface water between agricultural, urban, and environmental uses. Consider a single stream that provides surface water to three appropriative right holders and the environment. In a wet year, the stream is fed annually by 80 thousand acre-feet[6] (taf) of surface water. Alice Irrigation District diverts 48 taf annually at the top of the stream and began doing so in 1895. In 1910 near the bottom of the steam, Farmer Bob began diverting 18 taf each year to irrigate his land. Charlie City started diverting 24 taf in 1924 in the middle of the stream. Lastly, every year 8 taf of water flows out into the ocean providing vital ecosystem services that mediate saltwater intrusion and sustain endangered fish species.

Adding up the varying water uses, the 98 taf that is allocated every year appears to exceed the supply of 80 taf. However, recall that water systems reuse water, with return flows from upstream uses augmenting downstream supply. When Alice diverts and applies 48 taf on her crops, only 36 taf is lost through evapotranspiration and 12 taf returns to the stream. We will say that Alice has a *consumptive share* of 0.75 and that Bob, who unlike Alice uses flood irrigation instead of drip irrigation, has a consumptive share of 0.67, returning 6 taf to the system. Charlie City returns nothing to the system, instead disposing of treated wastewater directly into the ocean. With the reuse of 18 taf of return flow, all property rights and environmental uses are supported by the yearly flow of 80 taf.

Suppose that in a drought year, the stream will only see 56 taf. Figure 3.1 depicts how water is allocated in order of seniority.[7] Alice diverts her full claim of 48 taf, returning 12 taf. To ensure that Bob gets his allocation, Charlie is permitted to divert only 2 taf. Bob then diverts his full 18 taf right and returns 6 taf which undersupplies the environmental services relative to the wet year supply.[8]

6. An acre-foot is the standard measurement of stocks of water and is the amount of water it takes to cover an acre with a foot of water. Surface water is also measured as a flow in cubic-feet per second (cfs). For simplicity in this example we assume that water flows, is diverted, and returns at some constant rate throughout the year.

7. Seniority need not accord with stream order, though this is often the case in California (Hanemann et al. 2015).

8. It is possible for environmental water to be guaranteed in the appropriative water right system as an *in-stream use* (Chong and Sunding 2006). If the seniority of the appropriative water right superseded other rights in the stream, the in-stream environmental services would

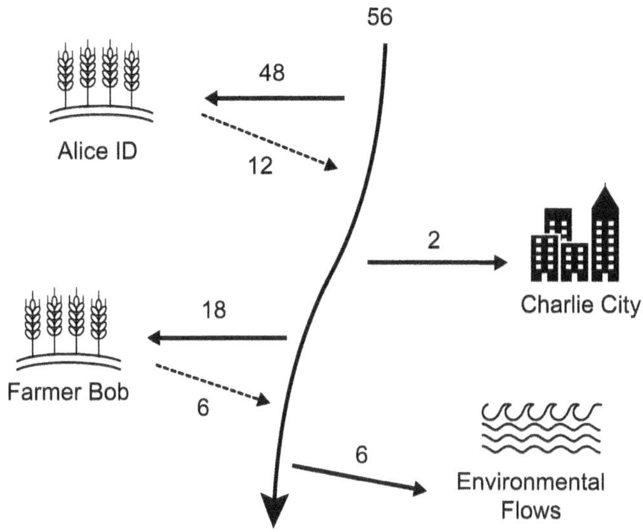

Fig. 3.1 Drought water allocations under an appropriative system

This simple example demonstrates the general principles of allocating water resources with appropriative property rights. Importantly, sustaining all the uses of water along the stream required the reuse of return flows in the system. This becomes especially important when users try to improve the drought year allocation by trading surface water between themselves. For example (see figure 3.2), suppose that in this drought year, Charlie City buys 12 taf from Alice and now diverts 14 taf. Alice, left with 36 taf, diverts her full claim and returns only 9 taf downstream. Unable to receive his full allocation, Bob can only divert 15 taf and returns 5 taf to the system—further draining environmental supplies. Interdependent surface water rights mean that, though beneficial to Charlie and Alice, this transaction infringes on other users and stream dependents.

If return flow dependence is not properly accounted for, trade changes uses in a way that creates externalities. Water reallocation that is beneficial during drought to the two traders can harm third parties that did not agree to the reallocation. Environmental water needs may be protected or may be the residual claimant of return flows. If they are not protected, these rights must compete with those of water right owners with strong economic incentives to protect their surface water claims (Chong and Sunding 2006, 253).

Despite its seeming complexity, our example is simplified compared to reality, because it depicts the structure of return flows as fixed and exog-

be guaranteed during the drought. In this example, we treat environmental water as not held in a specific property right.

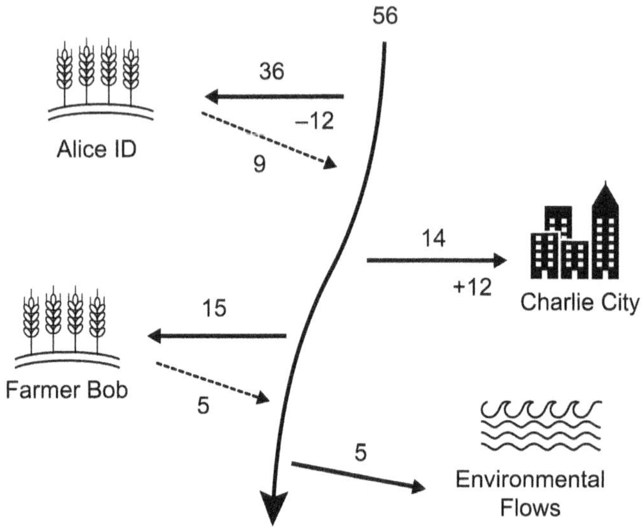

Fig. 3.2 Drought water reallocations with transfers under an appropriative system

enous, omitting various influences and water use decisions. In reality, consumptive shares and the externalities they imply can vary with temperature, crop choice, and irrigation technologies (Ward and Pulido-Velazquez 2008). If Alice or Bob chooses to grow different crops, their return flows could decrease, leaving someone downstream with less water. If Bob invested in drip irrigation, he may now have a consumptive share like Alice and return far less to the system. If Alice changed where she irrigated, the return flow could occur in a different season or to a different watercourse altogether. If there was a very hot season, evapotranspiration (evaporation plus plants' loss of water through their leaves) would increase and both Alice and Bob would consume more than the typical year.

Farmers frequently switch their portfolio of crops and invest in more efficient irrigation technologies (Huffaker and Whittlesey 2000), and as the climate crisis intensifies, weather patterns vary more and more across years (Rafey 2023). It would be hard to monitor all the relevant decisions made by water users, incorporate uncertain climatic variables, and guarantee that no user will be affected by the choices of upstream diverters, but property rights do not need to perfectly eliminate all externalities. Society can choose which physical interdependencies are recognized in property rights, understanding that this decision affects transaction costs. The optimal choice depends on the cost of measurement and surveillance and also on the complexity of water interdependence (Leonard et al. 2019).

The externalities from surface water allocation apply not only to the physical flow of water but also to local economic entities that depend on irrigation. In many agricultural communities throughout California, the local economy is driven by agricultural production which is in turn dependent on irrigation. If farmers decided to sell water and fallow their crops, the local labor market would lose jobs, companies supplying seeds, fertilizer, and farming equipment would lose sales, and in turn, other economic activity in the local economy like restaurants, movie theaters, etc. would lose business that was supported by the lost laborers/income.

These *pecuniary externalities* are not new to economists (Young 1986, 1147; Greenwald and Stiglitz 1986), however, the degree of dependence of agricultural communities on water resources raises its interest for policymakers. In fact, California's approval of water transfers includes an evaluation of the local economic impacts of a transfer. If a voluntary transfer between a buyer and seller is deemed too destructive to the seller's local economy, the transfer can be blocked by the regulators (Hanemann et al. 2015, 57). This concern for the local economic impact of water reallocation is motivated by the history of large transfers from agricultural communities to urban areas, none more notorious than the *water wars* between Los Angeles and the Owens Valley:

> In the early 20th century, Los Angeles purchased land and water rights in the Owens Valley to export the water to L.A. While L.A. handsomely rewarded most of the selling farmers, the resulting water transfer killed what was a thriving farming community and generated heated local protests. Since then, communities with marginal agricultural economies that use significant water have feared that water markets could siphon off their water for urban use, leaving the selling farmers economically better off but the local community to slowly die. (Thompson 2023)

Agricultural communities look to the Owens Valley experience as a warning against participation in water marketing, and this mentality contributes to additional regulatory and cultural barriers to trade. If transitional assistance had been made to compensate for local economic externalities, valuable water reallocation might be accomplished while maintaining trust in market mechanisms (Howe et al. 1990). Much work has been done to evaluate the magnitude of these pecuniary externalities. Zhang and Hatchett (1998) found an impact of $170,000 of net income loss and eight job losses per thousand AF traded out of the Central Valley. Other work suggests that "transfers involving less than a quarter of a region's water supply are unlikely to have a meaningful economic impact on the region" (Howitt 1994). While these estimates help inform state regulation of water transfers, most of the protection of communal dependence on surface water is adjudicated by irrigation districts.

Further complicating hopes for efficient water reallocation is that most farmers do not have their own appropriative water rights, which instead are allocated water by their irrigation district. Irrigation districts often have a portfolio of appropriative water rights, along with other entitlements, which they then distribute to their member irrigators.[9] Irrigation districts are managed by a board of directors elected by the members of or citizens within the district (Hanemann et al. 2015, 57). While individual farmers may find it profitable to sell their surface water to higher-value buyers, only the irrigation district typically is granted the power to sell water. Irrigation district board members caring about re-election may be wary of selling surface water for a variety of reasons, including the effect on the price of water, the potential loss of political power as the size of the water allocation is diminished, and pecuniary externalities on other voters in the water district (Thompson 1993). While irrigation districts may, in principle, contribute to efficiency by internalizing the pecuniary externality associated with transfers, many believe that the districts are too aggressive in their disruption of water reallocation (Womble and Hanemann 2020; Regnacq et al. 2016).

Evaluating a potential water transfer's local economic impact can be expensive and hard to measure, making it difficult to incorporate pecuniary externalities in a benefit-cost analysis. The practical result is that it falls to a complex combination of politically motivated stakeholders at various levels of governance to make binary decisions about the viability of any proposed water transfer (Womble and Hanemann 2020; Rosen and Sexton 1993).

Trade frictions in water management are reminiscent of the core market design problems discussed in the introduction. Surface water property rights exhibit a high degree of heterogeneity and extensive physical and economic interdependencies that require multilateral cooperation to achieve efficient allocations. Since the current system does not homogenize rights, internalize externalities, or limit transaction costs, reallocations of surface water do not resemble simple bilateral trades but instead appear more like major acts of diplomacy between several stakeholders.

3.3 Market Design Solutions for Water Property Rights

In this section, we step away from the current legal and regulatory regime and consider a possible endpoint of a change: what surface water property rights and market designs could overcome the structural frictions in water management? In order to promote efficiency through simple bilateral trades, any new arrangements would need to establish clear, tradeable property rights, limit both potential externalities and layers of regulatory approval, and leave the remaining details to market participants. As depicted in the previous section, there are currently important frictions that arise from the need for multilateral coordination to manage hydrological and economic

9. Most commonly irrigation districts allocate water proportional to acreage (Rosen and Sexton 1993).

dependencies. To minimize transaction costs, surface water property rights could be defined more homogeneously, allowing price competition among buyers and sellers to establish a public market price and reduce the space for costly haggling in bilateral transactions. To reduce externalities, property rights could be defined in terms of water consumed, rather than in terms of water diverted. Consumption rights reduce both trading externalities—because a user can sell only by reducing its net use, and externalities associated with users' decisions—because a user who plants a crop or adopts a technology that reduces its net consumption would be able to sell the water it saved. The advantages of homogeneity are particularly well illustrated by the crown jewel of water marketing in the world: the Murray Darling Basin in Australia (Rafey 2023; Hanemann and Young 2020; Turral et al. 2005). Below, we review these ideas more closely.

First, to reduce transaction costs, the heterogeneity of appropriative rights to surface water could be replaced with a homogenous consumptive right. Currently, it is very difficult to compare two different appropriative rights along the many dimensions in which they differ—location of use, purpose of use, seniority (year of first use), season of use, etc. (Thompson 2023, 5). A homogeneous entitlement to water that simply indicates source and quantity (Howe et al. 1986, 442) allows buyers and sellers to base their trades simply on quantity and price.

Second, to spread risk and promote agreement about the use of dams and other water infrastructure, surface rights could be designed to respond flexibly and uniformly to varying hydrological conditions. A system of proportionality, in which consumptive water rights are defined as a percentage of the water available in a given year, is a promising alternative to seniority-based allocation under an appropriative system partly because it creates the homogeneity needed to promote efficient trade (Livingston 1995, 206). Such systems seem to be popular among users who determine their own systems. For example, the State Water Project, Central Valley Project, and most irrigation districts allocate water to their users proportionally. A homogeneous system of rights was also implemented in several states in Australia, where water licenses were replaced with shares that entitle users to a proportion of any allocations made to a defined pool of water (Hanemann and Young 2020, Young 2014). This structure builds flexibility into the system, reduces the uncertainty faced by junior rights holders who are otherwise not guaranteed water in periods of low availability, and tends to homogenize the interests of users in decisions about investments in water storage facilities and about how much water to store or release in or from reservoirs each year.

This is still imperfect, because the consumption model does not exactly correspond to the facts of hydrology. Consumption-based property rights still leave room for hydrological externalities, so the market design could utilize *ex ante* adjudication about what trades are available between any pair of buyers and sellers or *ex post* compensation for economic damages, or both.[10] An *ex ante* adjudication system could include an easy-to-use public online platform, on which buyers and sellers input their locations of use and immediately learn the amount of water that can be traded (Raffensperger and Milke 2017; Regnacq et al. 2016; Colby et al. 2021).

There are two ways that something like this could be accomplished. First, the consumptive use could be clearly indicated in the water entitlement so that buyers know exactly how much net use is available from each seller (Johnson et al. 1981). Historically, granular information about the consumptive use of water has been costly to obtain. However, technological innovation in satellite imagery, like the OpenET platform, and increasingly sophisticated hydrological models have made it possible to continuously evaluate consumptive use at little cost (Melton et al. 2022; Thompson 2023).[11] Water entitlements could be legally attached to an account in the measurement system that automatically determines the consumptive use available for trade.

An alternative solution, adopted by the Murray-Darling Basin in Australia, provides more exchangeability among water entitlements by enforcing *exchange rates* across regions in the basin (Hanemann and Young 2020). When water is sold between hydrological regions, there is a fixed rate at which the water available for purchase is reduced. All hydrological externalities from inter-region transfers would be approximated for the whole region by a single factor. In this case, transaction costs and heterogeneity are significantly reduced as buyers and sellers need to know only their respective regions to determine how much water is available for transfer.

In both cases, regulatory management of hydrological externalities is approved *ex ante* to make clear and accessible to buyers and sellers what trading opportunities are available (Regnacq et al. 2016). The difference between these choices depends critically on the accuracy and reliability of hydrological measurement. If technology is too constrained for granular consumptive use determination, the exchange rate solution of the Murray-Darling Basin may be more desirable. However, entitlement-specific consumptive use measurement would better represent the space of trades that are nearly externality free.

If regionally homogenous consumptive shares are not a sufficiently good statistic for hydrological externalities and detailed information is too inaccurate or costly, the market could instead consider *ex post* compensation for economic externalities. Each water transfer could be subject to a tax that contributes to a general fund for injured third parties (Thompson 2023, 12).

10. Environmental damages may be more difficult to correct with ex post compensation, so ex ante solutions may be chosen for these.

11. While satellite remote sensing has been proposed as a viable solution to fill widespread gaps in monitoring of irrigation water use, the relative accuracy of different satellite-based technologies remains poorly understood, with evidence of large uncertainties when water use estimates are validated against in situ irrigation data (Foster et al. 2020).

While a transaction tax would introduce a wedge, this tax would be designed to efficiently internalize potential externalities and would be determined at the beginning of the water year, so that additional transaction costs would not be introduced for regulatory approval. The most important preconditions for such a system to succeed would be comprehensive hydrological monitoring and modeling so that lost water downstream can be attributed to water transfers rather than the normal happenings of a watershed (Colby 1990, 1190). If it was easy for users to claim harm when it was not the fault of an upstream trade, this system could unravel quickly.

The mix of mitigations between *ex post* compensation and *ex ante* adjudication, as with the choice of how to adjudicate consumptive use, will depend critically on the type of externality and the accuracy and cost of measurement. It is likely that different regions will be better served by different methods, so in this paper, we do not try to identify any best system to manage hydrological externalities. However, technological innovation has come a long way since the water management of the early 20th century, and solutions to these physical externalities are now available to support a new water market design.

Communal dependence on water and the political economy of water transfers highlight fundamental economic questions about governing the commons (Ostrom 2015). In other markets, gains from trade clearly dominate relatively small pecuniary externalities, but water is so crucial to both human consumption and irrigation that broadly efficient reallocation of water may cause serious harm to local communities (Thompson 2023; Chong and Sunding 2006; Livingston 1995). The current system to protect communities against harmful trading by requiring multilateral coordination between individual farmers and irrigation district board members on a case-by-case basis greatly increases transaction costs and does not effectively balance the gains from trade and potential economic externalities (Womble and Hanemann 2020; Regnacq et al. 2016).

To handle such concerns in the Murray-Darling Basin in Australia, farmers are subject to *exit fees* to sell water outside of their home irrigation districts. Exit fees, which are determined by the irrigation districts prior to the season, are uniform across trades and capped to not be unduly high (Hanemann and Young 2020, 120–21). This allows buyers to compensate agricultural communities through the irrigation district for perceived harm without requiring renegotiation or high transaction costs. Trading pairs have ex ante approval of the terms and conditions of a water transfer, greatly reducing transaction costs and the heterogeneity across particular trades.

One concern with such a solution is that there is not perfect pass-through of exit fees collected from the irrigation district to affected individuals. The exit fee mechanism could alternatively be implemented as a local tax on water exports that is redistributed to the residents. For example, some water trades in Arizona are subject to such a tax so that "the state government can adjust local government funding to account for water trade effects" (Chong and Sunding 2006). Additionally, since empirical work has suggested that the economic impact of a water transfer is small up to a quarter of a region's water supply, the rules of trade could bound the total amount of water that can be exported[12] (Howitt 1994).

A more aggressive policy would prevent irrigation districts from inappropriately blocking transfers by applying the *beneficial use doctrine.* Appropriative water rights in California and the American West are held in the public trust, and rights holders only have the usufructuary right to divert water for some "beneficial" use—a term that is flexibly defined (Thompson 2023). California could decide that an irrigation district cannot block the sale of water out of a district if the price is sufficiently higher than the district's price, as water being inefficiently withheld is not a beneficial use. Such a principle was invoked in a major transfer between the Imperial Irrigation District and San Diego related to the inefficient flood irrigation used in the district (Thompson et al. 2018). While such a policy tool might break through irrigation district barriers, it would certainly be subjected to a political battle.

Regardless of the exact mechanism, the design principle is clear. In order for a trading mechanism to avoid future situations like Owens Valley, irrigation districts and local communities would need to determine clear and uniform rules for how individual water right holders can transfer water out of the region. Buyers and sellers will struggle to reallocate water productively if they must renegotiate every potential trade with every potential affected group. If the magnitude of perceived economic harm is understood *ex ante* and managed consistently, bilateral agreements can be promoted by largely eliminating any uncertainty over how costly trade will be or whether trade will even be approved.

The potential solutions to both hydrological and economic externalities embed a few central themes. First, trading frictions are greatly reduced when water rights specify, without trade-by-trade negotiation or adjudication, how claims among the rights holder, potential buyer, and local communities are to be resolved. Establishing the explicit rules of trade will reduce transaction costs and create security in the water management system, as is necessary for low-conflict and voluntary market participation. With the market environment known, many willing bilateral trading pairs can transfer water according to the rules and guide water allocation toward efficiency.

3.4 Property Rights in Transition

The preceding discussion about how trade frictions create barriers to water markets and how rights systems can mitigate these frictions have been

12. Australia has a nationwide cap on transfers out of regions to address this concern (Chong and Sunding 2006).

widely discussed (Young 1986; Leonard et al. 2019; Thompson 2023). While most water economists agree that not only surface water rights reform is needed but also many details of the desired structure, change has still been stymied both because there is no realistic transition plan and because of the daunting administrative costs of such a change.

In the United States, water rights are constitutionally protected property: they cannot be seized or unfairly changed by a government entity without fair compensation (Sax 1990, 4). Two fundamental barriers to a full water property right transition are the enormous number of stakeholders with protected rights that would need to agree to a new system and the critical interdependencies among the existing rights. These barriers do not just make decentralized trade difficult but also create challenges to coordinated change.

Similar issues have been faced before in the use of radio spectrum, when the regulator's goal was to reduce the use of airwaves for television broadcast in order to make more capacity available for broadband communications and to impose fewer restrictions on use of those rights. One barrier to change was that each TV broadcaster had the right to be free of interference from other uses. TV broadcast and broadband cannot operate on adjacent frequencies without causing mutual interference, which makes any simple bilateral transaction between companies in the two industries useless. And, to avoid radio interference, there must always be a guard band between the two different uses, in which neither TV broadcast nor mobile broadband operates, so avoiding waste required ensuring that the total size of any guard bands is small. Although the challenges of change were great, the benefits were also clear: explosive growth in the demand for broadband services combined with the decline in over-the-air viewing as some 90 percent of television viewers had switched to using cable, satellite, or internet, made it obvious that changing the frequency allocations could unlock enormous value. The challenge was to find a way to use that value to convince and compensate those who would need to relinquish some rights.

A US presidential commission initiated the solution to this problem, proposing in the 2010 National Broadband Plan to run a "Broadcast Incentive Auction" in which broadcasters would be incentivized to surrender their rights voluntarily in exchange for cash. Broadcasters who chose not to sell their rights in the auction would retain a right to broadcast over the air but might be required to shift to a different broadcast channel. That meant the channels reassigned for broadband could be made contiguous and uniform across the United States and Canada, minimizing spectrum wasted on guard bands. Congressional legislation passed in 2012 authorized the Federal Communications Commission to run the auction. Milgrom's firm, Auctionomics, designed the process and provided critical software to execute it.

Planning for a successful Broadcast Incentive Auction entailed a series of steps. Once legal authorization was established, the next step was the *interference study*, which determined potential interference among broadcasters. This study used a mixture of measurement and modeling to create a map of the United States divided into one-kilometer square pixels and, for each pixel, an assessment of the signal strength of each broadcast location on each channel at the center of that pixel. The FCC determined the maximum allowable externality: channel assignments for eligible stations would be made so that no station interfered with more than 0.5 percent of the population served by another station.

Next, the FCC needed to determine which station rights had to be protected. For example, certain low-power broadcasters operating in otherwise unused frequencies had secondary licenses that were not entitled to protection or compensation in case their operations were interrupted.

There were technical challenges, too. Since the final allocation entailed finding acceptable channel assignments for all continuing stations, the FCC also needed fast algorithms that would run during the auction to check whether and how a given set of stations could be feasibly assigned to the given set of channels. During the auction that followed, the FCC sought to buy enough broadcast rights to allow the remaining stations to broadcast without interference in a specific, reduced set of channels. And, the FCC needed to decide, based on bids by both broadcasters and broadband users, how many channels to devote to broadcast TV and which frequencies to make available for broadband communications.

Although the preceding steps were technically complicated, the auction rules would need to be simple to avoid discouraging bidders from participating. New auction procedures were invented to make bidding simple and understandable, especially for broadcasters, while still guaranteeing that the resulting channel assignments would be technically feasible and nearly efficient, and could be purchased at prices that would be covered by broadband users' bids.[13]

The Broadcast Incentive Auction, which ran in 2016–17, was widely hailed as a success. When the dust had settled, the process had paid $10 billion to broadcasters who voluntarily sold their rights, raised $20 billion from companies that bought broadband licenses, and caused 70 MHz of new spectrum capacity to become available for wireless broadband communications.

There may be predictions that water users would resist a similar process,[14] echoing the skepticism expressed about the Broadcast Incentive Auction. Some broadcasters were public television stations or religious broadcasters whose missions, it was said, would not allow them to sell broadcast rights for cash. Yet the high prices offered for spectrum rights in big cities convinced even these mission-based broadcasters to participate. In Chicago, a

13. The new class of auctions designed for this purpose and their theoretical properties are both described in Milgrom and Segal (2020).

14. Leonard et al. (2019) and Colby et al. (2021) discuss water users' reluctance to participate in these mechanisms due to distrust of regulators.

religious broadcaster swapped its UHF station for a VHF station—a modest downgrade—plus hundreds of millions of dollars that it could use for its other outreach operations. In San Francisco, the public television network KQED that owned rights to use three broadcast channels discovered that by upgrading its technology, it could serve 99 percent of its viewers using just two channels, allowing it to sell the third channel for $95 million. It added those proceeds to its endowment to secure its future operations. In the end, the auction attracted ample participation from broadcasters and the sale of broadband rights generated more than enough revenue to pay them, with funds left over for the US Treasury.

A Water Incentive Auction is no less complicated than the Broadcast Incentive Auction, but can incorporate lessons that were learned. Both kinds of incentive auctions needed to be voluntary processes that would incentivize right holders to participate and convert one kind of right into a different kind. In the Broadcast Incentive Auction, TV broadcast rights were converted into a contiguous set of broadband rights covering the United States and Canada. Even if broadband companies could mitigate interference problems, the old individual broadcast rights would still be nearly useless to them. The engineering of broadcast networks requires using a wide band of contiguous frequencies over a large geographic area. So, for example, acquiring channels 47, 49, and 51 is very different from acquiring channels 46–48. Similarly, acquiring rights to use different frequencies in nearby cities is different from acquiring rights to use the same frequencies nationwide. Adjusting interference protections and "repacking" the remaining broadcasters—moving them onto new, equally usable channels—was a crucial part of the process.

We analyze a potential Water Incentive Auction that allows, but does not require, current appropriative property right holders to convert their limited diversion rights to the optimal endpoint discussed in the previous section—secure, transferable, homogenous, proportional, consumptive property rights that manage both hydrological and economic externalities with ex ante mitigation rules and ex post recourse for compensation.

The mechanism we consider constructs new water rights out of the pool of participating appropriative property rights. To encourage participation and preserve an entitlement that enjoys the security of very senior appropriative rights, the pool of water acquired by the mechanism might divide new water rights into three classes—high, medium, and low priority.[15] Depending on the total water flow each season, the total quantity of water within each class will adjust with higher priority classes receiving relatively more in drought years. Individual entitlements within a class will endow the right holder with a proportion of the class's total volume.

15. Water management in the Murray-Darling basin is an example of such a system, which offers both high and low priority entitlements.

Since priority classes are coarser than the current right-specific level of seniority, each trade in a class provides a simple benchmark for valuing subsequent trades. In a given year, users can lease the quantity of water determined by their class of rights to any other user. Right holders may also be able to make permanent transfers of their entitlement. While a water right's class will determine the total quantity that year, users would be able to trade across priority classes. Those that do not wish to participate will still be entitled to the water determined by current appropriative rights. However, non-participants will not enjoy the benefits of the new system and instead face the same restricted regime that does not allow changes in season, location of use, point of diversion or type of use. Non-participants will face the same awkward administrative process for transfers and continue to suffer limited adaptation to drought and illiquidity of their water rights, which prevent them from being used as security for loans. In contrast, holders of the new entitlements would be allowed to use those in new ways, such as selling the rights, storing the water in a reservoir, or offering the rights as security for a bank loan. Many users would likely find the new entitlement to be more valuable than their traditional rights even without additional compensation.

The major steps needed for a successful Surface Water Incentive Auction are similar to those that were required for the broadcast auction.

Once appropriate legal authorities are established, the crucial first step would be a hydrological study, playing a role similar to the interference study for the Broadcast Incentive Auction. Using a mix of measurement and modeling, the study would estimate how much water use in one area affects water supply in other areas. This hydrological study would determine both how the consumptive use of different users is to be determined to reduce local return flow externalities and the exchange rates between regions to recognize losses when water is transported. This hydrological model will also determine how priority classes will adjust to drought and will help to manage trade so that non-participating rights are largely unaffected. Property rights would entitle a user to a fixed consumptive quantity, but given the accuracy and cost of hydrological modeling, there are many different methods of consumptive monitoring that could be implemented (Colby et al. 2021).

For consumption rights to be effective, consumption needs to be measured, and satellite technology is one promising way to do that. At the end of the season, if property right holders consume more or less than their right, they could be compensated or charged for their deviation. Alternatively, farmers may be asked to report their crop choices before the irrigation season and their consumptive entitlement must match the expected evapotranspirative water needs for those crops in their region (Colby et al. 2021). In the first case, less oversight is required and farmers have more intertemporal flexibility for crop choice, but farmers are subject to potential costs related to overconsumption. In the latter, farmers are assured that their crop choices at the beginning of the season will not face punishment, but they must report and decide crop choices which the state must monitor, and if estimates are wrong, there is no recourse to reward/punish consumptive efficiency of the farmer.

Ultimately, the choice of method for determining consumptive use will depend on the accuracy of hydrological modeling, the political will for different kinds of surveillance, and the magnitude of externalities that can be ignored. In the TV interference study, a small level of interference was deemed admissible; in the water setting, a small level of return flow externalities could similarly be allowed.

One challenge for a Water Incentive Auction that is different from the broadcast model is that the pecuniary externalities are much larger. The economies of farming communities depend on water, making it important to decide about limits or taxes on out-of-region transfers. It may be unrealistic to ensure that all economic externalities will be addressed. Just as some low-powered broadcasters lost historical access without compensation, some water transfers might be allowed without compensation.

It is possible that new water consumption rights will be so attractive that many users would choose voluntarily to convert to those. One way to start the conversion process quickly and at low cost would be for the government to run a procurement auction (a "reverse" auction) offering to pay the first consumers who agree to convert their rights. The designer can create new rights out of the set of old rights successfully purchased in the auction. The creation of consumptive rights out of the pool of purchased legacy rights will involve estimates, so there may need to be an appeal procedure in which some non-participants claim that their rights have been harmed by the conversion of others. Since any losses suffered by a plaintiff would consist of reduced consumption, which could be remedied by purchases of consumption rights to water at market prices, the value of damages will be easy to estimate. If an appeals system is needed, it might be funded by a fee charged on water transactions.

Encouraging participation will be important for creating a robust new system of rights. Attracting participation from more appropriative rights increases the amount of water used to construct new rights which will make it easier to construct priority classes and protect non-participating rights. Because widespread participation has so many benefits, another possibility, similar to the Broadcast Incentive Auction, would include both forward and reverse auctions. In a forward auction, new water rights will be sold to willing buyers. Bidders in the forward auction might include growing cities that—seeking to secure future water supplies—will offer high prices that would imply significant compensation for sellers participating in the reverse auction. The availability of revenue from the forward auction would motivate participation by sellers who can find the least painful ways to reduce their water use. Current users who seek to convert their rights without significant changes to their operations would be permitted and encouraged to make "swap" bids, in which they act simultaneously as buyers and sellers in the auction (Milgrom 2007). Additional options could also be included to make participation safe and easy for swappers who seek the advantages of converting to the new rights without actually selling their rights.

The improved design of water rights makes trading simpler and would allow buyers and sellers to make more beneficial trades than in the current regime. With an active water market, the price of water would also help to inform regulation of users who decline to convert their rights. Traditional appropriative water rights require that any diverted water must be put to a "beneficial use," which is a standard that can be reset over time, using the market price as an objective standard. Holders of traditional rights whose uses are far less valuable than market prices could be subject to challenges that their uses are not beneficial.

3.5 Conclusion

The theory and practice of market design has evolved over its 25-year history. It is no longer just about algorithms but should now include rethinking property rights. Details of the rights specifications can affect both the ease of trade and the likelihood of externalities, as when a water transfer from a farm to a city reduces return flows to local aquifers and streams, harming other users. Trading can cause externalities that can involve many users, but giving veto power to too many users based on uncertain assessments about externalities, as in the current California regulatory regime, results in very high transaction costs and too little trade.

In this paper, we analyze some possible structures of property rights and a framework for promoting a transition. Replacing diversion rights with consumption rights would reduce externalities from changing uses of water and could be paired with reduced regulations, promoting beneficial trades and limiting negative externalities. There is a promising path to a voluntary transition, in which no protected user has to surrender their existing rights. And just as in the Broadcast Incentive Auction, a Water Incentive Auction could unlock enormous value, encourage ample participation, and promote much more efficient allocations.

References

Chong, H., and D. Sunding. 2006. "Water Markets and Trading." *Annual Review of Environment and Resources* 31(1): 239–64.

Coase, R. H. 1959. "The Federal Communications Commission." *Journal of Law and Economics* 2: 1–40.

Coase, R. H. 1960. "The Problem of Social Cost." *Journal of Law and Economics* 3: 1–44. http://www.jstor.org/stable/724810.
Colby, B. 1990. "Transactions Costs and Efficiency in Western Water Allocation." *American Journal of Agricultural Economics* 72(5): 1184–192. https://www.jstor.org/stable/1242530.
Colby, B., A. Walker, and M. O'Donnell. 2021. "Water Auctions: Design, Implementation, and Evaluation." Working Paper, Department of Agricultural and Resource Economics, The University of Arizona.
Dworczak, P., and E. Muir. 2023. "A Mechanism-Design Approach to Property Rights." Working Paper.
Foster, T., T. Mieno, and N. Brozović. 2020. "Satellite-Based Monitoring of Irrigation Water Use: Assessing Measurement Errors and Their Implications for Agricultural Water Management Policy." *Water Resources Research* 56(11): 1–19.
Greenwald, B. C., and J. E. Stiglitz. 1986. "Externalities in Economies with Imperfect Information and Incomplete Markets." *Quarterly Journal of Economics* 101(2): 229–64.
Hagerty, N. 2024. "Transaction costs and the gains from trade in water markets." Working Paper. Montana State University.
Hanemann, W. M. 2005. "The Economic Conception of Water." (No. 1557–2016–132978).
Hanemann, M., C. Dyckman, and D. Park. 2015. "California's Flawed Surface Water Rights." In *Sustainable Water: Challenges and Solutions from California*, edited by Allison Lassiter, 52–82. University of California Press.
Hanemann, M., and M. Young. 2020. "Water Rights Reform and Water Marketing: Australia vs the US West." *Oxford Review of Economic Policy* 36(1): 108–31. https://doi.org/10.1093/oxrep/grz037.
Heller, Michael A. 1998. "The Tragedy of the Anticommons: Property in the Transition from Marx to Markets." *Harvard Law Review* 111(3): 621–88. https://doi.org/10.2307/1342203.
Howe, C., J. Lazo, and K. Weber. 1990. "The Economic Impacts of Agriculture-to-Urban Water Transfers on the Area of Origin: A Case Study of the Arkansas River Valley in Colorado." *American Journal of Agricultural Economics* 72(5): 1200–1204. https://www.jstor.org/stable/1242532.
Howe, C., D. Schurmeier, and W. D. Shaw. 1986. "Innovative Approaches to Water Allocation: The Potential for Water Markets." *Water Resources Research* 22(4): 439–45.
Howitt, Richard E. 1994. "Empirical analysis of water market institutions: The 1991 California water market." *Resource and energy economics* 16(4): 357–371.
Huffaker, R., and N. Whittlesey. 2000. "The Allocative Efficiency and Conservation Potential of Water Laws Encouraging Investments in On-Farm Irrigation Technology." *Agricultural Economics* 24(1): 47–60.
Johnson, Ronald N., Micha Gisser, and Michael Werner. 1981. "The definition of a surface water right and transferability." *Journal of Law and Economics* 24(2): 273–288.
Kashner, Z. 2023. "Location Choice and Local Control of Wind Farms." Working Paper.
Leonard, B., C. Costello, and G. Libecap. 2019. "Expanding Water Markets in the Western United States: Barriers and Lessons from Other Natural Resource Markets." *Review of Environmental Economics and Policy* 13(1): 43–61.
Livingston, M. 1995. "Designing Water Institutions: Market Failures and Institutional Response." *Water Resources Management* 9: 203–20.

Melton, Forrest S., Justin Huntington, Robyn Grimm, Jamie Herring, Maurice Hall, Dana Rollison, Tyler Erickson, Richard Allen, Martha Anderson, Joshua B. Fisher, Ayse Kilic, Gabriel B. Senay, John Volk, Christopher Hain, Lee Johnson, Anderson Ruhoff, Philip Blankenau, Matt Bromley, Will Carrara, Britta Daudert, Conor Doherty, Christian Dunkerly, MacKenzie Friedrichs, Alberto Guzman, Gregory Halverson, Jody Hansen, Jordan Harding, Yanghui Kang, David Ketchum, Blake Minor, Charles Morton, Samuel Ortega-Salazar, Thomas Ott, Mutlu Ozdogan, Peter M. ReVelle, Mitch Schull, Carlos Wang, Yun Yang, and Ray G. Anderson. 2022. "OpenET: Filling a Critical Data Gap in Water Management for the Western United States." *Journal of the American Water Resources Association* 58(6): 971–94. https://doi.org/10.1111/1752-1688.12956.

Milgrom, P. 2007. "Package Auctions and Package Exchanges." *Econometrica* 75(4): 935–66.

Milgrom, P., and I. Segal. 2020. "Clock Auctions and Radio Spectrum Reallocation." *Journal of Political Economy* 128(1): 1–31.

Ostrom, E. 2015. *Governing the Commons: The Evolution of Institutions for Collective Action.* Cambridge University Press. https://doi.org/10.1017/CBO9781316423936.

Rafey, W. 2023. "Droughts, Deluges, and (River) Diversions: Valuing Market-Based Water Reallocation." *American Economic Review* 113(2): 430–71.

Raffensperger, J. F., and M. W. Milke. 2017. *Smart Markets for Water Resources: A Manual for Implementation.* Global Issues in Water Policy, vol. 12 Springer Cham.

Regnacq, C., A. Dinar, and E. Hanak. 2016. "The Gravity of Water: Water Trade Frictions in California." *American Journal of Agricultural Economics* 98(5): 1273–1564.

Rockström, J., M. Mazzucato, L. Andersen, S. Fahrländer, and D. Gerten. 2023. "Why We Need a New Economics of Water as a Common Good." *Nature*, March 22. https://www.nature.com/articles/d41586-023-00800-z?utm_source=Nature+Briefingandutm_campaign=2ca64d9ed4-briefing-dy-20230327andutm_medium=emailandutm_t erm=0_c9dfd39373-2ca64d9ed4-46602130.

Rosen, M., and R. Sexton. 1993. "Irrigation Districts and Water Markets: An Application of Cooperative Decision-Making Theory." *Land Economics* 69(1): 39–53.

Roth, A., and X. Xing. 1994. "Jumping the Gun: Imperfections and Institutions Related to the Timing of Market Transactions." *American Economic Review* 84(4): 992–1044.

Sax, J. 1990. "The Constitution, Property Rights and the Future of Water Law." *University of Colorado Law Review* 61(2).

Thompson, B. H., Jr. 1993. "Institutional Perspectives on Water Policy and Markets." *Calif. L. Rev.* 81: 671.

Thompson, B. H., Jr. 2023. "Water Markets Agonistes." In *A Research Agenda for Water Law*, 237–66. Elgar Research Agendas.

Thompson, Barton H. Jr., John D. Leshy, Robert H. Abrams, and Sandra Beth Zellmer. 2018. *Legal Control of Water Resources: Cases and Materials*, ed. 6. West Academic Publishing.

Turral, H. N., T. Etchells, H. M. Malano, H. A. Wijedasa, and P. Taylor. 2005. "Water Trading at the Margin: The Evolution of Water Markets in the Murray-Darling Basin." *Water Resources Research* 1(7): 1–8. https://doi.org/10.1029/2004WR00346.

Ward, F. A., and M. Pulido-Velazquez. 2008. "Water Conservation in Irrigation Can Increase Water Use." *Proceedings of the National Academy of Sciences* 105: 18215–18220.

Water Education Foundation. (n.d.). *Quantification Settlement Agreement.* Water Edu-

cation Foundation. https://www.watereducation.org/aquapedia/quantification-settlement-agreement.
Womble, P., and M. Hanemann. 2020. "Water Markets, Water Courts, and Transaction Costs in Colorado." *Water Resources Research* 56(4).
Young, M. D. 2014. "Designing Water Abstraction Regimes for an Ever-Changing and Ever-Varying Future." *Agricultural Water Management* 145: 32–38. https://doi.org/10.1016/j.agwat.2013.12.002.
Young, R. A. 1986. "Why Are There So Few Transactions Among Water Users?" *American Journal of Agricultural Economics* 68(5): 1143–151. https://doi.org/10.2307/1241865.
Zhang, B., and S. Hatchett. 1998. "Agricultural-to-Instream and Urban Water Transfers in the Central Valley of California: An Economic Reality Check." *American Agricultural Economics Association.*

4 Market Shaping to Combat Climate Change

William Arnesen and Rachel Glennerster

4.1 Market Failures in Innovation

If we are going to make meaningful progress against climate change, both in mitigation and adaptation, we will need innovations in virtually every aspect of our lives: from the crops we grow to the construction of our buildings, from the surface of roads to the vehicles we drive on them, from our landfills to our heating systems.

But the commercial incentives to create and scale up climate-friendly innovations are often incommensurate with the social value of those innovations. Across sectors, innovation has been found to generate extraordinarily high social returns. These large returns suggest that as a society we may be underinvesting in innovation. Innovation provides benefits not just to the innovating firm but also to consumers (through improved product quality and/or lower prices), imitating firms, and to broader society by enabling further technologies and businesses that build on these innovations. For instance, inventions like the Internet, human genome mapping, and the transistor enabled entire industries to be built on the backs of those earlier innovations. In a 2020 working paper, Jones and Summers found the average dollar of R&D spending in the United States yielded between $5 and $20 in social benefits domestically, with the benefits of the marginal dollar spent being similarly high (Jones and Summers 2020).

William Arnesen is a policy manager at the Market Shaping Accelerator at the Becker Friedman Institute for Economics at the University of Chicago.

Rachel Glennerster is president of the Center for Global Development, and a research associate of the National Bureau of Economic Research.

For acknowledgments, sources of research support, and disclosure of the authors' material financial relationships, if any, please see https://www.nber.org/books-and-chapters/new-directions-market-design/market-shaping-combat-climate-change.

Even under a patent system, firms capture a small percentage of the social value of innovation. Nordhaus (2004) found "only a minuscule fraction of the social returns from technological advances over the 1948–2001 period was captured by producers, indicating that most of the benefits of technological change are passed on to consumers rather than captured by producers." There are three main reasons why private investment in climate change innovation may fall below the social optimal: positive externalities, innovation spillovers, and the hold-up problem.

4.2 Externalities

Pollution, for the most part, is an unpriced externality. Except where a carbon or pollution tax fully reflects the social cost of carbon/pollution, firms that emit global warming–inducing particles into the atmosphere do not internalize the cost those emissions impose on the rest of the planet. Pollution reduction is a classic public goods problem. One cannot restrict the benefits of a cleaner atmosphere only to paying customers–the climate is a global public good.

Consider an innovation that produces clean cement (e.g., a cement that embodies half the emission of existing products) at the same price as the going market rate plus some small additional cost. Absent external incentives, private purchasers pursuing their narrow self-interest will opt for the conventional, more polluting cement: the benefits of the innovation are diffused across the rest of the globe, while the costs of purchasing the greener product are borne entirely by the purchaser. Aware of this dynamic, firms may be reluctant to invest in decarbonization innovation for fear that such efforts will struggle to be rewarded in the market.

4.3 Innovation Spillovers

Innovations by one firm can often result in benefits to other firms. A firm has little incentive to spend vast sums on research and development when most of the benefits of such innovation are enjoyed by other firms that do not compensate the original researcher for their efforts. In brief, what are some of the channels of spillovers?

First, there is direct copying. Not all innovations and techniques are patentable, or are cases where patents are unenforceable. Second, there may be demonstration effects to innovation, where one firm's successful innovation raises competitors' estimated probability of the profitability or success of that approach, incentivizing them to adopt or further pursue that method (Mansfield 1961). If a cement producer demonstrates a low-carbon cement plant using an alternative cement chemistry at a competitive price, while their specific processes may be patentable, the public existence of the successful innovation is a signal to other firms that they should consider redoubling their efforts into similar approaches. Third, people leave successful and innovative firms and join other firms (or start their own firms), bringing with them implicit knowledge about what does or does not work (Stoyanov and Zubanov 2012). Fourth, firms can share trade secrets with their business partners and suppliers, diffusing knowledge throughout the broader economic ecosystem (Fadeev 2023). Researchers have identified shared suppliers as an important route for knowledge diffusion, including in the specialized machine tools industry and the semiconductor industry (Rosenberg 1963; Lim 2009). Further, supplier innovation can influence buyers' innovation, and buyers' innovation can influence their supplier's innovations (Isaksson et al. 2016). Suppose a cement plant asks a supplier to produce a specialized piece of machinery that can handle their novel cement chemistry product. Now, when another company orders from the supplier for a similar innovation, the supplier is already competent at producing similar products.

A fifth channel is that new technologies can unlock new economics for other firms that might not have been previously possible. In the context of climate change, improvements in energy efficiency or improvements in energy technologies could lower overall prices, enabling other, more energy-intensive technologies in entirely different domains to become price-competitive in the market. The social surplus enabled by those other technologies was enabled by the initial innovation, but the original innovators are not compensated for those efforts.

These effects can be quite large. Bloom et al. (2013) find that due to spillovers, the social rate of return of innovation is 55 percent, and that "this implies under-investment in R&D, with the socially optimal level being over twice as high as the level of observed R&D."

4.4 Hold-Up Problem

The hold-up problem occurs when firms need to undertake unrecoverable investments, and buyers can exploit those sunk costs to extract value close to marginal costs. Would-be innovators, fearing this dynamic will result in a final price that is insufficient to recoup their sunk costs, shy away from investing large amounts in research and development.

Consider the following example from climate adaptation: heat-tolerant sorghum. Suppose a heat wave induced large-scale crop failure in sub-Saharan Africa. An inventor of heat-tolerant sorghum may face social or explicit government pressure to sell their product at cost (or to give it away), lowering the incentive to invest in inventing such a product.

4.5 Inefficiencies Associated with Patents

Patents do not fully prevent innovations from being copied by others, as discussed above: pharmaceutical companies have for example perfected the science of finding very similar molecules that deliver a similar impact to new drugs (so called "me too" drugs). However, even in cases where innovations are protectable by enforceable patents and spillovers are sufficiently modest, such that there exists a large commercial incentive to invest in innovation, patents do not produce a socially efficient innovation environment and it may still be desirable for the government to intervene. As patents provide a temporary monopoly for the innovator, they typically result in a higher price and lower quantity equilibrium than under a competitive market.

That poses two distinct complications for climate change innovation. First, time is at a premium. Carbon dioxide emitted today, unless removed through some net-negative process, will remain in the atmosphere and will contribute to warming for centuries. A patent system that delays meaningful deployment until the expiration of the patent may thus incur large social costs. Second, the higher prices may exclude low- and middle-income countries from adopting the new technology. Many of the most cost-effective forms of carbon abatement may exist in low- and middle-income countries building new infrastructure and structures for the first time, instead of retrofits that occur in richer countries (Glennerster and Jayachandran 2023). If the delay or higher prices result in pursuing fossil fuel-intensive infrastructure instead, that may create lock-in effects that are difficult to reverse later.

4.6 Market Failures Would Persist Even with Carbon Pricing

A price on carbon, whereby firms would be charged a fee or tax proportional to the amount of CO_2-equivalent emissions they produce that fully reflected the social cost of carbon, would help correct some of the aforementioned market failures. For instance, producing a metric ton of ammonia in the United States produces roughly 2.6 metric tons of greenhouse gas emissions (Liu et al. 2020). Depending on the carbon price, a producer could charge a higher pre-tax amount for a greener ammonia, since they would pay less in carbon fees and taxes. If the carbon price level is set equal to the social cost of carbon, then there would be no market failure stemming from unpriced externalities.

However, innovation for climate change would still be under-incentivized under such a regime because it would not address the other market failures discussed above: specifically, it would not address large knowledge spillovers and the hold-up problem associated with innovation for any green market with a small number of buyers. Third, the aforementioned analysis assumes that the carbon price is equal to the *global* social cost of carbon. Domestic social costs of carbon (the effect of a marginal unit of emissions on the polluting country itself) are often small fractions of the total global cost, even for large countries like the United States. As a result, if the carbon price is only set to the domestic social cost, then there will still be a large, unpriced global externality that results in inefficiently low global innovation.

4.7 General Push vs. Pull

Having established that commercial incentives for climate change innovation development and widespread dissemination are generally incommensurate with their social value, even under the existence of a patent scheme and carbon pricing, what tools do policymakers have to address this problem?

The standard toolkit governments and philanthropic organizations use is "push funding." "Push funding" refers to mechanisms where a sponsor pays for inputs (Kremer and Glennerster 2004). Examples of push funding include grants, equity investments in private firms, research and development tax credits, and public funding for national laboratories and basic science.

One drawback of this approach arises when there is considerable uncertainty from the planner about who to reward with this push funding, or when potential push recipients possess substantial amounts of asymmetric information (Kremer et al. 2020). Suppose the government wished to spend \$500 million for a series of small demonstration plants for near-zero carbon cement plants. As the technology largely does not yet exist, part of that funding would be for research to get the technology to a readiness level such that a small pilot facility could be built. While firms themselves know the state of their own private research and how close they are to being pilot-ready, the government may struggle to identify which plants are more or less promising. In a grant application, firms have every incentive to play up how certain their technological prospects are, making it difficult for the government to distinguish the lemons from the peaches. As a result, the government risks funding projects that are highly likely to fail, or leaving potentially highly likely projects out in the cold, all for want of an efficient means of differentiating the two.

An alternative approach is to use "pull funding." As mentioned previously, pull funding mechanisms increase the incentive to innovate by increasing the returns from innovation. A canonical example of pull funding is to use a prize, but it also encompasses volume guarantees and other "pay for results methods." If well designed, these mechanisms can sidestep the asymmetric information problem as firms will self-select out from participating if they believe their probability of success is too low. After all, they receive funding only if their innovations succeed.

However, different pull mechanisms have different advantages and drawbacks and are suited to combating different climate change challenges. There are also a lot of design details to get right if a pull mechanism is to be effective.

Perhaps the simplest form of pull mechanism is a prize: the sponsors set out the criteria for an innovation and the first one to come up with an innovation that meets the criteria is given a one-off, prespecified monetary reward. Prizes are frequently used, though they are often very small compared to the problem they are seeking to fix. We use the example of a prize for a novel cement chemistry to illustrate some of the economic challenges associated with prizes. To be effective, prizes need to be scaled to the size of the challenge and in practice are often far too small. If the US cement market is \$15 billion and a single cement plant costs \$1 billion, a \$100 million prize for inventing a novel cement chemistry is unlikely to induce many to participate and, most importantly, unlikely to lead to the large investment needed for mass adoption. Moreover, prizes often lack a crucial *market test*. Participants in prizes will optimize for winning the prize reward, which may differ subtly (or even substantially) from the preferences of consumers in hard-to-articulate ways. As a result, one may have to pay out a prize to an innovation that will do little to combat climate change, because the winning product met the terms of the prize but could not gain traction in the market.

It is difficult, or even impossible in some circumstances, to spell out all possible considerations that may be relevant to a consumer in a prize payout criterion without becoming so overly prescriptive as to exclude other promising efforts. For example, suppose one set a prize for decarbonizing cement that specified (a) a maximum threshold for embodied carbon, (b) a maximum price to produce, and (c) minimum performance standards (including performance under stress, heat, acidity, wind, and any other possible factor that may be relevant to the performance of cement). However, it turns out that the winning innovation—that meets all the specified criteria—ends up having such a long cure/set time that it is incompatible with existing construction industry practices and thus struggles to gain adoption. The prize funds were wasted. Conversely, if one did set maximum cure/set times, a prize competition may exclude a hypothetical variant that was vastly superior on global warming impact but whose cure time was slightly above the maximum allowed. The point is not that cure/set times in particular need to be accounted for in a prize, but that there are a wide range of possible factors that are relevant for market adoption but impossible for planners to specify in advance without being overly restrictive. What if the winning innovation requires such specialized expertise to build that it's infeasible at scale? What if the economics are contingent on a rare form of mineral that is uneconomical to mine at scale? One easy way to solve this problem is to use a market test: to link payouts to performance in the market.

One pull mechanism that incorporates a market test is the advance market commitment (AMC). An advance market commitment is a legally binding commitment for the sponsor to pay a subsidy per unit of a good sold into the market for a prespecified quantity, conditional on that good being invented and meeting some minimum performance requirements. One can also condition the AMC subsidy on the innovative firm agreeing to sell the product at a price close to the marginal cost of production even after the prespecified subsidized quantity is exhausted, thus solving the higher price problem from the patent monopoly. As a result, firms self-select into investing in R&D based on their own private information about their probability of success, since they only get paid if they succeed, and the planner does not need to specify every possible relevant criteria in advance.

An example of such an AMC is the pneumococcal AMC, where donors committed $1.5 billion for a pneumococcal conjugate vaccine (PCV) to target a strain of pneumococcus that afflicted children in low- and middle-income countries (Kremer et al. 2020). The AMC paid out a subsidy per dose, conditional on the vaccine meeting certain performance thresholds and the firm capping the price of the vaccine at $3.50/dose (Kremer et al. 2020). While knowing the counterfactual is impossible—one cannot observe a world in which the pneumococcal AMC did not exist—Kremer et al. show that rollout of PCV in eligible countries occurred faster than for a comparable rotavirus vaccine. Had PCV rollout occurred at the same pace as rotavirus vaccine rollout, "67 million fewer children under age 1 would have been immunized, amounting to a loss of over 12 million DALYs (disability adjusted life years)" (Kremer et al. 2020).

There are also conditions where an AMC is not the ideal policy response. Consider the case of accelerating COVID-19 vaccine innovation as was done by Operation Warp Speed in the United States. Athey et al. (2022) concluded that an advance market commitment might be dominated by other tools. One advantage of an AMC is that it results in firms self-selecting out of participation if they believe their probability of success is low. In the case of COVID-19, where the economic costs per day were so great, policymakers might have wanted to encourage even marginal participants to be investing their resources and efforts into developing vaccines. If one wanted to encourage marginal candidates to participate using an AMC, planners would have to set a very high subsidy rate in order to compensate marginal participants for their high risk of failure. However, it would be inefficient to also pay candidates with higher probabilities of success such a high subsidy rate. Moreover, without contracting explicitly on capacity, "the firm's commercial incentives are to save costs by investing in smaller capacity, fulfilling the order over a longer period but generating the same revenue from the contract" (Castillo et al. 2021). As a result, the policy that was chosen involved the government paying for capacity, essentially reimbursing firms for the costs of building out manufacturing capacity for vaccine candidates even prior to FDA approval. This mechanism also helped accelerate the pace of vaccine rollout, as firms had large numbers of doses ready to deploy soon after they received regulatory signoff.

4.8 Climate-Specific Considerations for Pull Mechanisms

Why are pull mechanisms relatively attractive when tackling many of the challenges in climate innovation?

One major reason is the uncertainty about the precise technological pathway to reduce emissions. Consider the case of carbon dioxide removal (CDR). There are many methods by which CO_2 molecules could be permanently removed from the atmosphere. There are engineered solutions such as direct air capture (DAC), where large fans pull in air that contacts with a sorbent, which selectively removes the CO_2 from the rest of the air. Others have attempted to use natural-based processes such as enhanced rock weathering, which entails using basaltic rocks that naturally react and combine with CO_2 in the atmosphere. There are processes as diverse as ocean alkalinity enhancement, direct ocean capture, soil carbon methods, and more.

CDR is not an outlier. For decarbonizing concrete, entrepreneurs have tried introducing waste materials to reduce the amount of polluting cement input that is required. Others are researching using cleaner heat sources, alternative binder chemistries, and even different cement chemistries themselves (such as using calcium silicate directly or magnesia instead of limestone). Within the green hydrogen space, there is a wide range of possible electrolyzer pathways (electrolyzers are machines that separate aqueous solutions into hydrogen and water), including simple alkaline electrolyzers, proton electron membrane electrolyzers, solid oxide electrolyzer, thermoelectric water splitting, photoelectrochemical water splitting, among others. It remains unclear which, if any, of the above pathways will prove to be most cost-effective at scale. Push funding that rewards specific firms pursuing specific techniques risks not only choosing the wrong firm, but also directing industry resources toward techniques that ultimately prove less successful. In a worst-case scenario, supportive infrastructure and industry familiarity evolves around these less successful approaches thanks to government subsidies, locking out more promising approaches from breaking into the market.

Key differences between vaccine development and climate interventions mean the AMC model must be adapted to the climate context. Firstly, the right model depends on the ratio of fixed costs to marginal costs. Vaccines have high research and development costs, high fixed costs of putting in place large manufacturing capacity, but relatively low marginal costs once a vaccine candidate has been approved and a factory built. In contrast, Direct Air Capture for carbon dioxide removal or current electrolysis methods of producing hydrogen use a lot of energy for each marginal unit of production. While there is hope that these marginal costs will decline over time, this is not guaranteed. Second, unlike a novel vaccine, green products often produce end products that are undifferentiated from their conventional competitors, limiting their ability to charge differentiated prices. If the green product has a higher marginal cost to produce than the conventional competitors, it might need to be subsidized indefinitely, unlike the vaccine sample where an AMC that covers the fixed cost of innovation would be sufficient. For instance, ideally, hydrogen produced using renewable energy and electrolyzers produces the identical product (H_2) from hydrogen produced using steam methane reforming. As a result, if the marginal cost of the greener approach exceeds the standard, conventional approach, then some permanent supportive policy might be necessary if the goal is to allow the green approach to remain cost competitive.

A third major differentiator is that one firm may not see innovation all the way from start to finish. In the pharmaceutical industry, financial structures exist such that firms can originate an idea (or take over a biotech company with an idea), examine its suitability, run clinical trials, and then manufacture and distribute the vaccine. For industrial decarbonization the process of identifying a low-carbon process and perfecting it to be produced at low cost at scale may require a series of multiple successive innovations and iterations. Solar is a good example of this. The first production of solar panels was expensive; costs declined and the product became lighter and easier to use only after hundreds or thousands of iterations of both product and manufacturing innovation. Many different firms have been part of this process of innovation, with each firm learning from the innovations of others. The initial innovators did not capture much of the final market. To achieve a cost-competitive net-zero cement, a firm may need to invent a novel cement chemistry, as well as new equipment and machinery to handle that new chemistry. They must then learn how to best optimize these complex plants to minimize cost. Under a simple pull design, a firm that achieves only one of these innovations may not be able to earn a return. For example, a firm that figures out how to make a novel cement chemistry work but cannot figure out how to optimize its manufacturing plant to approximate price parity with non-green cement would receive no reward. If one believes that the rewards of the early innovation (such as inventing the new cement chemistry) will ultimately spill over to another firm that refines the formula and optimizes other processes to ultimately take it over the finish line, then there will be little incentive to invest in that early innovation. A novel approach will be necessary to tailor optimal pull policy to climate change–specific problems: it is insufficient to directly replicate the lessons from pull designs in other domains.

4.9 Application Example: Cement

4.9.1 Background

In this section we attempt to apply these general principles to a specific example, in this case, cement. Cement is the primary input into concrete, which is the second-most-used material in the world after water. Concrete is used in everything from buildings to roads to dams and will all but certainly remain a critical part of the global economy for the near future.

However, cement is also highly pollutive, being responsible for roughly 7 percent of global emissions (US Department of Energy 2023). Cement comes from limestone rock, which is calcium carbonate. This rock is ground up and heated to form a substance called clinker, which is cooled and combined with other materials such as gypsum and raw limestone to form cement, which is in turn combined with water and other aggregates like sand to form concrete. Approximately 90 percent of the carbon intensity of concrete comes from the production of cement, hence the focus on cement itself in this section.

Only about half of the carbon intensity of cement comes from producing the heat and electricity involved in the clinker-making process. The other half comes from the *calcination* process, where the carbon embodied in the calcium carbonate is released as the rock is heated. This aspect of the production process may require unique policy measures. It is not merely a case of decarbonizing the industrial heat and electrical sectors and applying those gains to the cement industry.

There are currently several technologies that can help reduce the carbon intensity of cement from its current level of 0.8–0.9 tons of CO_2 per ton of cement produced (in the United States). One of the most common is to blend in supplementary cementitious materials (SCMs) into the cement, to reduce the amount of clinker used. These SCMs are often waste products, such as fly ash (a by-product of coal production) or slag (a by-product of steel production), or other common materials such as natural pozzolans. The performance of these blends tends to be very similar to standard cement (called Ordinary Portland Cement), with some blends having small differences such as higher strength but longer cure times. With little to no added costs, the Department of Energy estimates that this "low-hanging fruit" can reduce the carbon intensity of cement by up to 30–50 percent. However, achieving deeper decarbonization poses greater challenges still.

There are two other salient features of the cement industry that bear on its unique decarbonization challenges. First, cement is cheap by weight (~$130/ton) but highly expensive to transport. Combined with the extraordinarily high fixed costs in setting up a plant, this results in relatively few cement plants in any given area. There are currently only 96 cement plants in 34 US states (US Geological Survey 2023). As a result, even measures that have low costs per abated ton of CO_2 may lead to a large percentage impact on the price of cement. Second, government procurement drives roughly 50 percent of all demand in the United States, meaning that demand signals and regulatory changes from the government may have outsized effects on the overall market (US Department of Energy 2023).

4.10 Unique Challenges

There are three further features of the cement industry that make decarbonization particularly challenging.

First, capital expenditures to build cement plants are high, up to $1 billion per plant (US Department of Energy 2023). In order to recoup these large upfront expenditures despite thin margins, plants tend to last for on average

36 years (US Department of Energy 2023). Due to safety concerns and inertia in government procurement standards, customers and industry groups are often fairly reluctant to endorse the use of novel cement chemistries or processes (US Department of Energy 2023). The risk that government purchase subsidies may change over time adds to the challenge when plants are so long lived. Given these uncertainties, cement innovators may face high borrowing costs to finance the construction of large plants which will be hard to repay given the low margins in the industry unless there are long-term guaranteed market advantages for clean cement. One way for cement innovators to reduce uncertainties and potential borrowing costs would be to first build a pilot and demonstration plants to demonstrate their product's safety and cost-competitiveness before progressing to full commercial scale.

Second, the overwhelming majority of cement production occurs overseas (~98 percent) in low- and middle-income countries (>95 percent) (US Geological Survey 2023). China alone produces over half the world's cement (US Geological Survey 2023). As a result, merely eliminating cement emissions in the United States will have a limited impact on global emissions. Making global progress will require finding a process that can be cost-competitive enough with ordinary Portland cement that LMICs will ultimately choose to build the greener plants, rather than the OPC plants, even without external incentives. Processes such as adding carbon capture and sequestration (CCS) to existing cement plants may reduce the carbon intensity of that plant, but will necessarily be more expensive than cement without CCS, and are thus unlikely to be a cheap, exportable model for LMICs.

Third, because of the expense associated with transportation, demand for green cement needs to reach a critical mass in a sufficiently geographically small location to justify building a plant. It is not enough to have small amounts of distributed demand throughout the country. Even if the total demand is enough to be larger than the output of a single plant, if that demand is spread out through the 50 states then no one will find it worthwhile to build a plant in any specific location.

Finally, it is worth flagging that standard off-take agreements largely do not exist in the cement industry, as the primary purchasers of cement (ready-mix concrete plants, or RMC) are generally small family businesses that face uncertain and volatile demand in a boom-and-bust construction industry (US Department of Energy 2023). These RMC plants are also largely not big enough to make large, credit-worthy commitments to prospective cement plants.

4.11 Appropriateness of Pull

Despite these challenges, there are several attractive features of pull initiatives.

First, as mentioned, the government purchases roughly half of all cement in the United States (US Department of Energy 2023), meaning that tweaks to government procurement rules could influence large market decisions.

Second, there is considerable uncertainty about which technological approach will ultimately be most successful. There are many different kinds of alternative cement chemistries—magnesia, calcium silicate—and other approaches that use traditional limestone but combine them with novel SCMs, energy efficiency measures, green feedstock, and some CCS to eliminate emissions. It is unclear which approach will prove most promising.

Third, a market test is important. Billions of dollars could be spent on building pilot and demonstration plants, only to produce a cement that cannot be used at scale. Some of these provisions can be tested for—strength, performance under various weather conditions, etc.—but others are more subtle and cannot be evaluated without the overall market. As noted in section 4.7, there are many intersecting factors that may make a cement mixture look good on paper but ultimately of little practical value to the actual market.

We want to end with two other considerations associated with designing a pull mechanism for cement.

First, small incentives are highly unlikely to yield positive results: the returns to prize or pull funding are unlikely to be linear. A demand signal to purchase $10 million worth of cement with embodied carbon 50 percent below current baseline measures is unlikely to result in any new green plants (which can cost up to $1 billion), let alone investments in R&D, pilot and demonstration plants as well. If that money is claimed at all, it is likely to be captured by those who would have taken these steps without the prize/pull funding. A demand signal needs to be both large enough and credibly long-term enough to justify building a 10-figure capex plant with a 30-year lifespan.

Second, how do we handle the challenge of needing complementary innovations? As identified above, developing a novel cement process or chemistry may require a series of successive innovations. A firm that achieves only one may not be able to claim the final reward from an AMC or a prize. It might be able to sell its innovation to another firm that has a complementary innovation. But when it sets out on the R&D investment it may be unclear whether a firm with a complementary innovation will appear. In addition, it may worry that once it has invented the new innovation it will face a hold-up problem because the second firm knows the first innovation is worthless without the second innovation.

A program designer may be tempted to introduce intermediate targets: small rewards or prizes for reaching technical milestones that are on the path toward the end goal to solve this problem. While this might be the right approach in some situations, it comes with downsides. One challenge is identifying the correct intermediate targets. Suppose we want to optimize for two features: low-carbon and cost-competitiveness. Planners cannot merely give prizes to anyone who discovers a low-carbon cement blend, as many of those blends may be so expensive as to be wildly impractical. After all, the challenge is getting both of those factors at once, not merely achieving one of them. Identifying cost at the pilot stage, moreover, can be highly difficult: it is unclear at small size if the economics get worse or better as one scales. For instance, a novel plant reliant on new chemistries may seem to produce relatively cheap cement, but it may turn out that they are using a relatively rare and little-used input whose price would skyrocket if it started being used in multiple major cement plants simultaneously. Another plant may seem to produce rather expensive cement, but it may get much cheaper as economies of scale enable more efficient mining, milling, and processing. It is difficult at the intermediate stage to identify which plants will be economically feasible, and planners should be wary of prematurely rewarding firms with little path to future success.

4.12 Conclusion

The commercial incentive to innovate to combat climate change are generally incommensurate with the social returns of those innovations. This gap stems from several well-known market failures, including unpriced externalities, knowledge spillovers, and the hold-up problem. Existing mechanisms to correct those failures suffer from asymmetric information problems (push funding), monopoly problems (patents), and/or lack of incentives to do the detailed innovation for scale (small-scale prizes). Even the introduction of a carbon price, while correcting for some of the aforementioned market failures, would not, by itself, be sufficient to solve the market failures associated with innovation and the associated wedge between the social and commercial returns.

Pull funding—funding based on achieving identified results—may serve an important role in filling in some of these gaps. Many decarbonization tasks have sufficiently uncertain technological pathways, where identifying a target to hit and rewarding those who achieve it may be easier than specifying which firm or pathway should receive funding in advance. Each industry will require its own unique solution, however. As we see with the cement industry, using the same AMC structure used to incentivize pneumococcal vaccine research and capacity may not produce the desired result. Market designers need to be particularly conscious of balancing between (a) rewarding sufficient early innovations, such that firms that do necessary early innovations are rewarded, without (b) rewarding innovations that will ultimately be economically non-viable.

References

Athey, Susan, Juan Camilo Castillo, Esha Chaudhuri, Michael Kremer, Alexandre Simoes Gomes, and Christopher Snyder. 2022. "Expanding Capacity for Vaccines Against COVID-19 and Future Pandemics: A Review of Economic Issues." NBER Working Paper No. 30192. Cambridge, MA: National Bureau of Economic Research.

Bloom, Nicholas, Mark Schankerman, and John Van Reenen. 2013. "Identifying Technology Spillovers and Product Market Rivalry." *Econometrica* 81(4): 1347–1393.

Castillo, Juan Camilo, Amrita Ahuja, Susan Athey, Arthur Baker, Eric Budish, Tasneem Chipty, Rachel Glennerster, and others. 2021. "Market Design to Accelerate COVID-19 Vaccine Supply." *Science* 371(6534): 1107–9.

Fadeev, Evgenii. 2023. "Creative Construction: Knowledge Sharing and Cooperation Between Firms." Job Market Paper. https://evgeniifadeev.github.io/files/fadeev_jmp.pdf.

Glennerster, Rachel, and Seema Jayachandran. 2023. "Think Globally, Act Globally: Opportunities to Mitigate Greenhouse Gas Emissions in Low- and Middle-Income Countries." NBER Working Paper No. 31421. Cambridge, MA: National Bureau of Economic Research.

Isaksson, Olov H. D., Markus Simeth, and Ralf W. Seifert. 2016. "Knowledge Spillovers in the Supply Chain: Evidence from the High Tech Sectors." *Research Policy* 45(3): 699–706. https://doi.org/10.1016/j.respol.2015.12.007.

Jones, Benjamin, and Lawrence Summers. 2020. "A Calculation of the Social Returns to Innovation." NBER Working Paper No. 27863. Cambridge, MA: National Bureau of Economic Research.

Kremer, Michael, Jonathan Levin, and Chris Snyder. 2020. "Advance Market Commitments: Evidence from Theory and Experience." *AEA Papers and Proceedings* 110: 269–73.

Kremer, Michael, and Rachel Glennerster. 2004. *Strong Medicine: Creating Incentives for Pharmaceutical Research on Neglected Diseases*. New Jersey: Princeton University Press.

Lim, Kwanghui. 2009. "The Many Faces of Absorptive Capacity: Spillovers of Copper Interconnect Technology for Semiconductor Chips." *Industrial and Corporate Change* 18(6): 1249–1284. http://dx.doi.org/10.2139/ssrn.562862.

Liu, Xinyu, Amgad Elgowainy, and Michael Wang. 2020. "Life Cycle Energy Use and Greenhouse Gas Emissions of Ammonia Production from Renewable Resources and Industrial Byproducts." Green Chemistry. *Royal Society of Chemistry*. https://www.osti.gov/servlets/purl/1657142.

Mansfield, Edwin. 1961. "Technical Change and the Rate of Imitation." *Econometrica* 29(4): 744–66.

Nordhaus, William. 2004. "Schumpeterian Profits in the American Economy: Theory and Measurement." NBER Working Paper No. 10433. Cambridge, MA: National Bureau of Economic Research.

Rosenberg, Nathan. 1963. "Technological Change in the Machine Tool Industry, 1840–1940." *Journal of Economic History* 23(4): 414–43.

Stoyanov, Andrey, and Nikolay Zubanov. 2012. "Productivity Spillovers Across Firms through Worker Mobility." *American Economic Journal: Applied Economics* 4(2): 168–98.

US Geological Survey. 2023. "Cement." https://pubs.usgs.gov/periodicals/mcs2023/mcs2023-cement.pdf.

US Department of Energy. 2023. "Pathways to Commercial Liftoff: Low-Carbon Cement." https://liftoff.energy.gov/wp-content/uploads/2023/09/20230918-Pathways-to-Commercial-Liftoff-Cement.pdf.

5

Challenges in Designing Electricity Spot Markets

Mete Şeref Ahunbay, Martin Bichler, and Johannes Knörr

5.1 Introduction

Electricity markets globally, especially in Europe and extensive regions of the United States, have transitioned from being monopolistic to adopting a competitive wholesale market structure, a shift that primarily occurred in the 1990s. Presently, short-term electricity purchases in these jurisdictions are facilitated through power exchanges. These platforms are integral in establishing core pricing signals for both over-the-counter transactions and futures markets, as outlined by Shah and Chatterjee (2020). In the United States, notable examples of these power exchanges encompass the California Independent System Operator (CAISO), the Electric Reliability Council of Texas (ERCOT), the Midwest ISO (MISO), the New York ISO (NYISO), and the ISO New England (ISO-NE). These markets typically facilitate the trading of hourly products for the subsequent day in the day-ahead markets. After the day-ahead markets, the market operators use real-time markets in the United States (or intraday markets in Europe) to deal with changes in supply and demand that are closer to the actual dispatch. We will distinguish

Mete Şeref Ahunbay is a postdoctoral researcher in the Decision Sciences and Systems research unit of the Department of Computer Science at the Technical University of Munich.

Martin Bichler is head of the Decision Sciences and Systems research unit and a professor in the Department of Computer Science at the Technical University of Munich.

Johannes Knörr is a research assistant in the Decision Sciences and Systems research unit of the Department of Computer Science at the Technical University of Munich.

The financial support from the German Research Foundation (Deutsche Forschungsgemeinschaft, DFG) (BI 1057/10-1) is gratefully acknowledged. For acknowledgments, sources of research support, and disclosure of the authors' material financial relationships, if any, please see https://www.nber.org/books-and-chapters/new-directions-market-design/challenges-designing-electricity-spot-markets.

these types of *electricity spot markets* from *futures markets* where participants can hedge against longer-term price risks.

Spot markets are significant in size. In 2020, European coupled day-ahead markets alone cleared 1,530 TWh in 27 countries with average prices between 30 and 40 EUR/MWh (NEMO Committee 2021). Similarly, the cost of serving load amounted to $8.9 billion in the Californian market, covering 26,000 circuit miles, roughly 1,000 power plants, a population of 30 million, and about 9,700 pricing nodes (California ISO 2018, 2021). While many aspects of electricity market design are similar to other commodity markets, a few features stand out.

- First, at the moment of dispatch, demand and supply have to be balanced. Both excess and inadequate supply destabilize the voltage and frequency on the electricity grid, potentially leading to blackouts.
- Second, demand and supply meet on the nodes of the power grid, and excess supply can be shipped to neighboring nodes via transmission lines.
- Third, electricity markets are characterized by non-convex preferences. For example, electricity suppliers often incur fixed costs for starting up and running their generators. On the demand side, industrial customers typically need a certain volume of electricity over consecutive hours to finish production or maintain energy-intensive services. Such consumption profiles can sometimes be shifted over time, but the profiles themselves must not be altered. Non-convexities in the preferences of this sort lead to non-convex optimization problems that need to be solved in order to determine the efficient (welfare-maximizing) dispatch and prices. We will use the term *non-convex markets* in what follows.

The landscape of power systems is undergoing a transformation due to the influx of renewable energy sources (RES). A significant portion of this new capacity is attributed to Variable Energy Resources (VER) like solar and wind power. These energy sources, characterized by their inherent variability and unpredictability, necessitate the incorporation of flexible demand to ensure grid stability and reliability (Reihani et al. 2016). Demand response is the most immediately available way of increasing demand flexibility and the cheaper option compared to storage technologies today (EU 2016). For example, industrial processes for the production of pulp and paper are able to provide demand response with a duration of up to three hours without any notice time (EU 2016). Still, this flexibility comes at a cost, and bidders want lower prices if they provide more flexibility.

The traditional literature on electricity market pricing typically relies on the assumption of price-inelastic demand, but this assumption is unlikely to hold in the future (Herrero et al. 2020). It is expected that in the future we will see more price-responsive demand (Hytowitz et al. 2020). However, such price-sensitive bids for flexible demand make market design more challenging. First, new bid formats lead to additional non-convexities which can affect price formation. Second, prices that are individually rational and clear the market at the efficient dispatch cannot always be budget balanced anymore (Bichler et al. 2022). Overall, we move to an economy with many thousands of small generators and a more price-sensitive demand side that actively bids in electricity markets and offers flexibility to cope with variability in the supply (IRENA 2019, Hytowitz et al. 2020).

Such changes in the market have led to renewed interest in the design of electricity markets. We start out discussing standard notions of market equilibrium, before we survey the literature on electricity market pricing and some of the current research challenges.

5.2 Competitive Equilibrium on Markets

The literature on electricity markets draws on insights from general equilibrium theory. The Arrow-Debreu model shows that under convex preferences, perfect competition, and demand independence, there must be a set of competitive equilibrium prices (Arrow and Debreu 1954; McKenzie 1959; Gale 1963; Kaneko 1976). The results derived from the Arrow-Debreu model led to the well-known welfare theorems, representing important arguments for markets to be used as efficient or welfare-maximizing means to allocate scarce resources such as electricity. The first theorem states that any Walrasian equilibrium leads to a Pareto efficient allocation of resources. The second theorem states that any efficient allocation can be attained by a Walrasian equilibrium under the Arrow-Debreu model assumptions (Mas-Colell et al. 1995). Walrasian equilibrium prices are such that there is a single price for each product (i.e., prices for a package are *linear*) and this is the same price for all participants (i.e., *anonymous* prices with no price differentiation). The question is then whether electricity markets indeed admit a Walrasian equilibrium.

One feature of electricity markets is that they are based on a network with possibly thousands of spatially distributed nodes connected via transmission lines. To put it differently, we have a set of coupled markets and need to equalize supply and demand at each node.

Definition 1 (Ahunbay et al. 2023b). *A* ***coupled market*** *consists of a set of goods M, a set of transmission network parameters F, and a set of market participants $L = B \cup S \cup R$, partitioned into the set of buyers B, set of sellers S, and the set of transmission operators R. Each market participant $\ell \in L$ has preferences over bundles in $\mathbb{R}^{M \cup F}$, i.e., each buyer b has a valuation function $v_b : \mathbb{R}^{M \cup F} \to \overline{\mathbb{R}}$, each seller s has a cost function $c_s : \mathbb{R}^{M \cup F} \to \overline{\mathbb{R}}$, and each transmission operator r has a cost function $d_r : \mathbb{R}^{M \cup F} \to \overline{\mathbb{R}}$.*

Thus, we also need to price transmission lines in such coupled markets appropriately (Lété et al. 2022). For example, if a transmission line is congested, the price on two adjacent nodes should differ. Similarly, prices on all nodes should be identical if there is no network congestion. So, do the welfare theorems hold in coupled markets connected via transmission networks? Fortunately, the answer to this question is affirmative:

THEOREM 2.1 (The Welfare Theorems for Coupled and Convex Markets, Ahunbay et al. 2023b). *Let price vector* $p^* \in \mathbb{R}^{M \cup F}$ *and the allocation* $(z_\ell)^*_{\ell \in L}$ *be a Walrasian equilibrium, then this allocation maximizes social welfare. Conversely, if* $(z_\ell)^*_{\ell \in L}$ *is a welfare-maximizing allocation, then it can be supported by a Walrasian price vector* p^* *that forms a Walrasian equilibrium.*

However, this theorem, as well as the original welfare theorems, assumes convex preferences. As we discussed earlier, electricity markets have non-convex preferences and complex constraints. It is well known that only restricted types of valuations (e.g., substitutes valuations or unimodular demand types) allow for convex allocation problems and Walrasian equilibria (Kim 1986; Bikhchandani and Mamer 1997; Leme 2017; Baldwin and Klemperer 2019). Thus, we cannot expect Walrasian equilibria to exist on electricity spot markets.

This raises the question how prices can be computed in the presence of non-convex preferences for indivisible goods and which properties we can hope to achieve compared to Walrasian equilibria. Established market design desiderata are *efficiency* (i.e., maximization of welfare or gains from trade); *individual rationality* (i.e., participants should not make a loss); *budget balance* (i.e., the market operator should not make a loss or a gain); and *envy-freeness* (i.e., participants would not want a different allocation at the prices). These axioms are not only central to economic theory but are widely adopted and natural design desiderata for practical market design.

If the allocation problem is convex, dual variables for the convex allocation problem provide a principled way to determine competitive equilibrium prices that satisfy these desiderata (Bichler et al. 2020). In non-convex markets, it is well known that competitive equilibrium prices might need to be non-linear and personalized and such prices might not even exist (Bikhchandani and Ostroy 2002; Bichler and Waldherr 2019). Thus, in a combinatorial auction or exchange that allows for supply and demand bids on packages of items, each bidder might need to face a different price for the same package (personalized prices), and each package price could differ from the sum of the item prices in this package and the price of each package may differ from the sum of the prices of each constituent item (non-linear prices). In electricity markets, each item corresponds to electric power delivered at a certain hour and location, and the presence of non-convexities can render market clearing with linear and anonymous prices impossible. As a simple example, consider a single supplier with an (indivisible) sell bid of 2 MWh for $30, while there is one buyer asking for 1 MWh for at most $10, and another buyer asking for 1 MWh for $28. Linear and anonymous market prices could not be higher than \$10/MWh. As such there would be no trade and no gains from trade. Only with price differentiation would trade be possible.

However, non-linear and personalized prices would convey little information other than that a bidder has lost or won. Besides, prices should serve as a baseline for financial derivatives such as options or futures, which is hardly possible with non-linear prices that differ among participants. In other words, anonymity and linearity are important requirements for prices on electricity markets but also in other domains (Bichler et al. 2018). This has led to significant research on pricing in non-convex electricity markets.

5.3 State-of-the-Practice in Electricity Market Pricing

Let us now introduce the pricing rules used in electricity spot markets today. The literature on this subject is large, and we only focus on specific pricing rules that have been implemented in practice. The interested reader is referred to Liberopoulos and Andrianesis (2016) for an excellent survey on the topic.

Electricity spot markets are composed of varying levels of "demand" (load) and matching levels of "supply" (generation). Market participants submit supply and demand bids according to a certain *bid language* that determines the form of the allocation problem (which yields the efficient dispatch) and the pricing rule. Ideally, supply and demand curves at each traded time slice (e.g., hour) determine prices in equilibrium. However, sophisticated bid languages are required to express the technical constraints generators face, with consequences on the allocation problem (which yields the efficient dispatch) and the pricing rule (Herrero et al. 2020). For example, in markets in the United States, generators can express start-up or no-load costs, economies of scale (by means of piecewise-linear cost functions), or minimum-generation requirements. The resulting bid languages then translate into non-convex allocation problems (Herrero et al. 2020).

In 2005, the Pennsylvania, Jersey, Maryland Power Pool (PJM) introduced mixed-integer programming (MIP) in order to address these non-convexities and to determine the efficient allocation or dispatch (O'Neill et al. 2020). Since 2018, all Independent System Operators (ISOs) in the United States use MIPs to compute the efficient dispatch instead of the Lagrangian relaxation that was used before. The MIP used to solve the allocation problem on US electricity markets is also known as Direct Current Optimal Power Flow (DCOPF) problem. Dual prices as they are accessible for convex optimization problems are not available in such markets, which led to a fundamental question: How can market prices per hour be computed in such non-convex markets? What are meaningful prices in such non-convex markets and how can they be computed?

One approach followed by European day-ahead markets is to sacrifice efficiency. The EUPHEMIA algorithm that is used to clear European day-ahead markets first solves a welfare maximization allocation problem as a mixed-integer program and then iteratively tries to find linear and anonymous prices that clear the market. If such prices cannot be found, additional constraints are added to the welfare maximization problem (NEMO Committee 2020). However, it is unclear how much of the gains from trade are sacrificed this way. Furthermore, this approach inevitably leads to paradoxically rejected bids (Meeus et al. 2009). In particular, there are generators with an ask price that is less than the market price, yet they will not be dispatched. Such prices are thus not *envy-free* and hence do not constitute a Walrasian equilibrium. By its design as an iterative algorithm, EUPHEMIA further faces considerable computational challenges, magnified by the impending introduction of 15-minute market time units in the European electricity markets in 2025. We shall hence not further discuss this approach here, and focus on market designs that implement the efficient outcome, as in the United States.

Several pricing rules have been suggested aiming to mimic competitive equilibrium prices on such MIP-based electricity markets (Liberopoulos and Andrianesis 2016). Locational marginal pricing (LMP) rules of many ISOs are based on IP pricing (aka Integer Programming pricing), where the allocation problem is solved to optimality, the integer variables are fixed, and the prices are then derived from the dual variables of the demand-supply constraint of the resulting (convex) linear program (O'Neill et al. 2005). IP pricing computes anonymous and linear prices, but these prices do not constitute competitive equilibrium prices. Some generators might not maximize their individual profits and want to deviate, i.e., switch to a different dispatch at those prices, and IP prices are thus not *envy-free*. The latter is central to the definition of a competitive equilibrium and it leads to stability of the outcome. Importantly, besides a lack of stability, the generators often make a loss at the IP prices, i.e., prices are not even *individually rational*.

Another prominent pricing rule for electricity markets considered in academic literature is convex hull (CH) pricing (Hogan and Ring 2003; Gribik et al. 2007), which aims to minimize envy and thus implement a stable outcome and thus maximize the stability of the welfare optimal outcome at the expense of budget balance. We refer to incentives to deviate from the optimal outcome as lost opportunity costs, or LOCs. They describe the difference between each participant's profits under the welfare-maximizing allocation and the individual profit maxima each participant could obtain given the prices. With CH pricing, the market operator implements the optimal outcome and compensates participants for their LOCs (violating budget-balance). This way, market participants would not have an incentive to deviate. For certain bid languages, CH pricing is equivalent to Extended LMP (ELMP), a pricing rule used by some US ISOs. ELMP is based on the dual variables from the supply-demand constraint in the LP relaxation of the underlying DCOPF. However, market participants can also make a loss with ELMP, and they need to be compensated.

ISOs use personalized side-payments to address the fact that the public market prices from IP pricing or ELMP are neither envy-free nor individually rational. This effectively differentiates the linear and anonymous market prices from the payments of the market participants, which are then non-linear and personalized. LOCs are differentiated from *make-whole payments* (Schiro et al. 2016). LOCs describe payments that are so high that no generator would want to change its dispatch and envy-freeness is achieved. Such payments may be very large if the market contains non-convexities (Eldridge et al. 2020). However, electricity markets are highly regulated markets and as such there are alternative means to enforce stability other than high LOC payments. Actually, most ISOs only pay make-whole payments to ensure individual rationality of all generators and stipulate penalties that a generator has to pay if it indeed deviates from the optimal dispatch. In other words, they relax envy-freeness to only individual rationality requirements. We refer to such outcomes as having *penalty-based stability*.

However, even the make-whole payments are a significant concern (Hytowitz et al. 2020). The US Federal Energy Regulatory Commission (FERC) regulates the US wholesale power markets to promote just competition. In 2018, FERC found that the practices of several ISOs were unjust and ordered them to change their pricing because prices did not accurately reflect the cost of serving load (O'Neill et al. 2019). Moreover, make-whole payments are not reflected in the public price signals, which results in biased investment signals. This hence constitutes a problem for futures markets, where spot market prices serve as the key reference. This has led FERC to release several orders and notices on pricing, which argue that "the use of side-payments can undermine the market's ability to send actionable price signals."[1] Similarly, O'Neill et al. (2019) state that "the make-whole payments are not transparent to other market participants and are allocated too broadly to provide correct price incentives for market participants to make efficient entry and exit decisions as well as efficient investments in facilities and equipment." As a consequence, US ISOs continue to search for improvements in the pricing rules.

5.4 Dealing with Non-Convexities

In what follows, we discuss some of the current developments and research frontiers in electricity spot market design. We will discuss new ways to deal with non-convexities and approaches to deal with the volatility of supply in future electricity markets.

1. Energy Price Formation, Federal Energy Regulatory Commission (FERC) website, https://www.ferc.gov/industries-data/electric/electric-power-markets/energy-price-formation.

5.4.1 Non-Convexities in Supply and Demand

We have discussed that in non-convex markets, a Walrasian competitive equilibrium does not exist in general (Starr 1969; Bikhchandani and Mamer 1997). Current pricing rules as they were discussed in the previous section violate either envy-freeness or budget-balance or both. One might wonder whether existing pricing rules used in electricity markets can be improved upon. One way forward is to break down envy-freeness in the context of electricity markets and consider different types of LOCs (Ahunbay et al. 2023b).

Rather than minimizing LOCs as incentives to deviate, hereafter referred to as *global* LOCs (GLOCs), one may look at so-called *local* LOCs (LLOCs), and at the specific considerations required to price a coupled market. Specifically, in a coupled market, *transmission* has to be priced appropriately. For example, prices should only differ across a pair of nodes if there is *congestion* in the network and no further power may be transmitted from the node with the higher price to that with a lower price. Violations of this condition, i.e., price differences across uncongested branches, may result in a product revenue shortfall for transmission operators, which would require compensation. CH pricing does not satisfy this requirement (Schiro et al. 2016), but it is important to consider for a pricing rule.

It turns out that *local lost opportunity costs* describe a way to consider the quality of congestion prices. LLOCs measure incentives to deviate from the optimal allocation *under fixed commitment*.[2] In other words, LLOCs assume that the commitment decisions have been made but that generators can deviate from their assigned volumes in an attempt to improve their payoff. Interestingly, minimizing LLOCs also provides for the desired congestion signals in the network, in the sense that prices reflect the marginal value of additional transmission capacity.

Achieving low GLOCs, LLOCs, and MWPs (Make Whole Payments) are conflicting design goals and optimizing only one of these objectives comes at the expense of another. If MWPs are minimized, GLOCs can be unreasonably high and congestion signals become distorted leading to high LLOCs. Focusing only on LLOCs can also impose costs and lead to very high MWPs for some participants. This is striking, as IP Pricing and CH Pricing in fact correspond to minimizing respectively LLOCs and GLOCs. Ahunbay et al. (2023b) suggest the join pricing rule, which balances trade-offs between MWPs and LLOCs to minimize incentives of participants to locally deviate from the efficient outcome as well as their incentives to exit the market. Numerical experiments show that prices computed via this join require significantly less MWPs than traditional IP pricing and retain good

2. Commitment decisions on spot markets determine whether a generator is scheduled to produce electricity during a market time unit (a binary decision variable in the allocation problem) but not the production quantity (in megawatt hours [MWh]). Commitment decisions occur because many types of generators require a long time to turn on/off.

congestion signals with very low LLOCs at the same time. The approach can be computed efficiently and it requires no fine-tuning of objective weights. In electricity markets, where global incentives to deviate can be enforced by penalizing deviations, the join strikes a desirable balance, and the experiments show that the remaining incentives to deviate are low.

5.4.2 Non-Convexities from Non-Linear Power Flows

The literature on electricity market pricing so far focused mainly on non-convexities arising from the cost or valuation functions of market participants. The line losses are linearized leading to a mixed-integer linear program, the DCOPF. However, an accurate representation of the physics governing the transmission network would require the consideration of non-linear line losses. As a result, the allocation problem is accurately described instead as a non-linear and non-convex optimization problem referred to as Alternating Current Optimal Power Flow (ACOPF) problem (Molzahn and Hiskens 2019). This ACOPF is computationally intractable for the problem sizes that we observe in real-world electricity markets. This is the main reason why linearized network models such as the DCOPF are used for market clearing and pricing. In general, the optimal solution for DCOPF is generally neither AC-optimal nor AC-feasible. This requires market operators or transmission system operators (TSOs) to adjust the dispatch after the market clearing to reach a physically feasible outcome.

This issue is magnified by the transition to renewable energy sources (Lété et al. 2022). A decreasing number of thermal generators can supply reactive power and the consideration of reactive power on the transmission level is therefore crucial (Hemmati et al. 2013; Karmakar and Bhattacharyya 2020). Larrahondo et al. (2021) found that high integration of wind power contributes to the inaccuracies of the DCOPF by disregarding *reactive power*. As the number of thermal generators that can supply reactive power is also decreasing, the consideration of reactive power on the transmission level is crucial (Hemmati et al. 2013; Karmakar and Bhattacharyya 2020). There have been significant efforts to obtain tighter and more accurate relaxations of the ACOPF problem in an effort to leverage recent advances in convex optimization for real-world markets, which culminated in the ARPA-E Grid Optimization Competition.[3] However, errors in the optimization models due to linearization or simplifying assumptions remain a concern in virtually all electricity markets. For example, the revision of the European Capacity Allocation and Congestion Management (CACM) regulation requires accounting for "linearization errors" while calculating available capacities for trading (ACER 2021). A key problem of linearized models is the welfare loss arising from a poor approximation of ACOPF.

3. See ARPA-E's Grid Optimization (GO) Competition site at https://gocompetition.energy.gov/ for further details.

In recent years, substantial research has been devoted to finding tighter convex relaxations and approximations for the ACOPF problem (Molzahn and Hiskens 2019). This research focuses on the optimality of the solution and computational costs to obtain it. Tighter relaxations of ACOPF could lead to prices that better reflect scarcity in the physical network. However, the magnitude of these improvements is unclear. Bichler and Knörr (2023) study the impact of non-linear convex market clearing models on prices, MWPs, and LLOCs. More precisely, they consider the linearized DCOPF, a second-order conic (SOC) relaxation, and a quadratic convex (QC) relaxation (Molzahn and Hiskens 2019). For each relaxation, they compute market clearing prices via IP and CH pricing rules. The results show that different power flow models lead to substantial differences in the allocation. This of course has an impact on both welfare and prices.

As one would expect, tighter convex relaxations require substantially less redispatch compared to the standard DCOPF approximation. Moreover, MWPs, GLOCs, and LLOCs are on average lower for the final AC-feasible outcome. The tighter convex relaxations also lead to higher welfare of the final dispatch. However, welfare gains are not the most important argument for tighter convex relaxations of ACOPF. The numerical experiments show that the prices obtained from DCOPF are often substantially different from those of the non-linear relaxations, leading to biased scarcity signals that distort effective demand response and investment decisions. In contrast, the results of the SOC and QC relaxation, which both model reactive power and line losses more accurately, are almost identical. Prices obtained from DCOPF might be excessively high at some of the nodes, even though there is no congestion in the AC-feasible solution. In other words, the DCOPF leads to unnecessary price peaks at some of the nodes even though there is no congestion in the physical grid at all. Similarly, we might encounter congestion in the AC-feasible solution that the DC prices of adjacent nodes do not reflect. In a world with 100 percent renewables, where adequate demand response is even more important, this is a decisive disadvantage of standard DCOPF solutions compared to tighter non-linear relaxations.

5.4.3 Outlook

While increasing levels of storage suggest that the allocation problem becomes more convex, non-convexities will remain an important concern for a long time. Start-up costs of gas turbines, minimum operating levels, minimum run times and down times will also play a role in the foreseeable future. In this short paper, we could only discuss a few of the approaches to address different types of non-convexities on electricity markets. Other ideas revolve around the use of price differentiation or the use of two price vectors (O'Neill et al. 2019; Eldridge et al. 2020; O'Neill et al. 2016; Hytowitz et al. 2017; Milgrom and Watt 2021; Ahunbay et al. 2023a).

The volatility of renewable energy sources creates uncertainties in the day-ahead prices of electricity markets. Unlike dispatchable generators, which can ensure a specific amount of electricity production, wind and solar generators cannot provide such guarantees. Some authors suggest robust optimization to minimize cost in such stochastic environments (Zugno and Conejo 2015; Li et al. 2018; Silva-Rodriguez et al. 2022). Also stochastic clearing was suggested in the day-ahead market to better deal with the volatility of supply and demand in markets with large proportions of renewables (Zavala et al. 2017; Uçkun et al. 2015). How prices are determined in the presence of robust or stochastic market clearing is not yet well understood (Eldridge et al. 2021; Bertsimas and Koulouras 2024).

In particular in zonal markets such as the EU power market, the concept of local flexibility markets has been explored (Jin et al. 2020; Olivella-Rosell et al. 2018; Cramton 2022). The local flexibility market allows system operators to procure additional flexibility close to real time, which helps in managing unexpected grid conditions or fine-tuning the grid balance in response to real-time developments. After the day-ahead market has determined the initial energy dispatch based on expected supply and demand, local flexibility markets step in to address any emerging needs, such as intrazonal congestion or other grid constraints that were not fully resolved or anticipated in the day-ahead market. For example, a Distribution System Operator sends a request which includes specific requirements, such as the amount of load reduction or generation increase needed. Participants (e.g., households with batteries, electric vehicles, or small-scale generators) then submit bids indicating the amount of flexibility they can provide and at what price.

One of the concerns with such markets is gaming, which refers to participants' misrepresentation of their costs and valuations in order to increase their profit. The typical source of gaming arises from the structure of the market, which consists of forward markets, the day-ahead market, and the intraday market.

Poor choice of regulation can then allow for arbitrage between different markets, leading to what is known as *inc-dec gaming* in literature (Hirth et al. 2019). How a more *incentive compatible* and practical electricity market can be designed, in which participants have limited incentive to misrepresent their preferences, is an open problem. A deeper, related question is whether market participants can *learn* to game the market, and how the resulting market distortion may be limited. Byers and Eldridge (2022) show that generators may learn to self-schedule or self-commit to increase their own profit, using very simple learning algorithms with no particular knowledge of the market at large. Such strategic bidding results in increased profit for the generators with consumers bearing the additional cost. This motivates further investigation into whether such learned strategic behavior exists in practice, its effects on prices and efficiency, and how it may be limited.

Changes in electricity markets are not only relevant for market operators; they also impact generators, as well as industrial and retail consumers alike.

How to best design power markets such that they address the challenges of volatile supply of renewables continues to be a challenging research field at the intersection of computer science, economics, and operations research.

References

ACER. 2021. ACER recommendation 02–2021 on CACM 2.0: Annex 4-CACM reasoning. https://acer.europa.eu/Official_documents/Acts_of_the_Agency/Recommendations%20Annexes/ACER%20Recommendation%2002-2021%20on%20CACM/ACER%20Recommendation%2002-2021%20on%20CACM%20-%20Annex%204%20-%20CACM%20Reasoning.pdf.

Ahunbay M. Ş., M. Bichler, T. Dobos, and J. Knörr. 2023a. "Solving Large-Scale Electricity Market Pricing Problems in Polynomial Time." Technical University of Munich Working Paper.

Ahunbay M. Ş., M. Bichler, and J. Knörr. 2023b. "Pricing Optimal Outcomes in Coupled and Non-convex Markets: Theory and Applications to Electricity Markets." *ACM Conference on Economics and Computation.*

Arrow, K. J., and G. Debreu. 1954. "Existence of an Equilibrium for a Competitive Economy." *Econometrica 22(3):* 265–90.

Baldwin, E., and P. Klemperer. 2019. "Understanding Preferences: Demand Types, and the Existence of Equilibrium with Indivisibilities." *Econometrica* 87(3): 867–932.

Bertsimas, D., and A. G. Koulouras. 2024. "Adaptive Pricing in Unit Commitment Under Load and Capacity Uncertainty." *IEEE Transactions on Power Systems* 38(3).

Bichler, M., M. Fichtl, and G., Schwarz. 2020. "Walrasian Equilibria from an Optimization Perspective: A Guide to the Literature." *Naval Research Logistics (NRL).* Wiley Periodicals, LLC.

Bichler, M., V. Fux, and J. Goeree. 2018. "A Matter of Equality: Linear Pricing in Combinatorial Exchanges." *Information Systems Research* 29(4): 1024–1043.

Bichler, M., J. Knoerr, and F. Maldonado. 2022. "Pricing in Non-convex Markets: How to Price Electricity in the Presence of Demand Response." *Information Systems Research* 1 (to appear).

Bichler, M., and J. Knörr. 2023. "Getting Prices Right on Electricity Spot Markets: On the Economic Impact of Advanced Power Flow Models." *Energy Economics* 126: 106968.

Bichler, M., and S. Waldherr. 2019. "Computing Core-Stable Outcomes in Combinatorial Exchanges with Financially Constrained Bidders." *Proceedings of the 2019 ACM Conference on Economics and Computation*, 747–47. ACM.

Bikhchandani, S., and J. W. Mamer. 1997. "Competitive Equilibrium in an Exchange Economy with Indivisibilities." *Journal of Economic Theory* 74(2): 385–413.

Bikhchandani, S., and J. M. Ostroy. 2002. "The Package Assignment Model." *Journal of Economic Theory* 107(2): 377–406.

Byers, C., and B. Eldridge. 2022. "Auction Designs to Increase Incentive Compatibility and Reduce Self-Scheduling in Electricity Markets." arXiv preprint arXiv:2212.10234.

California ISO. 2018. ISO at-a-glance. https://www.caiso.com/Documents/CaliforniaISO-GeneralCompanyBrochure.pdf.

California ISO. 2021. "2020 Annual Report on Market Issues & Performance." https://www.caiso.com/documents/2020-annual-report-on-market-issues-and-performance.pdf
Cramton, P. C. 2022. "Local Flexibility Market." Technical Report, ECONtribute Discussion Paper.
Eldridge, B., B. Knueven, and J. Mays. 2021. "Efficient Prices Under Uncertainty and Non-convexity." *Optimization Online.* http://www.optimization-online.org/DBFILE/2021/04/8338.pdf.
Eldridge, B., R. O'Neill, and B. F. Hobbs. 2020. "Near-Optimal Scheduling in Day-Ahead Markets: Pricing Models and Payment Redistribution Bounds." *IEEE Transactions on Power Systems* 35(3): 1684–1694. http://dx.doi.org/10.1109/TPWRS.2019.2947400.
EU. 2016. "Impact Assessment Study on Downstream Flexibility, Price Flexibility, Demand Response & Smart Metering." Technical Report ENER/B3/2015–641.
Gale, D. 1963. "A Note on Global Instability of Competitive Equilibrium." *Naval Research Logistics Quarterly* 10(1): 81–87.
Gribik, P. R., W. W. Hogan, S. L. Pope, et al. 2007. "Market-Clearing Electricity Prices and Energy Uplift." Harvard Electricity Policy Group. https://hepg.hks.harvard.edu/publications/market-clearing-electricity-prices-and-energy-uplift.
Hemmati, R., R. A. Hooshmand, and A. Khodabakhshian. 2013. "State-of-the-Art of Transmission Expansion Planning: Comprehensive Review." *Renewable and Sustainable Energy Reviews* 23: 312–19. http://dx.doi.org/10.1016/j.rser.2013.03.015.
Herrero, I., P. Rodilla, and C. Batlle. 2020. "Evolving Bidding Formats and Pricing Schemes in USA and Europe Day-Ahead Electricity Markets." *Energies* 13(19): 5020.
Hirth, L., I. Schlecht, C. Maurer, and B. Tersteegen. 2019. "Cost- or Market-Based? Future Redispatch Procurement in Germany: Conclusions from the Project 'Beschaffung von Redispatch.'" https://www.bmwk.de/Redaktion/EN/Publikationen/Studien/future-redispatch-procurement-in-germany.pdf?__blob=publicationFile&v=2#:~:text=On%20the%20redispatch%20market%2C%20they,markets%20or%20as%20arbitrage%20trading.
Hogan, W. W., and B. J. Ring. 2003. "On Minimum-Uplift Pricing for Electricity Markets." Electricity Policy Group.
Hytowitz, Robin Broder, Bethany Frew, Gord Stephen, Erik Ela, Jessica Lau, Nikita Singhal, and Aaron Bloom. 2020. "Impacts of Price Formation Efforts Considering High Renewable Penetration Levels and System Resource Adequacy Targets." Golden, CO: National Renewable Energy Laboratory. NREL/TP-6A20-74230. https://www.nrel.gov/docs/fy20osti/74230.pdf.
Hytowitz, R. B., R. O'Neill, B. Eldridge, and A. Castillo. 2017. "Multi-Period Dual Pricing Algorithm in Non-convex ISO Markets." Working Paper. https://hobbsgroup.johnshopkins.edu/docs/papers/Hytowitz_DPAWorkingPaper_2017.pdf.
IRENA. 2019. *Innovation landscape for a renewable-powered future: Solutions to integrate variable renewables*. Summary for policy makers. International Renewable Energy Agency, Abu Dhabi. https://efficiencyforaccess.org/wp-content/uploads/IRENA-Innovation-Landscape-Report-2019P.pdf.
Jin, X., Q. Wu, and H. Jia. 2020. "Local Flexibility Markets: Literature Review on Concepts, Models and Clearing Methods." *Applied Energy* 261: 114387.
Kaneko, M. 1976. "On the Core and Competitive Equilibria of a Market with Indivisible Goods." *Naval Research Logistics Quarterly* 23(2): 321–37. http://dx.doi.org/10.1002/nav.3800230214.
Karmakar, N., and B. Bhattacharyya. 2020. "Optimal Reactive Power Planning in

Power Transmission Network Using Sensitivity Based Bi-Level Strategy." *Sustainable Energy, Grids and Networks* 23: 100383. http://dx.doi.org/10.1016/j.segan.2020.100383.
Kim, S. 1986. "Computation of a Large-Scale Competitive Equilibrium Through Optimization." *Computers and Operations Research* 13(4): 507—515.
Larrahondo, D., R. Moreno, H. R. Chamorro, and F. Gonzalez-Longatt. 2021. "Comparative Performance of Multi-period ACOPF and Multi-period DCOPF Under High Integration of Wind Power." *Energies* 14(15): 4540. http://dx.doi.org/10.3390/en14154540.
Leme, R. P. 2017. "Gross Substitutability: An Algorithmic Survey." *Games and Economic Behavior* 106: 294–316.
Lété, Q., Y. Smeers, and A. Papavasiliou. 2022. "An Analysis of Zonal Electricity Pricing from a Long-Term Perspective." *Energy Economics* 107: 105853. http://dx.doi.org/10.1016/j.eneco.2022.105853.
Li, H., X. Wang, F. Li, Y. Wang, and X. Yu. 2018. "A Robust Day-Ahead Electricity Market Clearing Model Considering Wind Power Penetration." *Energies* 11(7): 1772.
Liberopoulos, G., and P. Andrianesis. 2016. "Critical Review of Pricing Schemes in Markets with Non-convex Costs." *Operations Research* 64(1): 17–31.
Mas-Colell, A., M. D. Whinston, J. R. Green, et al. 1995. *Microeconomic Theory*, volume 1. New York: Oxford University Press.
McKenzie, L. W. 1959. "On the Existence of General Equilibrium for a Competitive Market." *Econometrica 27(1):* 54–71.
Meeus, L., K. Verhaegen, and R. Belmans. 2009. "Block Order Restrictions in Combinatorial Electric Energy Auctions." *European Journal of Operational Research* 196(3): 1202–1206. http://dx.doi. org/10.1016/j.ejor.2008.04.031.
Milgrom, P., and M. Watt. 2021. "Linear Pricing Mechanisms Without Convexity." https://mitchwatt.github. io/files/PricingMechanismsNonConvex.pdf.
Molzahn, D. K., and I. A. Hiskens. 2019. "A Survey of Relaxations and Approximations of the Power Flow Equations." *Foundations and Trends® in Electric Energy Systems* 4(1–2): 1–221. http:// dx.doi.org/10.1561/3100000012.
NEMO Committee. 2020. Euphemia Public Description. Technical Report.
NEMO Committee. 2021. CACM Annual Report 2020. https://www.nemo-committee.eu/assets/files/NEMO_CACM_Annual_Report_2020_deliverable_1_pub.pdf.
Olivella-Rosell, P., P. Lloret-Gallego, Í Munné-Collado, R. Villafafila-Robles, A. Sumper, SØ Ottessen, J. Rajasekharan, and B. A. Bremdal. 2018. "Local Flexibility Market Design for Aggregators Providing Multiple Flexibility Services at Distribution Network Level." *Energies* 11(4): 822.
O'Neill, R., R. B. Hytowitz, P. Whitman, D. Mead, T. Dautel, Y. Chen, B. Eldridge, A. Siskind, D. Kheloussi, D. Kolkmann, A. Smith, A. Castillo, and J. Mays. 2019. "Essays on Average Incremental Cost Pricing for Independent System Operators." Optimization Online. https://optimization-online.org/?p=23692
O'Neill, R. P., A. Castillo, B. Eldridge, and R. B. Hytowitz. 2016. "Dual Pricing Algorithm in ISO Markets." *IEEE Transactions on Power Systems* 32(4): 3308–310.
O'Neill, R. P., Y. Chen, and P. Whitman. 2020. "The One-Pass Average Incremental Cost Pricing Approach with Multi-step Marginal Costs, Ramp Constraints and Reserves." Working Paper.
O'Neill, R. P., P. M. Sotkiewicz, B. F. Hobbs, M. H. Rothkopf, and W. R. Stewart. 2005. "Efficient Market-Clearing Prices in Markets with Nonconvexities." *European Journal of Operational Research* 1(164): 269–85.
Reihani, E., M. Motalleb, M. Thornton, and R. Ghorbani. 2016. "A Novel Approach

Using Flexible Scheduling and Aggregation to Optimize Demand Response in the Developing Interactive Grid Market Architecture." *Applied Energy* 183: 445–55.

Schiro, D. A., T. Zheng, F. Zhao, and E. Litvinov. 2016. "Convex Hull Pricing in Electricity Markets: Formulation, Analysis, and Implementation Challenges." *IEEE Transactions on Power Systems* 31(5): 4068–4075. http://dx.doi.org/10.1109/TPWRS.2015.2486380.

Shah, D., and S. Chatterjee. 2020. "A Comprehensive Review on Day-Ahead Electricity Market and Important Features of World's Major Electric Power Exchanges." *International Transactions on Electrical Energy Systems* 30(7): e12360.

Silva-Rodriguez, L., A. Sanjab, E. Fumagalli, A. Virag, and M. Gibescu. 2022. "A Light Robust Optimization Approach for Uncertainty-Based Day-Ahead Electricity Markets." *Electric Power Systems Research* 212: 108281.

Starr, R. M. 1969. "Quasi-Equilibria in Markets with Non-convex Preferences." *Econometrica 37(1):* 25–38.

Uçkun, C., A. Botterud, and J. R. Birge. 2015. "An Improved Stochastic Unit Commitment Formulation to Accommodate Wind Uncertainty." *IEEE Transactions on Power Systems* 31(4): 2507–2517.

Zavala, V. M., K. Kim, M. Anitescu, and J. Birge. 2017. "A Stochastic Electricity Market Clearing Formulation with Consistent Pricing Properties." *Operations Research* 65(3): 557–76.

Zugno, M., and A. J. Conejo. 2015. "A Robust Optimization Approach to Energy and Reserve Dispatch in Electricity Markets." *European Journal of Operational Research* 247(2): 659–71.

6

Artificial Intelligence and Market Design
Lessons Learned from Radio Spectrum Reallocation

Kevin Leyton-Brown, Paul Milgrom, Neil Newman, and Ilya Segal

6.1 Introduction

The modern AI revolution has been fueled by computational processes that improve as they are allocated more data and more computing power. As computers have become faster and cheaper, and as data sets have grown larger, algorithmic approaches ranging from self-supervised neural networks to Monte Carlo Tree Search have exhibited skyrocketing performance. However, most mainstream market design approaches exhibit neither of these desirable scaling properties: purely theoretical analyses are unaffected by Moore's Law; rationality assumptions often make observations of actual bidder behavior irrelevant beyond the (worthwhile but narrow) question of estimating valuations via econometric techniques. How might we go further, leveraging cheap compute power and abundant data to complement the work of auction analysts? One path forward is running extensive simulations that leverage a high-fidelity market simulator and realistic models of participant preferences. A (mostly) recent literature has applied this approach across a diverse variety of domains, each with their own literature, includ-

Kevin Leyton-Brown is a professor of computer science and a Distinguished University Scholar at the University of British Columbia.

Paul Milgrom is the Shirley R. and Leonard W. Ely, Jr. Professor in Humanities and Sciences in the Department of Economics at Stanford University.

Neil Newman earned his PhD in computer science from the University of British Columbia and is currently a software developer with Auctionomics.

Ilya Segal is the Roy and Betty Anderson Professor in the Humanities and Sciences, and professor, by courtesy, in economics at the Graduate School of Business at Stanford University.

For acknowledgments, sources of research support, and disclosure of the authors' material financial relationships, if any, please see https://www.nber.org/books-and-chapters/new-directions-market-design/artificial-intelligence-and-market-design-lessons-learned-radio-spectrum-reallocation.

ing matching mechanisms for refugee resettlement (Delacrétaz et al. 2019); school assignment policies (Allman et al. 2022); dock allocation and rebalancing in bike sharing networks (Freund et al. 2018); patrolling strategies for wildlife protection (Yang et al. 2014); reallocating fishing licenses (Bichler et al. 2019); and matching in organ exchanges (Santos et al. 2017).

This chapter[1]—based on a talk given at the National Bureau of Economic Research Conference on New Directions in Market Design in May 2023—applies a qualitatively similar approach to the investigation of the Incentive Auction, a recent radio spectrum reallocation conducted by the Federal Communications Commission (FCC). There are many open questions in this setting: the auction's design was both novel and extremely complex (Leyton-Brown et al. 2017), and as a result it was not possible to thoroughly consider every potential design variation before the auction was run. Furthermore, the complexity of the setting presents a significant barrier to purely theoretical analyses. Our goal in this chapter is to show how a computationally intensive approach can be used to evaluate how well the auction design performed, particularly asking which elements of the design were most important and which variations of the design might have led to even better outcomes. Such insights can inform other important resource allocation problems that may leverage parts of the auction's design. More broadly, we hope this work will serve as an example for how AI can be employed to understand and evaluate alternative market designs in complex settings.

6.1.1 Evaluating Complex Auction Designs

To date, the design and analysis of auctions has relied primarily on theoretical tools. Such analysis becomes increasingly difficult as auctions become more complex,[2] e.g., as the number of goods at auction increases; as the number of parameters needed to describe valuation functions grows; as heterogeneity across bidders increases; etc. Nevertheless, the Incentive Auction's design was strongly informed by theoretical analysis, which has shown that deferred acceptance (DA) auctions have many good properties. DA auctions exhibit "unconditional winner privacy" (Milgrom and Segal 2020), meaning that winners are only required to reveal as much about their valuation as is necessary to prove that they are winners. When stations' bids are binary responses to a series of descending offers and when stations are all

1. This chapter substantially follows the paper "Incentive Auction Design Alternatives: A Simulation Study" by the same authors, published in 2024 in *Management Science: Revenue Management and Market Analytics*. Please refer to that paper for details regarding the setup of the experiments described here and for additional experimental results. The chapter also draws in places from "Deep Optimization for Spectrum Repacking," N. Newman, A. Fréchette, K. Leyton-Brown, *Communications of the ACM*, volume 61, number 1, pp. 97–104, January 2018.

2. For example, Kelly and Steinberg (2000) note of the Progressive Adaptive User Selection Environment (PAUSE) auction format that their design is "probably too complex to admit much theoretical analysis."

independently owned, DA auctions are obviously strategy-proof (Li 2017) and weakly group strategy-proof. When the sets of stations that can be jointly repacked form a uniform matroid, DA auctions repack the efficient set of stations (Bikhchandani et al. 2011); if furthermore bidder values are drawn independently from known distributions, scoring offers according to virtual values can implement the Myerson "optimal auction" (Milgrom and Segal 2020). In exchange for the universality of its findings, theoretical analysis necessarily relies on simplifications. Such simplifications can raise questions about the practical applicability of results.

A second approach for evaluating auction designs is data driven. There is a vast literature on laboratory and field experiments for auctions (Ferejohn et al. 1979; Rassenti et al. 1982; Kwasnica et al. 2005; Cason et al. 2011; Adomavicius et al. 2012). To our knowledge no such experimental data exist evaluating the Incentive Auction; indeed, it would be very challenging to conduct realistic experiments, given the real auction's long duration and extremely large number of participants. Data can also be obtained from an auction's practical deployment. There is an extensive structural estimation literature in auctions and matching markets. Such analysis has led to significant insights in data-rich domains such as school choice (Agarwal and Somaini 2018; Calsamiglia et al. 2020); highway procurement auctions (Krasnokutskaya and Seim 2011; Somaini 2020); timber auctions (Athey et al. 2011); and ad auctions (Athey and Nekipelov 2010). Unfortunately, only a single auction has been held to date using the Incentive Auction design, leaving us with only a single sample of past bids. We nevertheless leveraged this single datapoint to inform a valuation model, described below.

This chapter focuses on a third approach, computational simulations. This approach can verify whether theoretical findings from simplified models carry over to more complex, real-world settings without relying on the availability of rich historical data. Simulations are particularly well suited to studying market settings with complex clearing mechanisms (because such complexity tends to preclude "cleaner" analytical results) and uncontroversial models of agent behavior (because this reduces the risk that the model upon which the simulation relies will produce unrealistic behavior). The FCC conducted its own (mostly unpublished) internal simulations, leveraging a variety of techniques from operations research (Kiddoo et al. 2019).

The broader research community conducted simulation studies of the reverse auction at various points in the design process, differing in the fidelity with which they modeled the auction mechanism; the degree to which they made simplifications for computational reasons; and the valuation models they employed.

Before the auction mechanism was even finalized, Kearns and Dworkin (2014) used simulations to speculate on the amount of spectrum that might be reallocated. This work used a bidder model that consisted entirely of determining which bidders would participate, which they studied both using

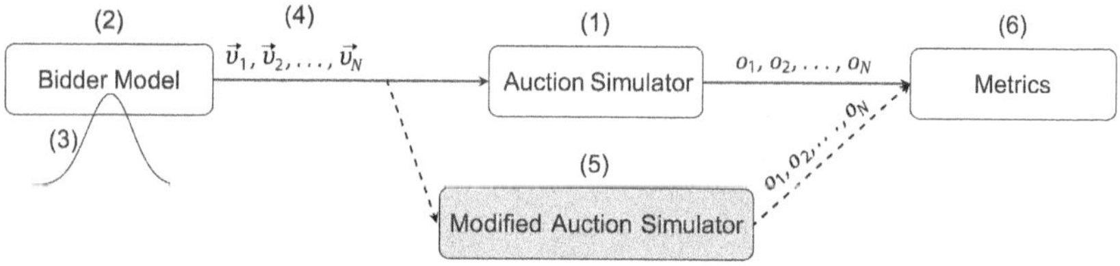

Fig. 6.1 An overview of our simulation approach. *N* samples from a bidder model are fed into both a modified and unmodified simulator. The two outcome sets are converted into metrics and compared on a per-sample basis.

independent coin flips for every bidder and more complex models in which affiliated bidders made correlated decisions. Later in the design process, Cramton et al. (2015) used simulations to lobby for design changes such as changing the methodology for setting opening prices. They leveraged a (non-public) valuation model developed through "discussions with many broadcasters, taking into account revenue data, historical station sales prices, station affiliation information, total market revenue, and other factors." After the auction concluded, Doraszelski et al. (2017) used simulations to estimate how profitable and how risky bidder collusion strategies might have been, restricting experiments to regional scale and furthermore employing approximations ("limited repacking") to speed up computation. They concluded that the auction could have mitigated the harm imposed by collusion by restricting the participation of affiliated bidders in the auction. This work leveraged a novel value model for bidders, which we discuss further in section 6.3.1.1 because we used it in our own simulations. The simulator used in this chapter more accurately simulates the actual reverse auction design than any other simulator of which we are aware.[3] Finally, Ausubel et al. (2017) performed a post-mortem analysis of the Incentive Auction in a similar vein to this chapter, but with a primary focus on the forward auction; we discuss one of their proposed amendments to the clearing algorithm in section 6.5.4.2.

6.1.2 Our Simulation Methodology

We employed, and can recommend, the following simulation methodology (see figure 6.1):

1. Build an auction simulator (choosing an appropriate level of abstraction, as auction rules are often incredibly complex).
2. Create a bidder model, exposing parameters that control both valuations and behavior.
3. Establish a probability distribution over parameters of the bidder model.

3. We make no comment about the fidelity of the FCC's own simulator, since details about it are not publicly available.

4. Identify many plausible auction scenarios by sampling repeatedly from this probability distribution.
5. Run paired simulations by holding this population of scenarios fixed and varying one or more elements of the auction design.
6. Compare outcomes across paired samples using predetermined metrics.

For the study described in this chapter we instantiated these steps as follows. First, we custom-built the simulator used in this chapter. Other Incentive Auction simulators have been used in previous work (surveyed below) but ours is the most comprehensive of which we are aware, both in terms of its scale (national) and its coverage of the auction rules (e.g., multi-stage auctions including VHF bands).[4]

Next, perhaps the most critical step in our methodology is the specification of a bidder model, describing both valuations and behavior for each bidder. Since we focus on the reverse auction, each of our bidders corresponds to a television station. We considered two different valuation models: (1) the only fully specified model from the literature of which we are aware; and (2) a model we created based on publicly released bid data. We ran simulations with both models and contrast the results to investigate the robustness of our findings. Realistically modeling agent behavior is perhaps easiest in settings giving rise to *obviously dominant* strategies (Li 2017). A strategy is obviously dominant if any time an agent might deviate from the strategy, the best it can do under the deviation is no better than the worst it can do by following the strategy. Descending clock auctions make truthful bidding obviously dominant for bidders who own a single broadcast station (but not for those who own multiple stations).[5] Unfortunately, the real reverse auction lacked obviously dominant strategies because stations could do more than just accept and reject an offer: they could also accept a lower price and downgrade to a VHF channel. We decided to study the problem by considering the assumptions both that VHF bidding could be abstracted away and that it could not. For the latter case, no equilibrium bidding strategy is known, let alone any model of how bidders would behave if they believed that some or all of their opponents were bidding out of equilibrium. Given the widespread belief that many bidders in this auction were unsophisticated, we modeled bidders as bidding truthfully and myopically (see section 6.3.2).

Finally, we restricted most of our comparisons to simulations that cleared the same amount of spectrum, considering two key metrics: the sum of values of stations removed from the airwaves (value loss) and the aggregate amount paid to stations (cost). When assessing design elements that did

4. Our simulator's code is freely available online at https://github.com/newmanne/SATFC.
5. An agent can deviate from truthful bidding in this setting either by (1) accepting an offer below its value, or (2) by rejecting an offer above its value. Since prices only descend, these deviations either lead to selling at a loss or not selling at all, thus having a best-case utility of zero. Since truthful bidding has a worst-case utility of zero, it constitutes an obviously dominant strategy in this setting.

affect the amount of spectrum cleared, we assumed that it was preferable to clear more spectrum, based on statements made by the FCC about the auction's intended goals (FCC 2012).

6.1.3 Questions Considered in Our Analysis

We ask one question about algorithmic design and three categories of questions about economic design.

1. *How important was it to optimize a solver for the computationally hard problems arising under the specific auction design?* Auctions can include problems that (in general) may not be solvable in a reasonable amount of time; a well-studied example is the winner determination problem in combinatorial auctions (Rothkopf et al. 1998). Exact solutions can be replaced with approximations, but this may degrade outcomes and incentives. We investigated station repacking, a hard problem that had to be solved repeatedly in the Incentive Auction. Was auction performance significantly improved by the FCC's use of a customized feasibility checker to determine whether a station could be repacked alongside the set of stations continuing over-the-air broadcasting? How large might that effect have been? Theoretical arguments sufficed to argue that incentives were robust to failures to solve repacking problems, but the way that such failures would have impacted cost and efficiency was harder to reason about. This question is important because the design of customized feasibility checkers required a nontrivial effort; such efforts should only be made in the future if they yield gains. We answer this question affirmatively in section 6.5.1, showing that substituting the custom feasibility checker with the best off-the-shelf alternative could have increased both average costs and value loss by more than 20 percent.
2. *How important was it to expand the set of products included in the Incentive Auction?* In the Incentive Auction, it would have been straightforward only to buy back licenses from stations broadcasting in the UHF band, since only UHF spectrum needed to be cleared. Instead—considerably increasing complexity—the FCC offered to purchase licenses from stations broadcasting in both the UHF and VHF bands and offered UHF stations the option of moving into the VHF band rather than going off-air. This increased the pool of stations eligible to participate in the auction by roughly 20 percent, with the potential both to increase efficiency (a lower-value VHF station could go off-air to make room for a UHF station) and to lower costs (c.f. Bulow and Klemperer's 1996 result that increasing competition can be more important to revenue than setting an optimal reserve price). Was the extra complexity justified by the outcomes? We found that it was (section 6.5.2): under straightforward bidding, not repacking the VHF band could have increased the auction's cost by 20–30 percent and decreased efficiency by 5–10 percent (with variation depending both on random sampling and the choice of value model).

3. *Was price discrimination effective at reducing payments to stations and increasing the number of channels cleared?* A canonical insight from revenue maximization (Myerson 1981) is that bidders with weaker valuation distributions should be boosted to increase competition with stronger bidders. The Incentive Auction attempted to do something similar, reducing initial price offers for stations that reached smaller populations of viewers. The reduced price offers, called "pops scoring," were politically contentious. In section 6.5.3, we show that the effects of scoring were not robust across value models. Under our new value model, pops scoring led to average costs 5 percent (2 percent) higher than head-to-head pricing when the VHF band was (was not) repacked. Under the value model from the literature, head-to-head pricing led to average costs that were 39 percent (5 percent) higher relative to pops scoring when the VHF was (was not) repacked.

4. *What was the impact of the FCC's method of determining supply?* The literature has studied various auction designs in which the seller can adjust supply after observing demand (Back and Zender 2001). In the Incentive Auction, the FCC separately ran forward and reverse auctions at a given clearing target; then, if forward-auction demand was insufficient to cover reverse-auction costs, the clearing target was lowered and a new stage of the auction began. This design was novel and received little advance comment from stakeholders. We compared it to a hypothetical auction having oracle access to the final clearing target. We found that the FCC's clearing procedure led to significantly higher costs and less efficient outcomes (section 6.5.4): across all experiments, the clearing procedure increased average value loss by 5–26 percent and average cost by 4–50 percent (with variation depending on random sampling, the choice of value model used, and whether the VHF band was repacked). We then introduce a new simple clearing procedure that performs nearly as well without knowing the final clearing target.

The rest of the chapter proceeds as follows. Section 6.2 describes the Incentive Auction in detail. Section 6.3 defines our valuation model and bidding model. Section 6.4 details our experimental setup, and section 6.5 reports our experimental findings.

6.2 The Incentive Auction

In this section we describe the Incentive Auction, focusing particularly on the reverse auction. We begin by describing the broad problem addressed by the Incentive Auction, and then introduce the station repacking problem. Solving repacking problems is a key subroutine within the reverse auction loop. We then proceed to the auction rules.

6.2.1 Radio Spectrum Reallocation

We begin by describing the context in which the Incentive Auction arose. Many devices, including broadcast television receivers and cell phones, rely on the transmission of electromagnetic signals. These signals can interfere with each other, so transmission is regulated: e.g., in the United States, by the Federal Communications Commission (FCC). Since electromagnetic spectrum suitable for wireless transmission is a scarce resource and since it is difficult for a central authority to assess the relative merits of competing claims on it, since 1994 the FCC has used *spectrum auctions* to allocate broadcast rights (see, e.g., Milgrom 2004). Many regulators around the world have followed suit. At this point, in the United States (as in many other countries), most useful radio spectrum has been allocated. Interest has thus grown in the *reallocation* of radio spectrum from less to more valuable uses. Spectrum currently allocated to broadcast television has received particular attention, for two reasons. First, over-the-air television has been losing popularity with the rise of cable, satellite, and streaming services. Second, the upper UHF frequencies used by TV broadcasters are particularly well suited to wireless data transmission on mobile devices—for which demand is growing rapidly—as they can penetrate walls and travel long distances (Knutson and Gryta 2014).

It was efficient from a resource allocation perspective for at least some broadcasters to sell their licenses to wireless internet providers willing to pay for them. However, two key obstacles made it unlikely that such trades would occur bilaterally and without government involvement, both stemming from the fact that wireless internet services require large, contiguous blocks of spectrum to work efficiently. First, a buyer's decision about which block of spectrum to buy would limit the buyer to trading only with broadcasters holding licenses to parts of that block; it could be hard or impossible to find such a block in which all broadcasters were willing to trade. Second, each of these broadcasters would have "holdout power," meaning the broadcaster could demand an exorbitant payment in exchange for allowing the deal to proceed. The likely result would have been very little trade, even if broadcasters valued the spectrum much less than potential buyers did.

A 2012 Act of Congress solved this problem. It guaranteed each broadcaster interference-free coverage in its broadcast area on *some* channel, but not necessarily on its currently used channel. This meant that if a broadcaster was unwilling to sell its license it could instead be moved to another channel, solving the holdout problem. To free up the channel that would permit this move to take place, broadcast rights could be bought from another station in the appropriate geographical area, even if this second station did not hold a license for spectrum due for reallocation. In what follows, we call such an interference-free reassignment of channels to stations a *feasible repacking*.

These trades and channel reassignments were coordinated via a novel spectrum auction run by the FCC between March 2016 and April 2017, dubbed the *Incentive Auction*. The result of the auction was to remove 14 UHF-TV channels from broadcast use, to sell 70 MHz of wireless internet licenses for $19.8 billion, and to make 14 MHz of spectrum available for unlicensed uses. With fewer remaining channels for TV stations, the TV spectrum needed to be reorganized; stations interfere with each other, so not all of them could be reassigned channels in the compressed TV band. Each station was either "repacked" in the leftover channels or voluntarily sold its broadcast rights, either going off the air or switching to a lower-quality band. These volunteers received a total of $10.05 billion to make repacking possible by yielding or exchanging their rights.

Roughly, the reverse auction began with a *clearing target,* or number of TV channels to decommission. Stations were approached one at a time with a series of decreasing price offers for their broadcast rights. When a station refused an offer, it exited the auction irrevocably and was guaranteed a spot in the leftover channels. As prices fell and more stations declined offers, the leftover channels became more and more congested. Before any station's bid was processed, a "feasibility checker" ensured that the station could still fit in the leftover channels alongside the exited stations without causing undue interference; if it could not, that station was "frozen," meaning that its price stopped falling and it was no longer eligible to exit the auction. The reverse auction further included a provision that allowed stations to exchange their broadcast rights for both a channel in a less desirable (VHF) band and monetary compensation. After the reverse auction concluded, a "forward" ascending clock auction was used to sell licenses in the cleared spectrum to mobile carriers. An outer-loop procedure iterated between reverse and forward auctions to identify the largest possible clearing target for which forward auction revenues exceeded costs.

6.2.2 The Reverse Auction

We now turn to a fuller and more formal summary of the auction mechanics. Prior to the auction, each television station $s \in \mathcal{S}$ in the United States and Canada[6] was assigned to a channel $c_s \in \mathcal{C} \subseteq \mathbb{N}$. The set of channels $\mathcal{C}$ can be partitioned into three equivalence classes, referred to as *bands*. Listed in decreasing order of desirability, these bands are: UHF (channels 14–51); high VHF ("HVHF," channels 7–13); and low VHF ("LVHF," channels 1–6). We use pre(s) to refer to a station's pre-auction band, sometimes called a station's home band.

Each station was only eligible to be assigned a channel on a subset of $\mathcal{C}$, given by a *domain* function $\mathcal{D} : \mathcal{S} \to 2^{\mathcal{C}}$ that maps from stations to these sets. The FCC determined pairs of channel assignments that would cause harmful interference based on a complex, grid-based physical simulation

6. Canadian stations did not bid in the auction but could be reassigned new channels.

("OET-69" FCC 2013); this pairwise constraint data is publicly available (FCC 2015a). Let $\mathcal{I} \subseteq (\mathcal{S} \times \mathcal{C})^2$ denote a set of *forbidden station–channel pairs* $\{(s,c), (s',c')\}$, each representing the proposition that stations s and s' could not concurrently be assigned to channels c and c', respectively.

The goal of the reverse auction was to remove some broadcasters from the airwaves and assign the remaining stations new channels from a reduced set $\overline{\mathcal{C}} = \{c \in \mathcal{C} \mid c < \overline{c}\}$. This reduced set is defined by $\overline{c} \in \mathcal{C}$; each choice of $\overline{c}$ corresponds to some clearing target. The actual Incentive Auction ended with $\overline{c} = 37$, allowing the higher numbered channels to be used for other purposes.

A *feasible assignment* is a mapping $\gamma : \mathcal{S} \rightarrow \overline{\mathcal{C}}$ that assigns each station a channel from its domain that satisfies the interference constraints: i.e., for which $\gamma(s) \in \mathcal{D}(s)$ for all $s \in \mathcal{S}$, and $\gamma(s) = c$ implies that $\gamma(s') \neq c'$ for all $\{(s,c),(s',c')\} \in \mathcal{I}$. As it turns out, interference constraints come in two kinds. *Co-channel constraints* specify that two stations may not be assigned to the same channel; *adjacent-channel constraints* specify that two stations may not be assigned to some pair of nearby channels. Thus, forbidden station–channel pairs are always of the form $\{(s,c),(s',c+i)\}$ for some stations $s,s' \in \mathcal{S}$, channel $c \in \mathcal{C}$, and $i \in \{0,1,2\}$.

Lastly, we define the *interference graph* as an undirected graph in which there is one vertex per station and an edge exists between two vertices s and s' if the corresponding stations participate together in any interference constraint: i.e., if there exist $c,c' \in C$ such that $\{(s,c),(s',c')\} \in I$. Figure 6.2 shows the interference graph for the United States and Canada.

We now describe a simplified version of the reverse auction in which only

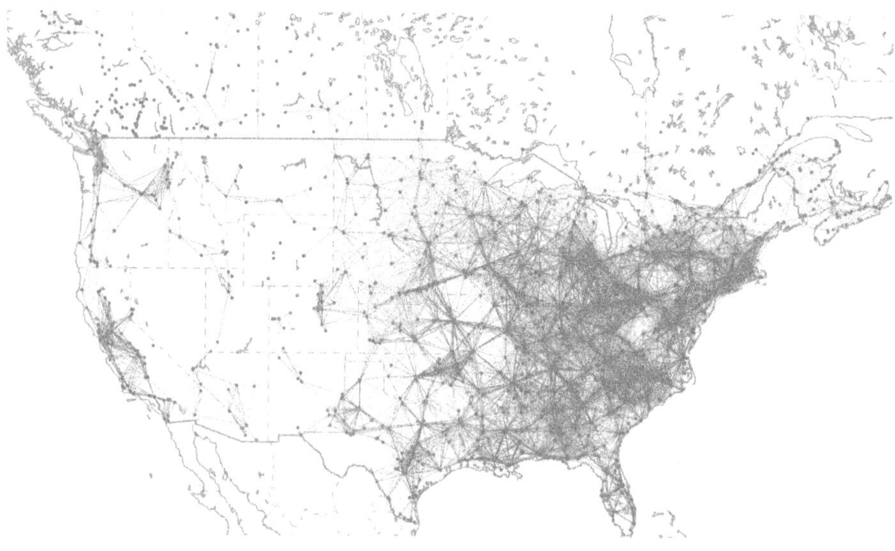

Fig. 6.2 Interference graph derived from the FCC's constraint data

the UHF band is repacked: only UHF stations participate in the auction and the only possible outcomes for each station are going off-air or continuing to broadcast in UHF. The real auction also repacked two VHF bands, but the inclusion of these bands complicates things significantly. The complete set of auction rules was published by the FCC in a 230-page document (FCC 2015b).

We begin by describing the reverse auction at a high level before giving more details about various key elements. First, stations respond to opening prices and decide whether to participate in the auction. Next, a solver finds an initial feasible channel assignment for all non-participating stations to minimize the number of channels required for those broadcasters, setting an initial clearing target $\overline{c}$. The auction then attempts to buy broadcast rights as necessary so that all stations remaining on air can fit into the available channels. It proceeds over a series of rounds, which consist of: (1) decrementing the clock and determining new prices, (2) collecting bids, and (3) processing bids.

A forward auction to sell the cleared spectrum follows the reverse auction. If sufficient revenue is raised in the forward auction, the Incentive Auction terminates; otherwise, the reverse auction resumes with a lower clearing target. We elaborate on each step of the reverse auction below.

6.2.2.1 Prices

Prior to the auction, the FCC used a *scoring rule* to assign a *score* (also sometimes referred to as a *volume*) to each station, which we denote by score (s). The score was used to determine individualized opening prices and was a function of both the station's interference constraints and the population of viewers that a station reached before the auction, which we denote by Population (s). We will have more to say about scoring rules in section 6.5.3.

The reverse auction is a descending clock auction. At the start of each round, the base clock price is reduced to $p_t = p_{t-1} - d_t$, where $d_t = \max[(p_{t-1}/20),(p_0/100)]$. Scores transform base clock prices to individualized station prices; this is, prices in each round $P_{s;t}$ are computed as $P_{s;t} = \text{score}(s) \cdot p_t$. We use $P_{s;\text{Open}}$ to refer to the auction's opening prices.

A "winning" station is one that ultimately goes off-air or moves to a different band. More specifically, if the final channel assignment is γ, s is winning if post(γ, s) $\neq$ pre(s), where post(γ, s) returns either the band to which s is assigned under γ or OFF if s is not assigned to a band under γ. We refer to the set of winning stations as S_{winners}. Throughout the auction, we track each station's "winning price" $\mathcal{P} : \mathcal{S} \rightarrow \mathbb{R}^+$. $\mathcal{P}(s)$ is the price that would have to be paid to s if the auction were to end immediately and s was a winning station. Initially $\mathcal{P}(s) = P_{s;\text{Open}}$.

6.2.2.2 Bidding

When only the UHF band is repacked, a bid in a given round corresponds to a binary decision. A station can accept $P_{s;t}$, indicating that it prefers to relinquish its broadcast rights and receive $P_{s;t}$. Alternatively, a station can

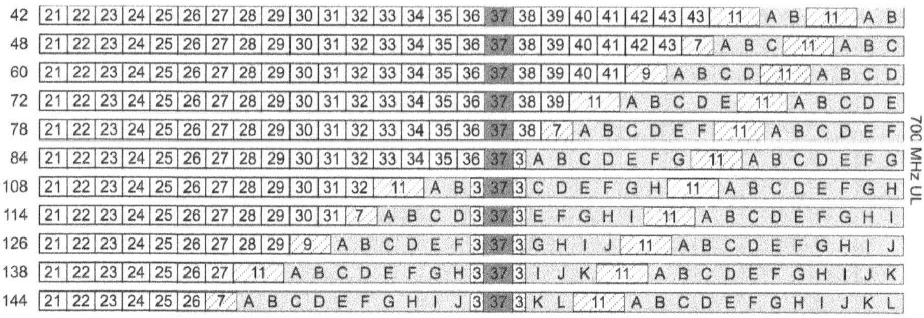

Fig. 6.3 The FCC's band plan for 600 MHz. Each row corresponds to a different clearing target and shows which channels would be repurposed and which would remain for TV broadcasting.

reject $P_{s;t}$, indicating that it prefers to continue to broadcast. If a station's bid to reject an offer is ever processed (as will be explained in the following section), it is said to have "exited" the auction. Such a station is never asked to bid again. An exited station receives no compensation and will continue to broadcast in its pre-auction band after the auction (albeit on a possibly different channel). We refer to the set of exited stations by S_{exited}.

6.2.2.3 Bid Processing

In the bid processing step, stations are considered one after another, in descending order of $[\mathcal{P}(s) - P_{s;t}]/[\text{score}(s)]$. When a station s is considered, first the feasibility checker is invoked to determine whether it is possible to repack s along with the exited stations: i.e., given a time limit, it tries to find a feasible assignment for $\{s\} \cup S_{\text{exited}}$. If the feasibility checker cannot repack s, its bid is not examined, and s is said to be "frozen." A station that is guaranteed to be frozen for the remainder of the stage is called a *provisional winner*; in a UHF-only auction, every frozen station is provisionally winning. In this case, $\mathcal{P}(s)$ is not reduced and s will no longer be asked to bid. If the feasibility checker can repack s, then $\mathcal{P}(s)$ is reduced and its bid is examined. If s bid to accept $P_{s;t}$, $\mathcal{P}(s)$ is lowered to $P_{s;t}$ and s remains "active," meaning it will be asked to bid again next round. If s bids to reject $P_{s;t}$, s permanently exits the auction.

6.2.2.4 Transitioning Between Auction Stages

A reverse auction stage ends when all stations are either frozen or have exited. Following each reverse auction stage is a forward auction stage where mobile carriers bid on licenses in the cleared spectrum. If the forward auction generates enough revenue to cover the costs of the reverse auction (the payouts to the winning stations $\sum_{s \in S_{\text{winners}}} \mathcal{P}(s)$),[7] the Incentive Auction termi-

7. Technically, the forward auction had to generate about $2 billion more: it also had to cover FCC expenses and the estimated costs of station retuning. In our examples and experiments, we ignore these additional requirements and only focus on the payments to winning stations.

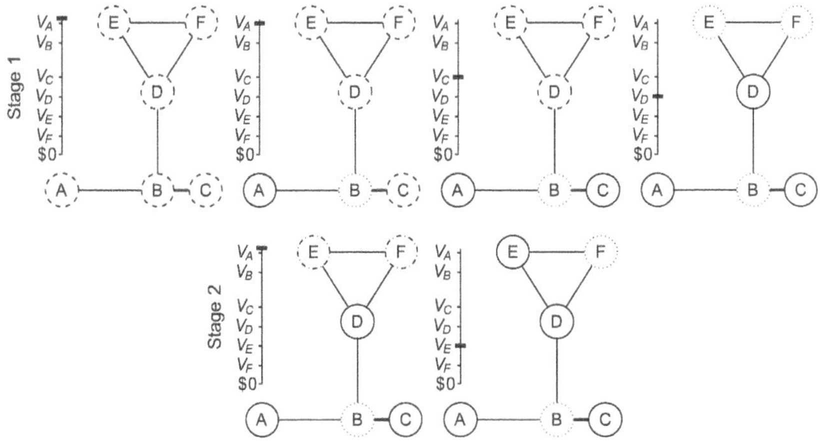

Fig. 6.4 An illustration of the reverse auction example described in section 6.2.3. Each row corresponds to a stage; a new image is drawn each time a station exits. Active stations are dashed, exited stations are solid, frozen stations are dotted, and stations with catch-up status are dash dotted. Connected stations cannot jointly broadcast on the same channel. *B* and *C* additionally cannot jointly broadcast on adjacent channels (shown by the thick bold edge between them). To the left of each image is the current clock price.

nates and each frozen station is paid $\mathcal{P}(s)$. An unsuccessful forward auction (one that does not raise sufficient revenue) triggers another stage of the reverse auction with a smaller clearing target.

The Incentive Auction thus determines the amount of spectrum to clear endogenously by iterating through stages of reverse and forward auctions that clear progressively less spectrum until a stage occurs in which the forward auction covers the costs of the reverse auction. When a new reverse auction stage begins, $\bar{c}$ is increased, expanding the set $\bar{\mathcal{C}}$. Given additional channels, some frozen stations may now be repackable; such stations are said to be in "catch-up" mode. At the beginning of a new reverse auction stage, the base clock p_t resets. A station in catch-up mode "unfreezes" if it can be repacked in the first round in which it would face a weakly lower price than the price at which it froze, $\mathcal{P}(s)$. Subsequent stages otherwise proceed like the initial stage.

6.2.3 Worked Example

Figure 6.4 illustrates the reverse auction through a worked example. Consider an auction setting with six stations *A*, *B*, *C*, *D*, *E*, *F* having valuations $V_A > V_B$, $V_C > V_D > V_E > V_F$. Assume that stations bid straightforwardly: they accept offers above their values and reject offers below their values. Let each station be identically scored (so starting prices are the same for all stations); thus, we can drop the station subscript when discussing prices, writing P_t instead of $P_{s;t}$. Assume that the feasibility checker is perfect, always finding a feasible assignment when one exists and always determining infeasibility otherwise. For convenience, let clock decrements be so small that we can model the clock as falling continuously. Let $\mathcal{C} = \{1,2,3\}$ and let $\mathcal{I}$ be structured so that all stations have co-channel constraints on every channel with each neighboring station according to the interference graph in figure 6.4. Let stations B and C additionally have adjacency constraints with each other due to their close proximity, prohibiting them from jointly broadcasting on adjacent channels.

Let $\bar{c} = 2$ initially, so that the auction begins trying to repack the stations into a single channel. Near the high opening prices, stations bid to remain off-air and their bids are processed because each station can exit. Nothing changes until $P_t < V_A$, at which point station A exits the auction. This movement freezes station B at price $\mathcal{P}(B) = V_A$, since A and B cannot both broadcast on the single channel. Other stations remain bidding and prices continue to fall until $P_t < V_C$ and C exits the auction. C's exit does not impact the other stations, so they continue to bid until $P_t < V_D$. At this point, D exits the auction, freezing E and F each $\mathcal{P}(E) = \mathcal{P}(F) = V_D$. Every station is now either frozen or has exited, so the stage ends. Stations B, E, and F are frozen at the end of the stage. If the Incentive Auction does not proceed to another stage, the total value removed from the airwaves will be $V_B + V_E + V_F$ and the total cost of freeing up two channels will be $V_A + 2V_D$.

Let us assume that in the forward auction, wireless carriers are unwilling to pay the repacking cost of $V_A + 2V_D$ to repurpose two channels worth of spectrum. The Incentive Auction then proceeds to a second stage where $\bar{c} = 3$: only one channel is cleared and two channels remain for repacking stations. Stations E and F can now be repacked alongside the exited stations and so enter catch-up mode. B cannot be repacked and remains frozen. P_t resets to a high value and then descends until $P_t < V_D$. At this point, E and F both transition from catch-up mode to bidding, since V_D was the price at which they froze. The auction continues until $P_t < V_E$, at which point E exits and freezes F at a price $\mathcal{P}(F) = V_E$. Again, all stations are either frozen or exited, so the second stage completes. Assuming the ensuing forward auction raises sufficient revenue, stations B and F will removed from the airwaves for a value loss of $V_B + V_F$ and a cost of $V_A + V_E$.

6.3 Value and Bidding Models

This section begins by describing two value models. The first follows Doraszelski et al. (2017); we created the second for this study, based on bid data released after the auction by the FCC. An advantage of considering two different value models is that we were able to compare simulation results under both settings to assess the robustness of our findings. We conclude the section by describing a model of how stations bid as a function of these values.

6.3.1 Value Models

Each station s has a value $v_{s,b}$ for broadcasting in each permissible band b. We normalize so that a station has no value for being off-air, i.e., $v_{s,\mathrm{OFF}} = 0$. Both models only provide $v_{s,\mathrm{UHF}}$, that is, home band values for UHF stations. For the two VHF bands in the auction, lower and higher VHF, we model a UHF station's value for switching to the HVHF band as $(2/3) \cdot v_{s,\mathrm{UHF}} \cdot \mathcal{N}(1,0.05)$ and similarly for the LVHF band as: $(1/3) \cdot v_{s,UHF} \cdot \mathcal{N}(1,0.05)$—i.e., roughly two-thirds and one-third of the station's UHF value with some multiplicative Gaussian noise. We generated values for VHF stations by computing a hypothetical UHF value and then applying the fractional reductions for VHF bands just described.

6.3.1.1 The MCS Value Model

Doraszelski et al.'s (2017) valuation model, which we dub the MCS (Max of Cash flow and Stick value) model, treats a station's value as the maximum of its cash flow value as a business and its stick value. The stick value represents the value of the broadcast license and tower, independent of the business; it can be more appropriate than cash flow when valuing noncommercial stations. Both of these were estimated from various sources including transaction data of station sales, advertising revenue, and station features.

6.3.1.2 A Novel Value Model based on Bid Data

Two years after the Incentive Auction concluded, the FCC released the auction bids. We used this data to construct a "realistic" model for station valuations. While the bids are not sufficient to reveal station values, they do allow us to infer bounds on values. In some cases these bounds are relatively tight, with upper and lower bounds separated by a single clock interval. Most of the time they are looser, in some cases, to an extent that does not allow us to improve on the trivial bound.

We inferred bounds on each UHF station's home band value, $v_{s,\mathrm{UHF}}$. We then used these bounds to fit a model. We assumed that value is proportional (in expectation) to population, $v_{s,\mathrm{UHF}} = \mathrm{Population}(s) \cdot n_s$. Here n_s is some number in units of \$/pop, sampled from an unknown cumulative distribution function (CDF) N. We computed a non-parametric maximum likelihood estimate of the distribution function N. Note that by definition $N(y_s) - N(x_s) + \Pr(x_s \leq n_s \leq y_s)$. Our goal was to maximize the product of these terms subject to constraints ensuring that N is a valid CDF. The results (figure 6.5) suggest that N is a log-linear function. Data were sparsest in the tails of the distribution, especially in the right tail, so we replaced the log-linear segments in both tails with Generalized Pareto Distributions (GPDs).

To generate UHF values, we multiply a station's population by a sample

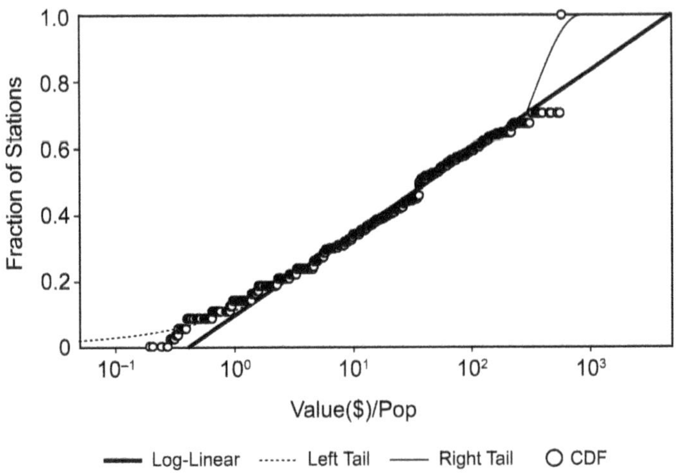

Fig. 6.5 CDF for our maximum likelihood estimate of *N* and its log-uniform distribution fit, plus generalized Pareto left and right tails

from the modeled distribution of N. In what follows, we refer to this model as the BD (bid data) model.

6.3.2 Bidding Model

We now describe our model of how stations bid. A station participated in our simulations if its opening price for going off-air exceeded its value for continuing to broadcast in its home band. After excluding 64 non-mainland stations, we considered 1813 stations eligible to participate in our simulations: 1407 UHF, 367 HVHF, and 39 LVHF.

In auctions with UHF options only, in which bidders are able only to remain off-air or to exit the auction, a single station faces a strategic situation in which its utility is "obviously" maximized by remaining off-air if the price exceeds its value and by exiting otherwise—that is, by bidding myopically (Li 2017). The situation when VHF options are included is no longer obvious in this sense, but we continue to assume for simplicity that when bidding in round t, a station selects the offer that myopically maximizes its net profit, $\arg\max_{b \in B_{s,t}} P_{s;b;t} + v_{s;b}$. We note that in the released bid data, only 52 percent (13 percent) of bids to move into LVHF (HVHF) were successful. Given that stations seeking to move to a VHF band faced a meaningful risk that their bid might fail to execute, some bidders might have benefited by bidding on VHF bands before it was straightforwardly optimal to do so. However, despite the potential drawbacks of straightforward VHF bidding, we are not aware of any behavioral rule that can be applied to all bidders and that is arguably more realistic.

6.4 Simulator Design and Experimental Considerations

As the reverse auction is simplest to reason about when only the UHF band is repacked, we ran both simulations that only repacked the UHF band and simulations that also repacked the VHF band. This allowed us to investigate which of our results generalize across settings. We ran simulations on both value models described in section 6.3. Unless otherwise stated, in every one of our experiments we took 50 samples per treatment. We gave feasibility checks 60 seconds to complete (as in the real auction, though of course we were unable to use exactly the same hardware) unless otherwise stated. Except when otherwise noted, we started our simulations at the 84 MHz clearing target (the clearing target at which the real Incentive Auction concluded; see figure 6.3 for more details on possible clearing targets) and ran auctions for only a single stage. We did this both because running multiple stages of the reverse auction is computationally expensive and because multi-stage simulations depend on additional assumptions about the forward auction. We do explore multi-stage auctions that begin from other clearing targets (including 126 MHz, the clearing target on which the Incentive Auction began) in section 6.5.4.

The Incentive Auction's design requires it to begin from a feasible channel assignment for the non-participating stations, however based on which stations participate, this will not always be possible. The FCC's rules therefore allowed a small number of stations to be assigned to channels *within* the spectrum that was otherwise resold (i.e., channels in $\mathcal{C} \setminus \bar{\mathcal{C}}$), even though doing so degrades the desirability of the mobile broadband licenses sold in the forward auction. Such stations are referred to as "impairing." We impair stations as necessary in our simulations to produce a valid starting assignment (for details, see the full paper).

We now explain how we compare simulated outcomes and discuss some simplifications our simulations make relative to the real auction process.

6.4.1 Metrics

One goal for the auction is efficiency: for any given clearing target, to maximize the total value of the stations that remain on the air, or equivalently, to minimize the total value of the stations removed from the airwaves. We focus on the latter definition—*value lost* instead of *value preserved*—because it is unaffected by value estimates for large, highly valuable stations that do not participate in the auction. That is, *value preserved* includes the values of easy-to-repack stations, even those that do not participate in any interference constraints, and leads to efficiency estimates near 100 percent when few stations go off-air relative to the number that remain on air, even when the number of stations going off-air is large relative to the number required by an optimal solution.

We define the *value loss* of an auction outcome as $\sum_{s \in \mathcal{S}} v_{s,\mathrm{pre}(s)} - v_{s,\mathrm{post}(\gamma,s)}$. Ideally, our metric for allocative efficiency would be the ratio of the value loss of a simulation's final assignment, γ, relative to an assignment from an efficient repacking γ^* that minimizes the value loss for a given value profile, i.e., $(\sum_{s \in \mathcal{S}} v_{s,\mathrm{pre}(s)} - v_{s,\mathrm{post}(\gamma,s)}) / (\sum_{s \in \mathcal{S}} v_{s,\mathrm{pre}(s)} - v_{s,\mathrm{post}(\gamma^*,s)})$. In general, however, γ^* is too difficult to compute, so we convert our absolute metric into a relative one by comparing the value loss between two simulations' final assignments (i.e., the ratio of value loss ratios, noticing that the denominators which depend on γ^* cancel out in this case).

Our second metric is the cost of reaching the specified clearing target: the prices paid to all winning stations, $\sum_{s \in \mathcal{S}_{\mathrm{winners}}} \mathcal{P}(s)$.

We use the terms *efficiency* and *cost* below as abbreviations that refer to value loss and the total payments made to broadcasters that go off-air or change bands. Outcomes with high efficiency (low value loss) and low cost are attractive. It is straightforward to compare two outcomes if they both clear the same amount of spectrum and one is both more efficient and cheaper; otherwise, any comparison requires a judgment call about how the two metrics should be traded off.

6.5 Experiments

Our experiments are divided into four categories, based on which element of the auction design they investigate: (1) repacking the VHF band in addition to UHF; (2) choosing the order in which stations are processed via a scoring function; (3) determining a clearing target by iterating between reverse and forward auction stages; and (4) determining which stations to freeze by checking the feasibility of station repackings.

6.5.1 Feasibility Checking

The feasibility checker determines if a given station can be repacked alongside the stations that have previously exited the auction. Feasibility checking was a large concern in the Incentive Auction because the station repacking problem is hard both theoretically—it is NP-complete—and in practice. When the feasibility checker cannot find a way to repack a station, either by proving that no repacking exists or by running out of time, a station freezes: it stops bidding and its compensation stops falling. The feasibility checker's quality therefore has a direct effect on both the cost and efficiency of the auction: if the feasibility checker fails to find an assignment that repacks a station when such an assignment exists, this station will freeze at an unnecessarily high price. If the station would otherwise never freeze at all, the value loss of the allocation is changed.

Do auctions achieve better efficiency and/or lower costs as the feasibility checker improves? Our intuition is that in general, better feasibility checking should lead to better results.

SATFC 2.3.1, the feasibility checker that was used in the Incentive Auction, was designed over several years (Fréchette et al. 2016; Newman et al. 2017). The solver is a prime example of AI empowering market design. It combines complete and local-search SAT-encoded feasibility checking with a wide range of domain-specific techniques, such as constraint graph decomposition. Automatic algorithm configuration techniques were applied to construct a portfolio of eight complementary algorithms from these various components. We now investigate whether the effort invested in making SATFC 2.3.1 was helpful, or whether a more off-the-shelf solution would have sufficed. To do so, we ran simulations in which we exchanged SATFC 2.3.1 with alternative solvers.

Newman et al. (2017) ran 22 solvers from ACLib (Hutter et al. 2014) (a library of solvers that support algorithm configuration) on a benchmark set of sampled station repacking problems from their reverse auction simulations.[8] The results are shown in figure 6.6. We selected certain solvers from this figure and ran simulations, using each as the feasibility checker. Specifically, we compared the following solvers:

- *SATFC 2.3.1*: the feasibility checker used in the Incentive Auction
- *Greedy*: a solver that simply checks whether a previous assignment can be augmented directly, without changing the assignments of any other stations (this algorithm is the simplest reasonable feasibility checker and thus serves as a baseline)
- *PicoSAT*: to our knowledge, alongside MIP approaches, the only other solver that has been used in publications on the Incentive Auction, probably because it was shown to be the best among a set of alternatives in an early talk at the FCC on the subject (Leyton-Brown 2013)
- *Gurobi* and *CPLEX*: MIP solvers initially considered by the FCC
- *Gnovelty+PCL*: the best performing of the 22 ACLib solvers on the benchmark data described above

Our experiments took just over two CPU years. Results are shown in figure 6.7. (In what follows, we typically present figures for repacking both UHF and VHF using the BD value model, but discuss our findings across all experimental settings.) Each point in the figure represents the outcome of one simulation, with its x-axis position denoting its efficiency and its y-axis position denoting its cost. Since it is difficult to show graphically which auctions use the same paired value profiles for even a modest number of samples, rather than plotting raw efficiency and cost on each axis we instead plot normalized efficiency and cost. That is, we select one setting (in this case, auctions that repack using SATFC 2.3.1) as the reference treatment, and

8. This benchmark can be downloaded at the University of British Columbia Computer Science Department website, https://www.cs.ubc.ca/labs/beta/www-projects/SATFC/cacm_cnfs.tar.gz.

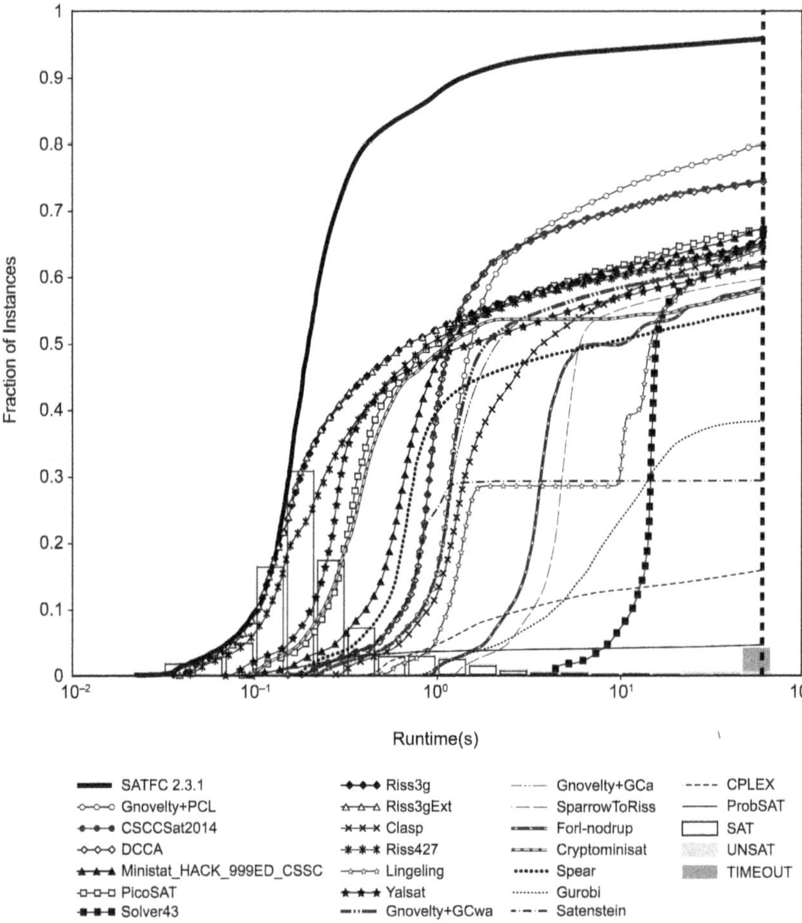

Fig. 6.6 Empirical Cumulative Density Function of runtimes for default configurations of MIP and SAT solvers and for SATFC 2.3.1 on a benchmark set of 10,000 non-trivial problems. Figure taken from Newman et al. (2017). The curves show fraction of instances solved (*y* axis) within different amounts of time (*x* axis; note the log scale). The legend is ordered by percentage of problems solved before the cutoff. The histogram indicates density of SAT and UNSAT instances binned by their (fastest) runtimes; unsatisfiable instances constituted fewer than 1 percent of solved instances.

then plot the ratio of the efficiency (cost) of each simulation from additional treatments relative to the corresponding simulation using the same value profile in the reference treatment. With this choice, the reference treatment always corresponds to the point (1, 1), represented in our figures by a diamond. For each treatment we also plot a star to indicate each metric's mean value. We observed that stronger feasibility checkers led to better outcomes

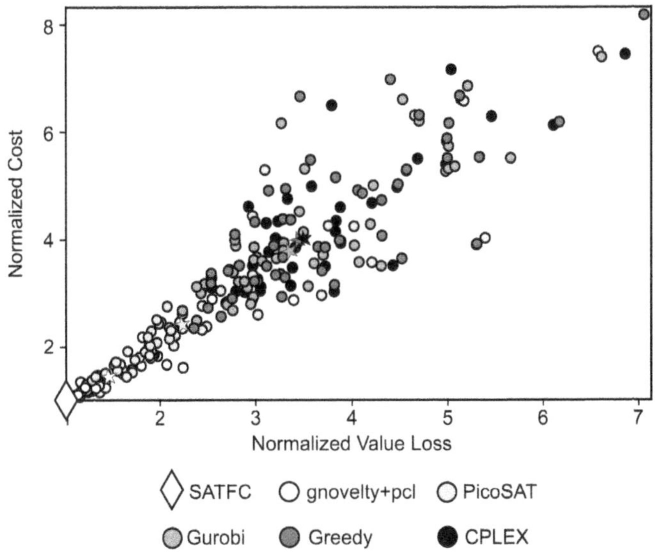

Fig. 6.7 Comparing auctions using different feasibility checkers

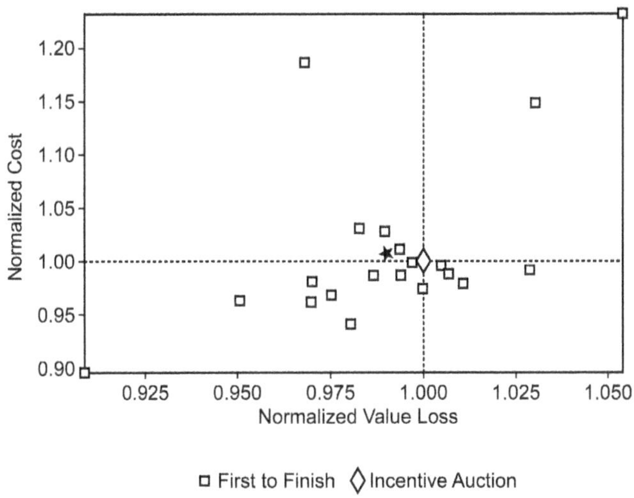

Fig. 6.8 Comparing the first to finish algorithm against the standard bid processing algorithm for single-stage 126 MHz auctions

according to both of our metrics: the relative rankings of the solvers in the benchmark study translated exactly into the relative rankings across both of our metrics, regardless of whether the VHF band was repacked and regardless of our choice of value model. In particular, we observed that SATFC 2.3.1 dominated all other solvers on both metrics, not only on average but in each individual simulation and across both value models. Reverse auctions run using the best off-the-shelf solver, *gnovelty+pcl*, cost between 1.22 and 1.45 times more on average (depending on bands being repacked and the value model used) and lost between 1.22 and 1.45 times as much broadcaster value as those based on SATFC 2.3.1.

6.5.2 Repacking the VHF Band

The Incentive Auction reduced only the number of UHF channels but repacked stations in three bands: UHF, HVHF, and LVHF. Repacking the two VHF bands offered the potential for cost savings and efficiency gains, as UHF stations might have been willing to accept a smaller payment to move to a VHF channel instead of going off the air and this could have constituted a net gain, even taking into account the need to compensate VHF stations for going off-air to make space. An optimal repacking for a given value profile can only become weakly more efficient when the VHF bands are included as more configurations of stations become available.

However, adding extra bands to the reverse auction complicated an otherwise elegant design. Stations no longer possessed obviously dominant strategies and might have benefited from reasoning about when to move between bands (a "ladder" constraint restricted movement from higher-value to lower-value bands). Price calculations became more involved as each option had to be priced appropriately. The bidding language had to be augmented with "fallback bids" that determine where a station goes if a move to a VHF band is unsuccessful. Also, unlike in UHF-only settings where freezing is permanent, VHF stations can freeze and later unfreeze within the same stage if other stations move out of their home bands, complicating bid processing. All of this extra complexity made the auction more difficult to explain to station owners, which mattered since some of the participants were relatively unsophisticated and encouraging them to participate was a first-order concern. It is thus sensible to ask whether the additional complexity was worthwhile. While repacking VHF raised the possibility of more efficient allocations, such gains might have been small, arising only under exotic bidding behavior, or have come at a high cost. We thus asked: What changes to efficiency and cost arise when VHF options are included and bidders bid straightforwardly?

To answer this question, we ran two sets of auctions: the first repacking both the VHF and UHF bands, the other repacking only the UHF band. Our results are shown in figure 6.9. The experiments took a little over one CPU year to run. Using both value models, we observed that repacking the VHF band led to a significant reduction in payments—on average, sampled UHF-only auctions cost 1.23 and 1.32 times as much as their VHF-repacking counterparts using the MCS and BD value models, respectively. The impact on efficiency was more modest and less uniformly positive. Under the MCS (BD) value model, sampled UHF-only auctions

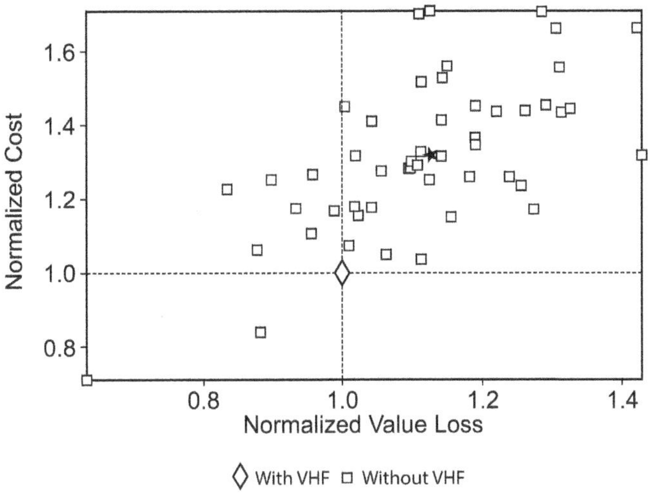

Fig. 6.9 Comparing auctions that only repack the UHF band against auctions that also repack VHF bands

experienced 1.05 (1.12) times higher value loss on average. On the whole, our simulations suggest that if bidders continued to bid straightforwardly despite the complex design, repacking the VHF band was an important design choice that likely led to lower costs and also somewhat more efficient outcomes.

6.5.3 Scoring Rules

Stations' starting prices in the Incentive Auction were not all the same: they were set proportionally to an assigned *score*, determined by a *scoring rule*. Under truthful bidding in a UHF-only auction, an unfrozen station will remain off-air for exactly as many rounds as it takes for its price to fall below its value, at which point it will exit. Using scoring to raise or lower a station's initial price relative to others is one control knob an auctioneer has over the order in which stations exit.

Theoretically, scoring performs two distinct functions. First, because every descending clock auction is equivalent to a greedy algorithm for packing stations into the broadcast spectrum, it may be possible to pack a larger and more valuable set of stations if the algorithm prioritizes stations that interfere with fewer neighbors. In the FCC's design, this was achieved by offering higher prices to stations with more "interference links" so that those stations would be less likely to exit. Second, scoring reduces an auction's expected cost by offering lower prices to stations that would be likelier to accept them, following Myerson (1981). In the FCC's design, this was implemented by reducing prices offered to stations serving smaller populations.

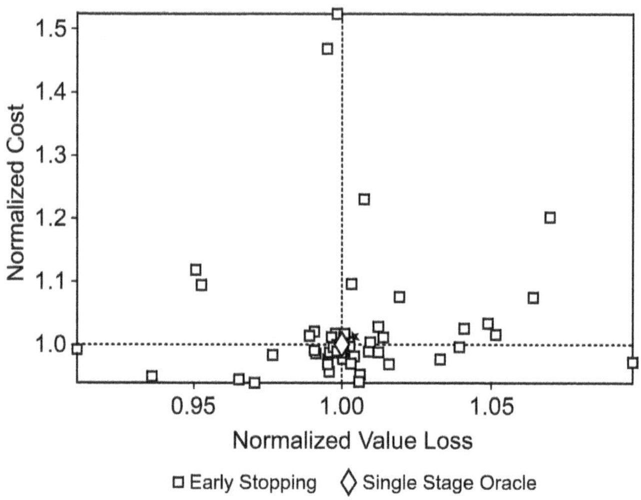

Fig. 6.10 Comparing early stopping auctions against single-stage auctions

(This design element was controversial: it was vigorously opposed by a coalition of owners of lower powered stations serving smaller populations, the "Equal Opportunity for Broadcasters Coalition," whose starting prices in the clock auction were reduced.) Overall, the two elements were combined by setting opening prices in proportion to the square root of the product of a station's population and its interference links.

In our experiments, we compared the following four scoring rules: (1) "Incentive Auction," the scoring rule used in the actual auction; (2) "Interference," the square root of a station's interference links; (3) "Population," the square root of a station's population; and (4) "Uniform," scoring each station identically. As in the actual auction, we normalized all scores so that the highest scoring UHF station had a score of 1 million.

We note a subtlety in these experiments: scoring rules impact prices, so simulations differing only in their scoring rules will not necessarily select the same set of impairing stations given the same value profile. To prevent "apples-to-oranges" comparisons across auctions clearing spectrum of varying quality, we disabled our impairment mechanism and ran simulations with high enough base clock prices to elicit full UHF-station participation. Running with no impairment mechanism corresponds to considering a world in which the FCC is unwilling to accept any degradation to the cleared spectrum.

Results for our simulations using the various scoring rules are shown in figure 6.10. Under the MCS value model, when the VHF band was repacked, we observed that simulations using only interference scoring cost 1.24 times as much and experienced 1.11 times as much value loss as simulations that combined population and interference scoring (the FCC's scoring rule). Uniformly scoring stations was not effective in this setting, with simulations averaging nearly 50 percent higher costs and 25 percent higher value loss. When only the UHF band was repacked, the scoring rule appeared to matter much less. Here, the interference scoring rule outperformed other scoring rules on average, with mean costs and value losses of 0.93 and 0.99 times respectively compared to corresponding simulations using the FCC's scoring rule. Under the BD value model, we observed much higher variance across simulations. If we nevertheless consider average performance, the FCC's scoring rule was outperformed in both metrics by every other scoring rule considered regardless of whether the VHF band was repacked. When the VHF band was repacked, the lowest value losses and costs were achieved, surprisingly, by the uniform scoring rule (94 percent mean value loss and 88 percent cost relative to the FCC's scoring rule). When only the UHF band was repacked, the lowest average value losses and costs were achieved by interference scoring (97 percent and 95 percent of the FCC scoring rule). On the whole, beyond a single setting (MCSMCS values and UHF + VHF repacking) we did not find robust evidence for population-based scoring. These experiments required 3.5 years of CPU time to run.

6.5.4 Multi-Stage Clearing

The Incentive Auction allowed for multiple stages of reverse followed by forward auctions in order to let market forces determine the appropriate amount of spectrum to clear. Each successive stage began with a reverse auction clearing a smaller amount of spectrum to achieve a lower overall cost than the previous stage. The actual Incentive Auction went through four stages.

One obvious practical drawback of a multi-stage approach is its impact on auction length: running multiple stages takes time. A less obvious concern is how the multi-stage approach impacted the final outcome. We turn to simulations, asking two questions: (1) What, if any, economic costs arose due to multi-stage clearing? (2) Would an "early-stopping" alternative to the reverse auction have performed better?

6.5.4.1 The Economic Impact of Multi-Stage Clearing

To assess the economic impact of multi-stage clearing, we ran experiments that began trying to clear 126, 114, 108, and 84 MHz of spectrum, each proceeding to follow the ordering of clearing targets selected by the FCC (see figure 6.3), and each terminating at 84 MHz, leading to four-, three-, two-, and single-stage auctions, respectively. These experiments took 31 years of CPU time.

A complicating factor in this comparison is that for any given value profile, the final set of impairing stations may differ based on the starting stage, which muddies the interpretation of cleared spectrum as a measure of per-

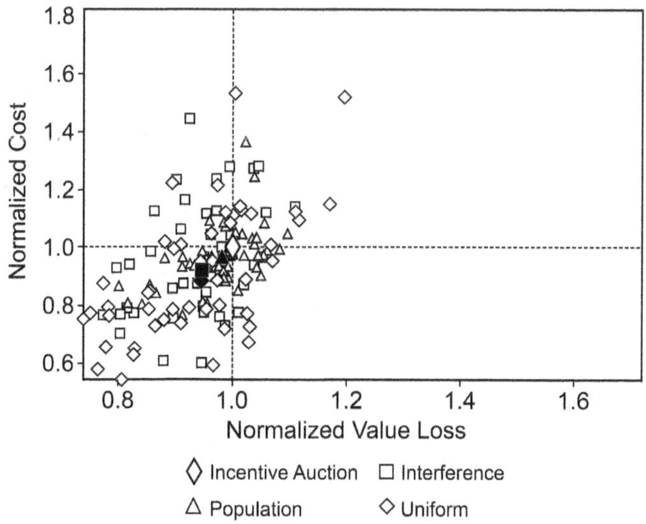

Fig. 6.11 Comparing auctions using four different scoring rules
Note: The black shapes indicate each metric's mean value.

formance. As above, we consider a world with high base clock prices to avoid impairments. Under this assumption we observed that running the auction through multiple stages degraded both cost and efficiency, especially when the VHF band was repacked (figure 6.11). In VHF-repacking simulations using the MCS (BD) model, on average four-stage auctions cost 1.50 (1.19) times as much as their single-stage counterparts and had 1.26 (1.14) times the value loss. The results were similar but less dramatic in magnitude for UHF-only auctions. In UHF-only simulations using the MCS (BD) model, four-stage auctions cost roughly 5 percent (10 percent) more and had roughly 5 percent (10 percent) additional value loss compared to perfectly forecasting the clearing target. In all cases, even if the exact stage was not perfectly selected, starting the auction closer to the final stage would also have yielded significant improvements to both metrics on average.

6.5.4.2 *Early Stopping*

The results just presented led us to ask: Is there any other way the FCC could have determined a clearing target endogenously with less impact on cost and efficiency? We suggest an approach that we call *early stopping*: for each candidate clearing target, conduct the forward auction before the corresponding reverse auction, and stop each reverse auction as soon as its cost exceeds the forward auction revenue. To see why this would help, consider again our example in figure 6.4, but now imagine that the auctioneer knows going into the first reverse auction stage that the forward auction revenue is some number less than V_A. Once station B freezes at a price of V_A, the provisional cost exceeds the forward auction revenue. Under the early stopping scenario, the first reverse auction stage would immediately stop and so station C would not exit. Then, in the second stage, station B would exit next and the outcome would exactly match that of an auction in which the clearing target had initially been set to the second stage target. In general, continuing the reverse auction instead of aborting can only result in more stations exiting, limiting flexibility in later stages. The original design proposed that the forward and reverse auctions be run in parallel, but due to finite staffing resources, the auctions had to be sequenced. We note that early stopping represents a potential algorithmic improvement even over the original parallel design.

Early stopping does not always outperform the original design; it is possible to construct examples where the commitments made in earlier stages are better than those made in later stages. To test whether early stopping might help in practice, we ran two sets of experiments. The first set compared early stopping auctions against single-stage stations that "knew" the correct clearing target. The second set compared the amount of spectrum cleared by early stopping auctions to auctions using the original design. Both of these experiments required forward auction revenues as inputs. We had little data to use for modeling these revenues—one observation for each of the four clearing targets that were reached in practice—so we adopted a convenient regression model. Unlike previous experiments where we assumed a predetermined number of stages, we now determined the auction's end by comparing forward auction revenues to clearing costs. This meant that auctions could end at any stage, so the amount of spectrum sold could differ across paired simulations. We assume that clearing more spectrum is preferable to clearing less, noting the FCC's stated goals. We ran early stopping auctions with an initial clearing target of 126 MHz (corresponding to the first stage of the real auction) and following the 600 MHz band plan (see figure 6.3) from that point on.

Once these experiments completed, we determined the final stage of each early stopping simulation and ran a corresponding single-stage auction in order to assess the "penalty" due to early stopping vs. perfect forecasting of the clearing target. The results are shown in figure 6.12. For computational reasons, we only ran UHF-only simulations; even so, the experiments took more than 15 CPU years overall. To avoid making comparisons between different qualities of spectrum, we disabled our impairment mechanism and let prices start as high as required for full participation. We observed that in both value models, early stopping performed well relative to single-stage auctions, with increases to average cost and value loss of no more than about 1 percent. These results are particularly encouraging when compared to the multi-stage experiments described earlier, in which we observed significant gaps between multi-stage clearing and perfect forecasting.

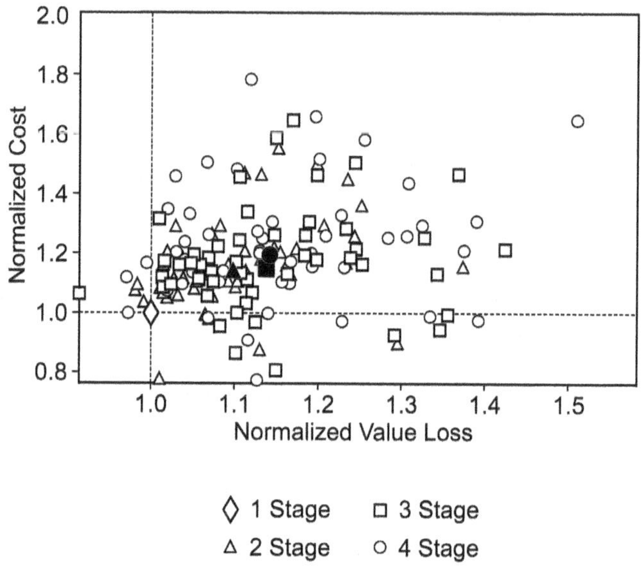

Fig. 6.12 Comparing auctions running through 1–4 stages, ultimately ending on the same clearing target

Note: The black shapes indicate each metric's mean value.

We next ran simulations that compared early stopping to the original clearing procedure to determine which cleared more spectrum. Under both value models, on average more mobile licenses were created when by early stopping than the original algorithm—0.50 and 0.22 extra licenses under the BD and MCS models, respectively. Early stopping also led to shorter auctions, averaging 30 percent and 76 percent of the rounds required by the original algorithm under BD and MCS, respectively.

We conclude by reflecting on some concrete numbers from the real auction. At the end of the first round of the first stage, payments to frozen stations already exceeded $50 billion; when the stage finished, these payments were $86 billion. In the subsequent forward auction, revenues were only $23 billion. Early stopping would have terminated the reverse auction during the very first round of bidding. The first reverse auction stage took one full month to resolve. This month, and possibly more time in future stages, would have been saved if early stopping had been implemented.

6.6 Conclusions and Reflections on the Intersection Between AI and Market Design

High fidelity, computationally intensive simulations are an approach for quantitatively contrasting candidate market designs which offer a key advantage: the quality of answers provided by such simulations will improve with both available computational resources and available market data. We outlined a six-step simulation methodology and instantiated it in the context of the Incentive Auction to investigate previously unanswerable questions about the cost and efficiency of certain alternative designs. To validate the robustness of our results, we used two quite different value models: one from the empirical economics literature and another that we constructed to rationalize public bid data. Our main findings were that: the specialized feasibility checker developed for the auction significantly improved both cost and efficiency; repacking VHF led to significantly lower costs and more efficient outcomes; the performance of pops scoring relative to other scoring rules varied widely based on the value model and whether the VHF band was repacked; the multiple stage clearing rule substantially both increased costs and reduced efficiency; and a simple amendment to the clearing algorithm could nearly eliminate multi-round inefficiency. We hope these specific insights can help to inform future auction designs. More broadly, our analysis demonstrates the practicality[9] and promise of large-scale computational analysis of the simulated behavior of candidate market designs in highly complex settings.

Of course, simulations are not the only way that AI can be applied to market design. We offered a second example in passing when discussing SATFC: this algorithm was automatically designed using algorithm configuration and algorithm portfolio techniques, achieving state-of-the-art performance by leveraging data characterizing realistic problem inputs. Some additional ways in which AI can impact the design of practical markets include helping to overcome search frictions problems when matching with an interested counterparty is hard, and helping participants express complex or non-linear preferences.

The recent success and wide adoption of large language models (LLMs) is leading many to dream bigger. The fundamental catch is counterfactuals: most machine learning techniques find patterns in independent and identically distributed samples, whereas most market design aims to optimize over possible worlds for which no prior data exist. We nevertheless foresee various ways in which machine learning approaches in general, and LLMs in particular, could be useful for market design. The first is by using machine learning to improve individual components of a market-design pipeline. We have already discussed how econometric methods can be used to fit

9. Altogether, our final experiments took more than 60 CPU years to run. Writing this chapter consumed perhaps 200–300 CPU years of compute in total, since we often found ourselves needing to rerun experiments as we uncovered bugs, changed parameters, or refined our experimental questions. We do not provide these CPU time numbers with the goal of impressing the reader with how much compute power we used. Instead, we hope (a) to give other researchers a sense of the scale of experiments that we consider necessary for answering questions like the ones we tackled here, and (b) to reassure the reader that we ran more or less the largest experiments that were practically feasible.

valuation distributions to data. Similarly, observational data could be used to fit models of bidding behavior (e.g., drawing on approaches from behavioral game theory, for instance Camerer 2003; Wright and Leyton-Brown 2017). Second, machine learning could also be used to improve individual components of a market itself. LLMs could be used to elicit preferences, to conduct rich automated negotiations (e.g., Bakhtin et al. 2022), and even to serve as user interfaces on top of messy markets in which bidders might hold complex preferences (e.g., eBay, ad markets). Third, machine learning can be used in a principled way to directly attack the problem of reasoning about counterfactuals. Causal inference has been a hot area for over a decade (e.g., Bottou et al. 2013; Wager and Athey 2018). Reinforcement learning simulations of economic systems are becoming rich enough to answer market design questions in some cases (e.g., Zheng et al. 2022). LLMs even offer the prospect of serving as a cheap proxy for human subject experiments (Aher et al. 2023; Horton 2023). Fourth, and finally, AI is likely to give rise to a new application domain for market designers. Important open questions include how to monetize LLMs (via, e.g., product placement or sponsored recommendations); how to defend LLMs against strategic manipulation (e.g., non-sponsored recommendations or prompt injection attacks); how to structure partnerships between custom LLMs and broader algorithmic services within which they are embedded; and how to price access to LLMs (particularly given the existence of a complex quality/cost trade-off).

References

Adomavicius, Gediminas, Shawn P. Curley, Alok Gupta, and Pallab Sanyal. 2012. "Effect of Information Feedback on Bidder Behavior in Continuous Combinatorial Auctions." *Management Science* 58: 811–30.

Agarwal, Nikhil, and Paulo Somaini. 2018. "Demand Analysis Using Strategic Reports: An Application to a School Choice Mechanism." *Econometrica* 86(2): 391–444.

Aher, Gati, Rosa I. Arriaga, and Adam Tauman Kalai. 2023. "Using Large Language Models to Simulate Multiple Humans and Replicate Human Subject Studies." In *Proceedings of the 40th International Conference on Machine Learning (ICML'23)*, vol. 202. JMLR.org, Article 17, 337–371. https://dl.acm.org/doi/10.5555/3618408.3618425.

Allman, Maxwell, Itai Ashlagi, Irene Lo, Juliette Love, Katherine Mentzer, Lulabel Ruiz-Setz, and Henry O'Connell. 2022. "Designing School Choice for Diversity in the San Francisco Unified School District. In *Proceedings of the 23rd ACM Conference on Economics and Computation*, 290–91.

Athey, Susan, and Denis Nekipelov. 2010. "A Structural Model of Sponsored Search Advertising Auctions." In *EC '10: Proceedings of the 11th ACM conference on Electronic commerce.* https://dl.acm.org/doi/10.1145/1807342.

Athey, Susan, Jonathan Levin, and Enrique Seira. 2011. "Comparing Open and

Sealed Bid Auctions: Evidence from Timber Auctions." *Quarterly Journal of Economics* 126(1): 207–57.
Ausubel, Lawrence M., Christina Aperjis, and Oleg Baranov. 2017. "Market Design and the FCC Incentive Auction." Working Paper.
Back, Kerry, and Jaime F. Zender. 2001. "Auctions of Divisible Goods with Endogenous Supply." *Economics Letters* 73(1): 29–34.
Bakhtin, Anton, Noam Brown, Emily Dinan, Gabriele Farina, Colin Flaherty, Daniel Fried, Andrew Goff, Jonathan Gray, Hengyuan Hu, et al. 2022. "Human-Level Play in the Game of Diplomacy by Combining Language Models with Strategic Reasoning." *Science* 378(6624): 1067–1074.
Bichler, Martin, Vladimir Fux, and Jacob K Goeree. 2019. "Designing Combinatorial Exchanges for the Reallocation of Resource Rights." *Proceedings of the National Academy of Sciences* 116(3): 786–91.
Bikhchandani, Sushil, Sven De Vries, James Schummer, and Rakesh V Vohra. 2011. "An Ascending Vickrey Auction for Selling Bases of a Matroid." *Operations Research* 59(2): 400–413.
Cason, Timothy N., Karthik N. Kannan, and Ralph B. Siebert. 2011. "An Experimental Study of Information Revelation Policies in Sequential Auctions." *Management Science* 57: 667–88.
Bottou, Léon, Jonas Peters, Joaquin Quiñonero-Candela, Denis X. Charles, D. Max Chickering, Elon Portugaly, Dipankar Ray, Patrice Simard, and Ed Snelson. 2013. "Counterfactual Reasoning and Learning Systems: The Example of Computational Advertising." *Journal of Machine Learning Research* 14(101): 3207–3260. http://jmlr.org/papers/v14/bottou13a.html.
Bulow, Jeremy, and Paul Klemperer. 1996. "Auctions Versus Negotiations." *American Economic Review* 86(1): 180–94.
Calsamiglia, Caterina, Chao Fu, and Maia Güell. 2020. "Structural Estimation of a Model of School Choices: The Boston Mechanism Versus Its Alternatives." *Journal of Political Economy* 128(2): 642–80.
Camerer. Colin F. 2003. *Behavioral Game Theory: Experiments in Strategic Interaction*. Princeton University Press.
Cramton, Peter, Hector López, David Malec, and Pacharasut Sujarittanonta. 2015. Design of the Reverse Auction in the FCC Incentive Auction. https://cramton.umd.edu/papers2015-2019/cramton-reverse-auction-design-fcc-comment-pn.pdf.
Delacrétaz, David, Scott Duke Kominers, and Alexander Teytelboym. 2019. "Matching Mechanisms for Refugee Resettlement." Working Papers 2019–078. Human Capital and Economic Opportunity Working Group, December.
Doraszelski, Ulrich, Katja Seim, Michael Sinkinson, and Peichun Wang. 2017. "Ownership Concentration and Strategic Supply Reduction." NBER Working Paper No. 23034. Cambridge, MA: National Bureau of Economic Research.
FCC. 2012. "In the Matter of Expanding the Economic and Innovation Opportunities of Spectrum Through Incentive Auctions." *Notice of Proposed Rulemaking*, FCC 12–118, 10 2012.
FCC. 2013. "Office of Engineering and Technology Releases and Seeks Comment on Updated OET-69 Software." *FCC Public Notice*, DA 13–138, February.
FCC. 2015a. Repacking Constraint Files. Accessed November 20, 2015. http://data.FCC.gov/download/incentive-auctions/Constraint_Files/.
FCC. 2015b. "Application Procedures for Broadcast Incentive Auction Scheduled to Begin on March 29, 2016." *FCC Public Notice*, DA 15–1183, 10.
Ferejohn, John A., Robert Forsythe, and Roger G Noll. 1979. "An Experimental Analysis of Decision Making Procedures for Discrete Public Goods: A Case Study

of a Problem in Institutional Design." *Research in Experimental Economics*, edited by V. L. Smith, 1–58. JAI Press.

Fréchette, Alexandre, Neil Newman, and Kevin Leyton-Brown. 2016. "Solving the Station Repacking Problem." In *AAAI Conference on Artificial Intelligence*, 702–9.

Freund, Daniel, Shane G. Henderson, and David B. Shmoys. 2018. "Minimizing Multimodular Functions and Allocating Capacity in Bike-Sharing Systems." *Production and Operations Management* 27(12): 2346–2349.

Horton, John J. 2023. "Large Language Models as Simulated Economic Agents: What Can We Learn from Homo Silicus?" National Bureau of Economic Research Working Paper Series 31122. http://www.nber.org/papers/w31122.

Hutter, Frank, Manuel López-Ibáñez, Chris Fawcett, Marius Lindauer, Holger H. Hoos, Kevin Leyton-Brown, and Thomas Stützle. 2014. "AClib: A Benchmark Library for Algorithm Configuration." In *Conference on Learning and Intelligent Optimization (LION)*, 36–40. Springer.

Kearns, Michael, and Lili Dworkin. 2014. "A Computational Study of Feasible Repackings in the FCC Incentive Auctions." arXiv:1406.4837 (cs), June.

Kelly, Frank P., and Richard Steinberg. 2000. "A Combinatorial Auction with Multiple Winners for Universal Service." *Management Science* 46: 586–96.

Kiddoo, Jean L., Evan Kwerel, Sasha Javid, Melissa Dunford, Gary M. Epstein, Charles E. Meisch Jr., Karla L. Hoffman, Brian B. Smith, Anthony B. Coudert, Rudy K. Sultana, et al. 2019. "Operations Research Enables Auction to Repurpose Television Spectrum for Next-Generation Wireless Technologies." *INFORMS Journal on Applied Analytics* 49(1): 7–22.

Knutson, Ryan, and Thomas Gryta. 2014. "Verizon, AT&T May Face Bidding Limits in Spectrum Auction." *Wall Street Journal*, April 18. Accessed December 12, 2016. http://www.wsj.com/articles/SB10001424052702304626304579510154106120342.

Krasnokutskaya, Elena, and Katja Seim. 2011. "Bid Preference Programs and Participation in Highway Procurement Auctions." *American Economic Review* 101(6): 2653–2686.

Kwasnica, Anthony M., John O. Ledyard, David Porter, and Christine DeMartini. 2005. "A New and Improved Design for Multiobject Iterative Auctions." *Management Science* 51: 419–34.

Leyton-Brown, Kevin. 2013. "The Viability of Exact Feasibility Checking." Talk at the Stanford Institute for Economic Policy Research Conference on the Design of the U.S. Incentive Auction for Reallocating Spectrum Between Wireless Telecommunications and Television Broadcasting, February. https://www.cs.ubc.ca/~kevinlb/talks/2013-Feasibility-Testing.pdf.

Leyton-Brown, Kevin, Paul Milgrom, and Ilya Segal. 2017. "Economics and Computer Science of a Radio Spectrum Reallocation." *Proceedings of the National Academy of Sciences* 114(28): 7202–7209.

Li, Shengwu. 2017. "Obviously Strategy-Proof Mechanisms." *American Economic Review* 107(11): 3257–87.

Milgrom, Paul. 2004. *Putting Auction Theory to Work*. Churchill Lectures in Economics. Cambridge University Press.

Milgrom, Paul, and Ilya Segal. 2020. "Clock Auctions and Radio Spectrum Reallocation." *Journal of Political Economy* 128(1): 1–31.

Myerson, Roger B. 1981. "Optimal Auction Design." *Mathematics of Operations Research* 6(1): 58–73.

Newman, Neil, Alexandre Fréchette, and Kevin Leyton-Brown. 2017. "Deep Optimization for Spectrum Repacking." *Communications of the ACM* 61(1): 97–104.

Rassenti, S. J., V. L. Smith, and R. L. Bulfin. 1982. "A Combinatorial Auction Mechanism for Airport Time Slot Allocation." *Bell Journal of Economics* 13(2): 402–17.

Rothkopf, Michael H., Aleksandar Sasa Pekec, and Ronald M. Harstad. 1998. "Computationally Manageable Combinational Auctions." *Management Science* 44: 1131–147.

Santos, Nicolau, Paolo Tubertini, Ana Viana, and João Pedro Pedroso. 2017. "Kidney Exchange Simulation and Optimization." *Journal of the Operational Research Society* 68(12): 1521–1532.

Somaini, Paulo. 2020. "Identification in Auction Models with Interdependent Costs." *Journal of Political Economy* 128(10): 3820–3871.

Wager, Stefan, and Susan Athey. 2018. "Estimation and Inference of Heterogeneous Treatment Effects Using Random Forests." *Journal of the American Statistical Association* 113(523): 1228–1242.

Wright, James R., and Kevin Leyton-Brown. 2017. "Predicting Human Behavior in Unrepeated, Simultaneous-Move Games." *Games and Economic Behavior* 106: 16–37.

Yang, Rong, Benjamin Ford, Milind Tambe, and Andrew Lemieux. 2014. "Adaptive Resource Allocation for Wildlife Protection Against Illegal Poachers." In *International Conference on Autonomous Agents and Multi-Agent Systems*, page 453–60.

Zheng, Stephan, Alexander Trott, Sunil Srinivasa, David C Parkes, and Richard Socher. 2022. "The AI Economist: Taxation Policy Design via Two-Level Deep Multiagent Reinforcement Learning." *Science Advances* 8(18): eabk2607.

7

Influencing Policy and Transforming Institutions
Lessons from Kidney/Liver Exchange

Tayfun Sönmez and M. Utku Ünver

7.1 Introduction

In 1984, the US Congress passed the *National Organ Transplant Act* (NOTA) to address the shortage of transplant organs and improve the organ allocation process. This landmark legislation led to the establishment of the *Organ Procurement and Transplantation Network* (OPTN), entrusted with maintaining a national transplantation registry. NOTA specified that a private organization should operate this network under a federal contract. Since 1986, the *United Network for Organ Sharing* (UNOS), a non-profit organization, has been fulfilling this important role.

In 2000, the US Department of Health and Human Services (HHS) implemented a *Final Rule*, outlining comprehensive regulations governing OPTN's structure and operations.[1] According to this Final Rule, OPTN is required to form a board of directors consisting of

(i) approximately 50 percent transplant surgeons or transplant physicians;
(ii) at least 25 percent transplant candidates, transplant recipients, organ donors, and their family members;

Tayfun Sönmez is a professor of economics at Boston College.
M. Utku Ünver is a professor of economics at Boston College.
The material presented in this paper is based on a presentation given by Sönmez in May 2023 at the "New Directions in Market Design" conference in Washington, DC. The authors would like to disclose that they have not received any research support and have no significant financial relationships that could influence the content or findings presented in this paper. For acknowledgments, sources of research support, and disclosure of the authors' material financial relationships, if any, please see https://www.nber.org/books-and-chapters/new-directions-market-design/influencing-policy-and-transforming-institutions-lessons-kidneyliver-exchange.

1. The Final Rule is available at the National Archives Code of Federal Regulations web page, https://www.ecfr.gov/current/title-42/chapter-I/subchapter-K/part-121, last accessed on 08/26/2024.

(iii) representatives of organ procurement organizations, transplant hospitals, voluntary health associations, transplant coordinators, histocompatibility experts, non-physician transplant professionals, and the general public.

Despite OPTN's primary mission of ensuring efficient and equitable organ procurement and allocation, the current composition of the OPTN Board of Directors, guided by the Final Rule, lacks representation from fields such as market design, operations research, or computer science—areas where researchers possess the expertise to design complex allocation systems. In our view, recognizing this crucial expertise gap is essential, given OPTN's mission. At the same time, policy recommendations from experts in these formal disciplines must align with the institution's overarching goals to receive serious consideration from decision-makers.

Many initiatives in US transplantation policy could significantly benefit from expertise in market design. Before exploring how persuasion strategies can be incorporated into market design research to enhance its potential influence on real-life policies, let's briefly discuss three of these initiatives.

Liver Exchange in the US: Living-donor organ exchange, utilized for kidneys and livers, involves a process where a group of patients, some or all of whom have medically incompatible donors, engage in a donor swap to ensure that each recipient receives a compatible transplant. In the United States, kidney exchange programs have thrived since the mid-2000s, but liver exchange is a more recent development.[2] In a significant move, UNOS, in collaboration with 15 top-tier transplant centers in the United States, initiated the first national liver exchange pilot program on January 13, 2023.[3] Unfortunately, after failing to generate any transplants, the pilot program was discontinued on November 30, 2023.[4]

This setback faced by UNOS is in an area where market designers have a lot of experience. In the case of kidney transplantation, while the practice of donor exchange existed in the United States before market designers took an interest, it thrived globally with their contributions. In section 7.2, we explore the strategies that helped achieve this policy impact. Furthermore, as discussed in section 7.2.8, the results from the first two and a half years of a single-center liver exchange program in Turkey—which quickly established itself as a global leader—highlight the potential importance of input from market design experts. This suggests that such expertise could have been equally vital for the UNOS liver exchange pilot program.

2. According to a *UT Health* story published on February 4, 2020, titled "Called 1st in U.S.: Living Liver Donors Kindly Swap to Save 2 Recipients," the first liver exchange in the United States took place in April 2019.

3. Refer to the *UNOS News* story titled "UNOS launches first national liver paired donation pilot pro- gram," dated January 13, 2023, last accessed on 08/29/2024.

4. See the blogpost "UNOS ends its liver exchange pilot program" by Alvin Roth, dated November 30, 2023, last accessed on 08/29/2023.

A New System for Allocating Deceased Donor Organs: To enhance the fairness of the current system for allocating deceased donor (DD) organs, OPTN has been developing a new system called "continuous distribution." The multifaceted objectives of this system, as outlined by OPTN, are as follows:[5]

- Prioritize the sickest candidates first to reduce waitlist deaths.
- Improve long-term survival after transplant.
- Increase transplant opportunities for patients who are medically harder to match.
- Expand transplant opportunities for candidates with distinct characteristics, such as those under the age of 18 or prior living donors.
- Promote the efficient management of organ placement.

The new system is structured as a *priority point system*, with the aim of simultaneously considering multiple factors crucial for a successful transplant within the organ offer process. The objective is to establish a system that not only prioritizes urgency but also incorporates various medical and demographic factors, ensuring a comprehensive and equitable allocation of organs.

While OPTN promotes the new system as more equitable than the current one, it has raised concerns among specific groups. Living donors, currently enjoying the highest priority under the existing system, express anxiety that their status may now become just one of several factors determining priority under the new system.[6] This potential shift also raises concerns about the negative impact on the supply of living-donor transplant organs. In an open letter dated March 13, 2023, the president of the American Society of Nephrology, Michelle A. Josephson, issued an important warning to officials in OPTN:[7]

> It would be a massive violation of trust to living donors to alter the prioritization they were promised and would almost certainly be a substantial deterrent to anyone considering living donation today and in the future.

In the design of such allocation systems, there is often an oversight of *incentive considerations* when not guided by experts in market design. This is another setting where expertise from market design can be very valuable.

OPTN Modernization Initiative: In March 2023, a significant shift in

5. For more details, visit the Organ Procurement and Transplantation Network site, "Creating a More Fair and Patient-Focused System for Organ Allocation," https://optn.transplant.hrsa.gov/policies-bylaws/a-closer-look/continuous-distribution/, last accessed on 11/19/2023.

6. Refer, for instance, to the *STAT News* opinion piece by Martha Gershu titled "Living kidney donors rely on a promise to protect our future health. We're scared it will go away," published on 03/22/2023, last accessed on 08/29/2024.

7. The open letter, dated March 13, 2023, from the American Society of Nephrology is available in https://www.asn-online.org/policy/webdocs/23.3.13ASNOPTNLKD.pdf, last accessed on 11/18/2023.

transplantation policy occurred with the introduction of the OPTN Modernization Initiative by the White House. This landmark initiative signaled the government's commitment to breaking UNOS's monopoly in US transplantation policy.[8]

The drive behind this initiative to revamp the current system stems from several concerns related to UNOS, including

- too many organs being discarded, damaged, or not collected;
- issues with faulty technology risking transplant procedures;
- lack of accountability for underperforming entities.

An article in *the Washington Post* on March 22, 2023, titled "Troubled U.S. Organ System Targeted for Overhaul," sheds light on the proposed federal reform (Bernstein 2023). One of the main objectives in the proposed reform is to increase transparency in the complex process of patient and organ matching. Bernstein (2023) outlines another noteworthy feature as follows:

> HRSA [Health Resources and Services Administration], however, is proposing a "modular" system of improvements that could be tested independently of one another and gradually integrated into a new structure while the old one is still running. This setup would also enable each component to be improved individually, without having to rewrite the entire program.

This transformative initiative also presents numerous opportunities for market designers. However, to impact policy, these ideas must not only be innovative but also transparent and seamlessly harmonize with the broader system.

In our experience, market designers are more likely to succeed in influencing policy and transforming institutions if their policy recommendations, supported by research, strongly align with the mission of the institution. In section 7.2, we discuss how we benefited from this approach for over two decades in designing living-donor organ exchange clearinghouses. We then conclude in section 7.3 by discussing how these experiences helped shape a broader institution design framework, *minimalist market design* (Sönmez 2023), which we used to persuade decision-makers to enhance their institutions in various settings.

7.2 Policy Relevance of Research in Market Design: Lessons from Living-Donor Organ Exchange

What factors contribute to the potential success of market design research in this field? Drawing on insights from our extensive collaborations with policymakers and experts across various disciplines since the late 1990s, we focus on the area of living-donor organ exchange. In this section, we

8. For detailed information, see the press release from the Health Resources and Services Administration (HRSA), dated 03/22/2023, last accessed on 08/29/2024.

articulate our perspective on the factors that are pivotal to the effectiveness of market design research in shaping policy.

One of the most unexpected applications of market design, which has significantly elevated the visibility and success of the field, is *kidney exchange* (Roth, Sönmez, and Ünver 2004, 2005b, 2007). Within a few years after its introduction as a market design application, our formal approach transformed living donor kidney donation in many countries (Purtill 2018). Within a decade, it started saving more than a thousand lives annually (Rose 2019). This success was "unexpected" not only because kidney transplantation was far beyond the traditional scope of economics but also because assistance from economists came from "outsiders" rather than being actively sought.

How did three economists manage to develop the tools for and help establish the infrastructure which regularly touches so many lives? In our view, the key was convincing stakeholders (e.g., policymakers, system operators) that we could assist them in enhancing their institution

1. in aspects they care about;
2. by using the tools with which they are familiar (or at the very least they are comfortable to use);
3. without creating any new issues.

To have a realistic chance of influencing policy, an aspiring market designer must possess a deep understanding of the mission of the institution. In this regard, the history of the institution can often provide valuable insights. For an outsider aspiring design economist, another crucial prerequisite for enhancing an institution is to have a *practical* and *transparent* plan for its improvement. Policy aspirations often carry substantial implications for viable designs, thereby shaping the underlying research program.

7.2.1 Paired Kidney Exchange and List Exchange

To provide practice guidelines for transplant physicians, primary care providers, and health care planners, a *Consensus Statement on the Live Organ Donor* was issued in 2000 by representatives of several professional transplantation societies (Abecassis et al. 2000). Two instruments aimed at overcoming medical incompatibilities between kidney patients and their willing living donors, namely a *paired kidney exchange* and a *list exchange*, were prominently discussed in the Consensus Statement.

Paired Kidney Exchange (PKE): A donor who is medically incompatible with their patient can often be compatible with another patient. Similarly, a patient who is incompatible with their donor may be compatible with another patient's donor. In such cases, patients can find a medically compatible donor by exchanging their donors. The process by which two patients mutually exchange their donors, ensuring a medically compatible transplant for each, is referred to as *paired kidney exchange* or *2-way exchange*.

The concept of PKE was initially proposed in 1986 by Dr. Felix Rapaport, a renowned transplant surgeon who served as the editor of *Transplantation Proceedings* for over three decades (Rapaport 1986). Globally, it was first implemented in South Korea in 1991 (Park et al. 1999). In the United States, the first PKE took place in Rhode Island in 2000 (Anderson et al. 2015).

List Exchange (LE): The second kidney exchange mechanism entails an indirect exchange between an incompatible pair and the deceased-donor (DD) list. In this scenario, a donor, incompatible with their intended recipient, contributes a kidney to a patient on the DD list. As a reciprocal arrangement, the incompatible patient gains priority in the DD list, facilitating a mutually beneficial exchange.

Initially discussed in Ross and Woodle (2000), LE stands out for its organizational simplicity. While orchestrating a PKE necessitates the coordination of two mutually compatible patient-donor pairs, LE can be arranged whenever an incompatible pair expresses interest in this kidney exchange form. However, as thoroughly explored in Ross and Woodle (2000), a significant ethical concern surrounds LE: it has the potential to be detrimental to blood type O patients on the DD list.

To comprehend this concern, it is essential to recall the principles of blood type compatibility. There are four blood types: A, B, AB, and O. Blood type AB patients can receive a kidney of any blood type. Blood type A or B patients can accept a kidney of their own blood type or one from blood type O. On the other hand, blood type O patients can only receive a kidney from blood type O donors. This natural limitation places blood type O patients at a disadvantage.

As Ross and Woodle (2000) pointed out, the disadvantage for blood type O patients without willing donors may be exacerbated by LE. This is because blood type O patients, who are already at a disadvantage due to their limited compatibility, may be further disadvantaged by participating in LE. Specifically, blood type O patients who are blood type–incompatible with their potential donors are particularly likely to benefit from this form of kidney exchange, highlighting the intricate ethical considerations inherent in the use of LE.

Among these two forms of kidney exchange, PKE garnered widespread approval in the Consensus Statement, being deemed "ethically acceptable." To forestall scenarios wherein a donor contributes a kidney to another patient through PKE, only for their own intended donor to face potential transplant challenges later on due to the other donor reneging or becoming unavailable, the Consensus Statement urged for the simultaneous execution of all four operations. In contrast, the Consensus Statement underscored the ethical apprehensions associated with LE (Abecassis et al. 2000).

7.2.2 Early Phases of Kidney Exchange in New England

Approved by the UNOS Board of Trustees in Fall 2000, the first kidney exchange program in the United States was established in New England

(UNOS Region 1) in February 2001 (Delmonico et al. 2004). In addition to PKE, which received broad support from the transplantation community, New England also included LE in its program despite the ethical concerns. This decision was defended by its leadership as follows:

> This exchange program has a clear utilitarian goal: to have more recipients undergo successful transplantation by expanding the pool of compatible live donors. (Delmonico et al. 2004)

However, Delmonico et al. (2004) centered much of its discussion on the ethical concerns, particularly focusing on the precautions implemented to mitigate the adverse impact of LE on blood type O patients listed for transplantation. Consequently, the New England kidney exchange program operated under the guidance of two fundamental ethical principles: *utilitarianism* and *equity*.[9]

In its initial phases, despite being the less favored type of kidney exchange, the majority of transplants facilitated by the New England program were through LE. Between February 2001 and December 2003, the program orchestrated 17 LE transplants, in contrast to only 8 transplants coordinated across four PKEs during the same period. One significant factor directly contributing to the limited number of transplants from PKE was the absence of a patient-donor database accessible by all 14 participating centers, a shortcoming rectified through our initiatives in the Fall of 2004.

While arranging an LE does not necessitate a patient-donor database, the organization of such exchanges also presented operational challenges in New England. A prerequisite for LE eligibility was to ensure that no PKE was feasible between the patient and any other patient registered in all 14 transplant centers in the system.

> [. . .] The duration that the RTOC [Renal Transplant Oversight Committee] will wait for a live donor exchange pair to come forward from another center has not been regulated, although the general practice has been to ask such pairs to wait a minimum of one month, in order to avoid flooding the system with "unnecessary" list exchanges. If no such pair is identified, the center can proceed with the live donor list exchange process. (Delmonico et al. 2004)

Amid the challenges faced by New England's kidney exchange program, in the Fall of 2003 we presented Roth, Sönmez, and Ünver (2003) to Dr. Francis Delmonico, who served as the Medical Director of the New England Organ Bank.[10] During this encounter, we expressed our interest in collabo-

9. Health equity, as defined by the *Centers for Disease Control and Prevention*, is the state in which everyone has a fair and just opportunity to attain their highest level of health. Achieving this necessitates societal efforts to address historical and contemporary injustices, overcome economic and social obstacles to health and health care, and eliminate preventable health disparities.

10. A shorter version of Roth, Sönmez, and Ünver (2003) is later published as Roth, Sönmez, and Ünver (2004).

rating to enhance their kidney exchange program. Surprisingly, Delmonico exhibited a keen interest in our initiative. As we will discuss in more detail in section 7.2.6, his strong opposition to the Global Kidney Exchange (GKE) initiative, led by Mike Rees from Alliance for Paired Donation and Alvin Roth in the following years, suggested that our meticulous attention to medical ethics considerations in Roth, Sönmez, and Ünver (2003) might have been pivotal in shaping his openness to our proposal.

7.2.3 Early Market Design Research on Kidney Exchange

While we were faculty members at Koc, University in İstanbul, Ünver visited Alvin Roth at Harvard University for the academic year 2002–2003. During his visit, Roth pointed out that the model for *house allocation with existing tenants*, initially introduced in Abdulkadiroğlu and Sönmez (1999) and further explored in Sönmez and Ünver (2005), has an unconventional application in kidney transplantation.

Motivated by the efficient and incentive-compatible allocation of campus housing units, Abdulkadiroğlu and Sönmez (1999) introduced a mechanism known as *You Request My House–I Get Your Turn (YRMH–IGYT)*, which allocates two types of houses to two types of individuals. One type of individual, termed existing tenants, had the option to retain their current houses if they chose to do so. The other type of individuals, referred to as newcomers, did not have any claim to specific houses. The two types of houses included the occupied houses of existing tenants and the vacant houses that did not belong to any specific individuals.

In the context of kidney transplantation:

- Patients with living donors correspond to existing tenants.
- Living-donor kidneys correspond to occupied houses.
- Patients on the deceased-donor (DD) list correspond to newcomers.
- DD kidneys correspond to vacant houses.

Existing tenants can retain their current houses in Abdulkadiroğlu and Sönmez (1999), and similarly, patients with living donors can hold onto their donors. Just as newcomers have no claim on any specific house, patients on the DD list also do not have any claim on any specific kidney. Finally, as in the case where all individuals collectively own all vacant houses in house allocation, all patients collectively own all deceased donor kidneys.

Drawing on these analogies, the YRMH-IGYT mechanism finds direct application in kidney exchange. By overseeing claims for "unattached" houses, which could be either vacant or vacated during the procedure, through an exogenous priority list, the YRMH-IGYT mechanism organizes two distinct types of transactions: *cycles* and *chains*. In a cycle, existing tenants exchange their occupied houses, with PKE corresponding to a cycle involving only two patients with living donors. In a chain, an individual exchanges their priority for an "unattached" house, and the remaining individuals trade their currently occupied houses. LE corresponds to a chain involving one patient with a living donor and the highest-priority patient on the DD list.

While employing exogenous priority lists, such as in YRMH-IGYT, was a viable approach for regulating chains in kidney exchange, we observed that alternative *chain selection rules* might alleviate, and even eliminate, the adverse impact of LE on blood type O patients on the DD list. Leveraging this insight, we addressed both goals of the transplantation community in Roth, Sönmez, and Ünver (2003, 2004) through a generalization of the YRMH-IGYT mechanism, rather than merely framing kidney exchange as a direct application of Abdulkadiroğlu and Sönmez (1999).

7.2.4 The Birth of a Partnership Between Economists and Medical Doctors

Our informed and cautious approach resonated with Delmonico, who subsequently made the following requests as prerequisites for a potential collaboration:

1. Considering the scale of simulated welfare gains from our system, we should eliminate the more controversial LE altogether.
2. Due to logistical constraints, we should restrict the kidney exchange to PKE, i.e., two-way exchanges.
3. To prevent a situation where patients and hospitals might compete for donors with specific characteristics, we must assume that patients are indifferent between all compatible donors.[11]

We accommodated all requests in Roth, Sönmez, and Ünver (2005b) which formed the basis of the New England Program for Kidney Exchange (NEPKE). Approved by the Renal Transplant Oversight Committee of New England in September 2004, NEPKE became the first kidney exchange system that adapted analytical techniques from market design and optimization (Roth, Sönmez, and Ünver 2005a).

Our team coded and ran NEPKE's software for several years. Our partnership resulted in a number of additional breakthroughs.

Larger Cycles: Analyzing New England data, it became evident early on that the incorporation of three-way exchanges is particularly crucial from a utilitarian standpoint (Roth, Sönmez, and Ünver 2007). We successfully persuaded our medical partners to integrate three-way exchanges into the NEPKE software and jointly advocated for it within the broader transplantation community (Saidman et al. 2006).

Non-Directed Donor Chains: In collaboration with our NEPKE partners,

11. Strictly speaking, rather than suggesting a formal structure on patient preferences, Delmonico indicated that he is not in favor of a system where patients rank compatible donors. In his view, compatibility information should be sufficient to effectively run a kidney exchange system.

we introduced and advocated for the non-simultaneous implementation of chains, particularly when initiated with a non-directed living donor kidney (Roth et al. 2006). Although NEPKE did not incorporate non-directed donor chains, a second kidney exchange program we supported during its early years, Alliance for Paired Donation (APD), did (Anderson et al. 2015). Today, a sizable part of the welfare gains from kidney exchange in the United States are due to non-directed donor chains (Agarwal et al. 2019).

7.2.5 The Role of Compatible Pairs in Living-Donor Organ Exchange

Currently, the majority of kidney exchange programs worldwide restrict participation to incompatible patient-donor pairs. This limitation results in a significant welfare loss worldwide, particularly posing a challenge for blood type O patients with donors of blood types A, B, or AB. The challenge arises because, unless there is tissue-type incompatibility with their patients, blood type O donors are medically compatible with their designated patients.

Importantly, our initial paper on kidney exchange successfully navigated this challenge. In Roth, Sönmez, and Ünver (2003, 2004), preferences, assumed to depend on blood type compatibility, tissue-type compatibility, and donor age, were considered strict. Consequently, Roth, Sönmez, and Ünver (2003, 2004) incorporated a built-in mechanism for compatible pairs to participate in kidney exchange.

In contrast, Roth, Sönmez, and Ünver (2005b), developed at the request of Delmonico, and enabling our collaboration, imposed a limitation by restricting participation to incompatible pairs. As a result, the intrinsic mechanism in Roth, Sönmez, and Ünver (2003, 2004) for compatible pairs to engage in kidney exchange was forfeited in Roth, Sönmez, and Ünver (2005b). Since NEPKE served as a blueprint for kidney exchange programs subsequently launched in the United States and many other countries, the end result was a substantial efficiency loss. Sönmez et al. (2020) estimates that the number of kidney exchange transplants in the United States could increase by as much as 160 percent if blood-type-compatible pairs were included in kidney exchange.

Various policies have been proposed in academic literature and the field to incorporate blood-type-compatible pairs into living-donor organ exchange.

7.2.6 Global Kidney Exchange

One direct approach to incorporating blood-type-compatible pairs into kidney exchange pools in high-income countries, such as the United States, is proposed and implemented, albeit with limited success, through the GKE program (Rees et al. 2017). GKE offers funding for a kidney transplant procedure to recipients from low- and middle-income countries in exchange for a living donor who facilitates a cycle or NDD-chain of transplants in the high-income country. As depicted in figures 1A and 1B of Rees et al. (2017), the main idea involves including blood type-compatible pairs who cannot afford transplantation in a low- and middle-income country into the kidney exchange pool for the high-income country.[12]

Despite strong promotion by Michael Rees from APD and Alvin Roth, GKE has led to a relatively modest number of transplants. Between January 2015 and February 2022, 17 international patients facing financial barriers to direct transplantation facilitated kidney transplants for 35 US patients through GKE, resulting in a total of 52 kidney transplantations (Rees et al. 2022). In contrast, the number of kidney exchange transplants in the United States during the same time frame exceeded 6,000.[13]

Why did GKE account for only about 0.5 percent of kidney exchange transplants in the United States from January 2015 to February 2022? The answer lies in the strong opposition to GKE within the transplantation community.[14]

Many contend that GKE undermines various ethical norms in transplantation. The persuasion strategies employed during the initial interactions between our team of market designers and members of the broader transplantation community are either bypassed under GKE or have shown limited effectiveness. Delmonico, a pivotal figure in the initial collaboration between market designers and medical professionals, played a central role in the opposition against GKE. He not only co-authored a comment titled "Opposition to Irresponsible Global Kidney Exchange" in the *American Journal of Transplantation* (Delmonico and Ascher 2017) but he also spearheaded an ethical objection to GKE through his position as the Executive Director of the *Declaration of Istanbul Custodian Group* (DICG).[15]

According to DISG:

1. GKE is deceptive.
2. GKE program exploits poor countries and individuals.
3. Helping poor patients in exchange for "donated" organs constitutes organ trafficking.
4. GKE increases the risk that organs will come from paid sources.

12. In figure 1A of Rees et al. (2017), a blood type A patient with a blood type O donor, facing financial barriers for direct transplantation, engages in a two-way exchange with a blood type O patient from a high-income country who has a blood type A donor. In figure 1B of Rees et al. (2017), a blood type B patient with a blood type O donor, confronting financial barriers for direct transplantation, participates in a five-way exchange with four blood type–incompatible pairs from a high-income country.

13. Data available at the Organ Procurement and Transplantation Network website, https://optn.transplant.hrsa.gov/data/view-data-reports/national-data/, last accessed 08/29/2024.

14. Refer to Ambagtsheer et al. (2020) for an extensive analysis of the opposition to GKE, involving organizations and professional groups such as the *Council of Europe Committee on Organ Transplantation,* the *European Union's National Competent Authorities on Organ Donation and Transplantation,* and the *Declaration of Istanbul Custodian Group.*

15. See the "Statement of the Declaration of Istanbul Custodian Group Concerning the Ethical Objections to the Proposed Global Kidney Exchange Program", last accessed 08/26/2024.

Based on similar ethical concerns, GKE has also faced criticism and opposition from other key groups, such as the Council of Europe Committee on Organ Transplantation[16] and the European Union's National Competent Authorities on Organ Donation and Transplantation.[17]

We abstain from taking a position on whether the sharp criticisms of GKE by these groups are justified or not, as many of these objections fall beyond our expertise. What is relevant for our purposes is that GKE faced substantial criticism from various organizations, indicating a level of ineffectiveness in achieving the intended welfare gains from kidney exchange. The contrast between the early success in kidney exchange and the opposition to GKE underscores the importance of adopting a cautious approach when establishing partnerships with policymakers and experts in other disciplines.

7.2.7 Incentivized Kidney Exchange

In contrast to GKE, where certain blood type compatible patient-donor pairs are compelled to join kidney exchange through direct means, Incentivized Kidney Exchange (IKE) (Sönmez and Ünver 2015; Sönmez et al. 2020) adopts a more nuanced strategy to achieve the same objective. The primary idea involves incentivizing such pairs to participate in kidney exchange by offering the patient a priority increase in the DD list in the event of another renal failure in the future. This incentive is valuable, as a kidney from a living donor typically lasts about 15 to 20 years on average.

Since 2021, more than 1,100 patients in the United States have received transplants annually through kidney exchange. According to Sönmez et al. (2020), for every 10 percent increase in incentivized pairs in the United States, the number of kidney exchange transplants could rise by approximately 180. Therefore, the number of kidney exchange transplants in the United States could potentially double if 60 percent of compatible pairs were incentivized.

The ethical aspects of this policy have been favorably discussed by several members of the Canadian transplantation community in Gill et al. (2017). In principle, IKE could be considered for potential implementation as part of the ongoing reform of the UNOS-DD allocation system discussed in section 7.1. However, since the allocation of living donor kidneys and deceased donor kidneys is managed separately in the United States, the adoption of a policy that links the management of these two sources of transplant kidneys requires a broader consensus at the national level.

For another solid organ, the liver, recent efforts have been more effective at incentivizing blood type–compatible pairs to participate in donor exchange through localized policies.

16. See the "CD-P-TO Position Statement on Global Kidney Exchange Concept," last accessed 08/26/2024.

17. See the "Statement on a Proposed Concept of Global Kidney Exchange," last accessed 08/26/2024.

7.2.8 Developing and Implementing Best Practices in Liver Exchange

The key challenge in encouraging blood type–compatible pairs to participate in kidney exchange is the absence of a widely accepted and ethically sound "biological" incentive mechanism to motivate these pairs to swap their donors.

In contrast, liver exchange presents several "biological" incentive mechanisms, primarily due to size compatibility requirements (Ergin et al. 2020; Yilmaz et al. 2024). One such mechanism relates to the varying donor risks associated with left-lobe versus right-lobe donation.

In living-donor kidney transplants, an entire kidney is transplanted. In contrast, living-donor liver transplants involve dissecting the liver and using only a portion—typically the right lobe, left lobe, or segments 2–3 of the left lobe. To ensure patient safety, the standard practice is to transplant a liver graft that comprises at least 40 percent of the patient's original liver volume. Since the right lobe usually accounts for 60–70 percent of the liver's volume, it is often the only viable option for most patients with blood type–compatible living donors and is, therefore, commonly chosen.

However, historically, donor mortality and morbidity rates have been three to five times higher for right-lobe donations compared to left-lobe donations. Ergin et al. (2020) argue that this substantial difference in donor risk could serve as the basis for a "biological" incentive mechanism, encouraging a significant number of compatible patient-donor pairs to consider joining a liver exchange pool. By participating in an exchange with another pair that includes a relatively smaller patient, a donor may secure a transplant for their co-registered patient while opting to donate the less risky left lobe (or segments 2–3 of the left lobe) instead of the higher-risk right lobe.

Expanding on this intrinsic biological incentive, Ergin et al. (2020) introduced an additional ethical argument in favor of liver exchange and formulated an efficient and incentive-compatible liver exchange mechanism.

Building on the ideas presented in Ergin et al. (2020) and refining them further using best practices learned from our kidney exchange experience, we reached an agreement with the leadership of the Liver Transplantation Institute at İnönü University (Malatya, Turkey) in September 2019 to establish and run a single-center liver exchange system.[18]

Our collaboration brought to light the fact that there are other, and likely more significant, "biological" incentives for blood type–compatible pairs to participate in liver exchange. For example, the anatomical structure of the smaller left lobe of many potential donors is often unsuitable for transplan-

18. The Liver Transplantation Institute at İnönü University, located in Malatya, Turkey, is the highest-volume liver transplant center in Europe and one of the largest worldwide, performing about 250 to 300 living-donor liver transplants annually. For comparison, the annual number of living-donor liver transplants in the United States reached a record high of 658 in 2023.

tation, whereas pediatric patients frequently need a transplant involving all or part of the left lobe. Hence, the existence of patient-specific size compatibility requirements has provided us with several avenues to encourage the inclusion of blood type–compatible pairs in the system.

After a three-year delay caused by administrative hurdles and the COVID-19 pandemic, the pilot phase of the *Banu Bedestenci Sönmez Liver Paired Exchange (BBS-LPE) System* was launched in June 2022.[19] The pilot continued until August 2023. Despite a magnitude 7.8 earthquake that struck the region in February 2023, 15 liver exchange transplants, including the world's first four-way liver exchange, were successfully completed during this phase (Yilmaz et al. 2023).

The BBS-LPE system was publicly announced in late July 2023, marking the end of its pilot phase and significantly enhancing its visibility and impact. By mid-February 2025, the system had facilitated 214 additional liver exchange transplants, bringing its total to 229.

During this period, the BBS-LPE system achieved several world-first milestones, including a five-way liver exchange in October 2023, a six-way exchange in January 2024, and, most recently, a seven-way exchange in July 2024 (Yilmaz et al. 2024). In March 2024, it became the first liver exchange program to surpass 100 transplants, and by January 2025, it was the first to exceed 200 transplants.

For context, fewer than 250 liver exchange transplants had been reported worldwide in the two decades before the BBS-LPE system's implementation, from 2002 to 2022. Although the first liver exchange was performed over 20 years ago at South Korea's ASAN Medical Center in 2003 (Hwang et al. 2010) to increase the supply of liver grafts, no program before the BBS-LPE accounted for more than 2 percent of liver transplants at participating centers.[20]

In stark contrast, with 64 transplants, the BBS-LPE system accounted for 27.7 percent of the 231 living-donor liver transplants performed at the Liver Transplantation Institute at İnönü University in 2023 (Yilmaz et al. 2024). Further improving its performance in 2024, it contributed 122 trans-

19. The system is named in memory of Banu Bedestenci Sönmez, the late wife of the first author, who passed away in August 2016. More information about the system, including the latest statistics on liver exchange transplants it has facilitated, can be found on the Banu Bedestenci Sönmez Liver Paired Exchange System website, https://caprazkaracigernakli.inonu.edu.tr/en, last accessed on 02/13/2025.

20. Despite the first liver exchange taking place at South Korea's ASAN Medical Center in 2003, the number of liver exchange transplants in South Korea remained at 52 from 2002 to 2018, representing only 0.4 percent of all living donor liver transplants performed in the country during that period (Kim 2022). We are aware of only two other liver exchange programs globally that have reported more than 10 liver exchange transplants to date. The highest number is reported from Medanta Hospital in India, with 91 transplants conducted from 2009 to 2022 (Soin et al. 2023). Another program in India reported by Agrawal et al. (2022) conducted 34 liver exchange transplants between 2012 and 2021, accounting for 1.45 percent of the living donor liver transplants in that program.

plants, making up 45.2 percent of the 270 living-donor liver transplants—an unprecedented achievement for any living-donor organ exchange system, including kidney exchange programs.

The system enabled transplants for 45 patients with incompatible donors in 2023, resulting in a 24.2 percent increase in the total number of living-donor liver transplants that year. In 2024, it facilitated transplants for 86 patients with incompatible donors, leading to a 46.7 percent increase in living-donor liver transplants.[21]

These statistics highlight that within just two years, the BBS-LPE system became the world's leading liver exchange program, driven by the adoption of several best practices developed over time. The system's success can be attributed to the incorporation of multiple "biological" incentive mechanisms that encouraged participation from compatible pairs, as well as its capability to perform up to seven simultaneous liver transplants.

As of mid-February 2025, the BBS-LPE system is responsible for all reported liver exchanges worldwide involving more than three pairs, including

- nine 4-way exchanges;
- four 5-way exchanges;
- five 6-way exchanges;
- two 7-way exchanges.

Moreover, with 21 three-way exchanges, it has conducted all but two of the three-way liver exchanges reported to date.[22]

7.3 Conclusion: Integrating Persuasion Strategies into Market Design

Over the past three decades, the field of *market design* has come to the forefront, witnessing active engagement from researchers in auction theory and matching theory. Their involvement has been pivotal in shaping and reshaping economic and social institutions.

Two of the earliest success stories in market design are commonly recognized as the first *spectrum auction* conducted by the Federal Communication Commission (FCC) in 1994,[23] and the subsequent redesign of the National Resident Matching Program algorithm that matches graduating medical

21. Nineteen patients in 2023 and thirty-six in 2024 participated in liver exchange either to receive a more favorable transplant or altruistically to benefit patients with incompatible donors.

22. Outside of the BBS-LPE system, only two other three-way exchanges have been documented in academic literature or media: the world's first three-way exchange from Pakistan (Salman et al. 2023) and another from India (Soin et al. 2023).

23. Prominent contributors to the design of the Federal Communication Commission's (FCC) spectrum auction encompass renowned auction theorists. Notable among them are John McMillan, who served as a consultant directly for the FCC, along with Paul Milgrom and Robert Wilson, who provided their expertise as consultants for Pacific Telesis (McMillan 1994).

students to residency programs in the United States, led by Alvin Roth in 1995 (Roth and Peranson 1999). These instances exemplify "commissioned" market design, where the imperative for change is acknowledged, and experts are specifically enlisted to drive the transformation. In contrast, "aspired" market design, as exemplified by *kidney exchange* and *liver exchange,* involves offering unsolicited reform advice as external critics.

Below we outline some essential distinctions between commissioned versus aspired market design.

Commissioned Market Design:

1. The imperative for change is already established, minimizing (if not entirely eliminating) the need for a persuasion strategy.
2. Market designers are selected based on their track record of success, affording them significant autonomy in various facets of the design.
3. Custom-made theory is not obligatory; a convincing case can be built through experimental, empirical, or computational methods.

Aspired Market Design:

1. The need for change is not established, facing resistance and skepticism.
2. A compelling persuasion strategy is crucial, as past success may not sway stakeholders with vested interests.
3. Custom-made theory aligning with stakeholders' goals becomes pivotal in the persuasion stage.

Since the late 1990s, the distinctions between commissioned and aspired market design have significantly shaped our research and policy strategies. Our engagements in *kidney exchange* and *school choice* (Balinski and Sönmez 1999; Abdulkadiroğlu and Sönmez 2003) during this period culminated in the development of the *minimalist market design* paradigm (Sönmez 2023). In our experience, this paradigm uniquely benefits *aspiring* market designers contributing insights as external critics.

Essentially, *minimalist market design* ingrains a persuasion strategy into its core. Three pivotal tasks define this paradigm:

1. **Identify the *mission* of the institution:** Uncover the fundamental objectives of policymakers, system operators, and other stakeholders. Notably, these goals may diverge from the primary objectives of mainstream economics research. Historical insights into the institution's evolution can prove instructive.
2. **Evaluate the existing institution against these objectives:** Assess whether the current institution aligns with the identified objectives. If not, the potential for impactful policy changes arises. To realize this potential in a successful redesign, pinpoint the *root causes* of the shortcomings.
3. **Address failures through minimal interference:** Intervene *only* in the flawed aspects of the deficient institution, akin to a surgeon's "minimally

invasive" procedure. This focused approach aligns with the medical principle of "first do no harm," ensuring precise adjustments that optimize the chances of a successful and influential transformation.

Building upon the success of our methodology in kidney exchange (outlined in this chapter) and in school choice during the early 2000s, we systematically applied this paradigm across diverse contexts, consistently achieving success in influencing policy and enhancing real-life institutions. A compelling testament to the effectiveness of our approach is also evident in our experience with liver exchange, as discussed in section 7.2.8.

In a similar vein, Pathak et al. (2024) and Greenberg et al. (2024) present case studies on the *pandemic allocation of scarce medical resources* and the *branching process of US Army cadets*, illustrating the efficacy of minimalist market design for policy success in these applications. Additional instances that underscore the informativeness and relevance of this paradigm include school choice implementations in Chicago and England (Pathak and Sönmez 2013) and the implementation of court-mandated affirmative action policies in India (Sönmez and Yenmez 2022).

References

Abdulkadiroğlu, Atila, and Tayfun Sönmez. 1999. "House Allocation with Existing Tenants." *Journal of Economic Theory* 88(2) 233–60.

Abdulkadiroğlu, Atila, and Tayfun Sönmez. 2003. "School Choice: A Mechanism Design Approach." *American Economic Review* 93(3): 729–47.

Abecassis, M., et al. 2000. "Consensus Statement on the Live Organ Donor." *JAMA* 284(22): 2919–26.

Agarwal, Nikhil, Itai Ashlagi, Eduardo Azevedo, Clayton R. Featherstone, and Ömer Karaduman. 2019. "Market Failure in Kidney Exchange." *American Economic Review* 109(11): 4026–70.

Agrawal, Dhiraj, Sanjiv Saigal, Shekhar Singh Jadaun, Shweta A. Singh, Shaleen Agrawal, and Gupta. 2022. "Paired Exchange Living Donor Liver Transplantation: A Nine-year Experience from North India." *Transplantation* 106(11): 2193–2199.

Ambagtsheer, Frederike, Bernadette Haase-Kromwijk, Frank J. M. F. Dor, Greg Moorlock, Franco Citterio, Thierry Berney, and Emma K. Massey. 2020. "Global Kidney Exchange: Opportunity or Exploitation? An ELPAT/ESOT Appraisal." *Transplant International* 33(9): 989–98.

Anderson, Ross, Itai Ashlagi, David Gamarnik, Michael Rees, Alvin E. Roth, Tayfun Sönmez, and M. Utku Ünver. 2015. "Kidney Exchange and the Alliance for Paired Donation: Operations Research Changes the Way Kidneys Are Transplanted." *Interfaces* 45(1): 26–42.

Balinski, Michel, and Tayfun Sönmez. 1999. "A Tale of Two Mechanisms: Student Placement." *Journal of Economic Theory* 84: 73–94.

Bernstein, Lenny. 2023. "Troubled U.S. Organ Transplant System Targeted for Overhaul." *Washington Post*, March 22. https://www.washingtonpost.com/health/2023/03/22/transplant-system-overhaul-unos/.

Delmonico, Francis L., and Nancy L. Ascher. 2017. "Opposition to Irresponsible Global Kidney Exchange." *American Journal of Transplantation* 17(10): 2745–2746.

Delmonico, Francis L. et al. 2004. "Donor Kidney Exchanges." *American Journal of Transplantation* 4(10): 1628–1634.

Ergin, Haluk, Tayfun Sönmez, and M. Utku Ünver. 2020. "Efficient and Incentive-Compatible Liver Exchange." *Econometrica* 88(3): 965–1005.

Gill, J. S., K. Tinckam, M. C. Fortin, C. Rose, K. Shick-Makaroff, K. Young, J. Lesage, E. H. Cole, M. Toews, D. N. Landsberg, and J. Gill. 2017. "Reciprocity to Increase Participation of Compatible Living Donor and Recipient Pairs in Kidney Paired Donation." *American Journal of Transplantation* 17(7): 1723–1728. https://www.sciencedirect.com/science/article/pii/S160061352225045X.

Greenberg, Kyle, Parag A. Pathak, and Tayfun Sönmez. 2024. "Redesigning the US Army's Branching Process: A Case Study in Minimalist Market Design." *American Economic Review* 114(4): 1070–1106. 10.1257/aer.20211743.

Hwang, Shin, et al. 2010. "Exchange Living Donor Liver Transplantation to Overcome ABO Incompatibility in Adult Patients." *Liver Transplantation* 16(4): 482–90.

Kim, Jong Man. 2022. "Increasing Living Liver Donor Pools: Liver Paired Exchange Versus ABO-Incompatible Living Donor Liver Transplantation." *Transplantation* 106(11): 2118–2119.

McMillan, John. 1994. "Selling Spectrum Rights." *Journal of Economic Perspectives* 8(3): 145–62.

Park, K., J. I. Moon, S. I. Kim, and Y. S. Kim. 1999. "Exchange Donor Program in Kidney Transplantation." *Transplantation* 67(2): 336–38.

Pathak, Parag A., and Tayfun Sönmez. 2013. "School Admissions Reform in Chicago and England: Comparing Mechanisms by their Vulnerability to Manipulation." *American Economic Review* 103(1): 80–106.

Pathak, Parag A., Tayfun Sönmez, M. Utku Ünver, and M. Bumin Yenmez. 2024. "Fair Allocation of Vaccines, Ventilators and Antiviral Treatments: Leaving No Ethical Value Behind in Healthcare Rationing." *Management Science* 70(6): 3999–4036.

Purtill, Corinne. 2018. "How AI Changed Organ Donation in the US." *QUARTZ*, September 10. https://qz.com/1383083/how-ai-changed-organ-donation-in-the-us.

Rapaport, Felix T. 1986. "The Case for a Living Emotionally Related International Kidney Donor Exchange Registry." *Transplantation Proceedings* 18(3): Suppl. 2: 5–9.

Rees, M. A., et al. 2017. "Kidney Exchange to Overcome Financial Barriers to Kidney Transplantation." *American Journal of Transplantation* 17(3): 782–90.

Rees, Michael, et al. 2022. "The First 52 Global Kidney Exchange Transplants: Overcoming Multiple Barriers to Transplantation." *Transplantation* 106(9S): S469.

Rose, Ian. 2019. "How an Economist Helped Thousands Get a New Kidney." *BBC*, December 17. https://www.bbc.com/news/business-50632630.

Ross, Lainie Friedman, and E. Steve Woodle. 2000. "Ethical Issues in Increasing Living Kidney Donations by Expanding Kidney Paired Exchange Programs." *Transplantation* 69(8): 1539–1543.

Roth, A. E., T. Sönmez, M. U. Ünver, F. L. Delmonico, and S. L. Saidman. 2006. "Utilizing List Exchange and Nondirected Donation through 'Chain' Paired Kidney Donations." *American Journal of Transplantation* 6(11): 2694–2705.

Roth, Alvin E., and Elliott Peranson. 1999. "The Redesign of the Matching Market for American Physicians: Some Engineering Aspects of Economic Design." *American Economic Review* 89: 748–80.

Roth, Alvin E., Tayfun Sönmez, and Utku Ünver. 2003. "Kidney Exchange." NBER Working Paper No. 10002. Cambridge, MA: National Bureau of Economic Research.

Roth, Alvin E., Tayfun Sönmez, and Utku Ünver. 2004. "Kidney Exchange." *Quarterly Journal of Economics* 119(2): 457–88.

Roth, Alvin E., Tayfun Sönmez, and Utku Ünver. 2005a. "A Kidney Exchange Clearinghouse in New England." *American Economic Review* 95(2): 376–80.

Roth, Alvin E., Tayfun Sönmez, and Utku Ünver. 2005b. "Pairwise Kidney Exchange." *Journal of Economic Theory* 125: 151–88.

Roth, Alvin E., Tayfun Sönmez, and Utku Ünver. 2007. "Efficient Kidney Exchange: Coincidence of Wants in Markets with Compatibility-Based Preferences." *American Economic Review* 97(3): 828–51.

Saidman, S. L., A. E. Roth, T. Sönmez, M. U. Ünver, and F. L. Delmonico. 2006. "Increasing the Opportunity of Live Kidney Donation by Matching for Two- and Three-Way Exchanges." *Transplantation* 81(5): 773–82.

Salman, Saad, Muhammad Arsalan, and Faisal Saud Dar. 2023. "Launching Liver Exchange and the First 3-Way Liver Paired Donation." *JAMA Surgery* 158(2): 210–11.

Soin, A. S., et al. 2023. "Simultaneous 3-way Paired Exchange Liver Transplantation Without Nondirected Donation: Novel Strategy to Expand the Donor Pool." *Transplantation* 107(6): e175–e177.

Sönmez, Tayfun. 2023. "Minimalist Market Design: A Framework for Economists with Policy Aspirations." Monograph, ArXiv, https://arxiv.org/abs/2401.00307.

Sönmez, Tayfun, and M. Utku Ünver. 2005. "House Allocation with Existing Tenants: An Equivalence." *Games and Economic Behavior* 52(1): 153–85. https://doi.org/10.1016/j.geb.2004.04.008.

Sönmez, Tayfun, and M. Utku Ünver. 2015. "Enhancing the Efficiency of and Equity in Transplant Organ Allocation via Incentivized Exchange." Available at SSRN: https://ssrn.com/abstract=2551344.

Sönmez, Tayfun, M. Utku Ünver, and M. Bumin Yenmez. 2020. "Incentivized Kidney Exchange." *American Economic Review* 110(7): 2198–2224.

Sönmez, Tayfun, and M. Bumin Yenmez. 2022. "Affirmative Action in India via Vertical, Horizontal, and Overlapping Reservations." *Econometrica* 90(3): 1143–176.

Yilmaz, Sezai, Tayfun Sönmez, M. Utku Ünver, Volkan Ince, Sami Akbulut, Burak Isik, and Sukru Emre. 2023. "The First 4-way Liver Paired Exchange from an Interdisciplinary Collaboration Between Health Care Professionals and Design Economists." *American Journal of Transplantation* 23(10): 1612–1621.

Yilmaz, Sezai, Tayfun Sönmez, M. Utku Ünver, Volkan Ince, Sami Akbulut, Kemal Baris Sarici, and Burak Isik. 2024. "Enhanced Role of Multi-Pair Donor Swaps in Response to Size Incompatibility: The First Two 5-Way and the First 6-Way Liver Paired Exchanges." *American Journal of Transplantation* 24(10): 1881–1895.

8 Matching Hospital Resources with Patients in Need

Fanyin Zheng

Hospitals provide care for the most urgent and most severe sub-populations. In the United States, hospitals contribute to over 30 percent of total national health care expenditures.[1] However, how care is delivered in hospitals largely remains a black box in the economics literature. This chapter provides several examples demonstrating the complexity of allocating hospital resources to patients and highlights the need for more studies in this area using market design tools.

At a high level, matching hospital resources to patients in need is a complex problem for several reasons. First, the allocation involves multiple parties, including patients and their families, physicians and nurses from potentially multiple units of the hospital and different specialized areas of care, as well as hospital management and administration teams. Coordinating these parties to reach a decision in a timely fashion is non-trivial. Second, these parties might have different preferences, incentives, and sometimes competing objectives when making allocation decisions regarding hospital resources. Patients and their families are likely to focus on their own health outcomes subject to their financial constraints. Physicians, as the primary decision-makers, are responsible for their assigned patients only, rather than the broader patient population. Some physicians might have their own practices and, therefore, face distorted incentives. Management and administration staff might prioritize the hospital's overall objective. Hospitals might also

Fanyin Zheng is an associate professor at Imperial Business School, Imperial College London.
For acknowledgments, sources of research support, and disclosure of the author's material financial relationships, if any, please see https://www.nber.org/books-and-chapters/new-directions-market-design/matching-hospital-resources-patients-need.

1. See "National Health Expenditures 2023 Highlights," Centers for Medicare & Medicaid Services, https://www.cms.gov/files/document/highlights.pdf.

have their own preferences when allocating medical resources. For instance, many hospitals in the United States prioritize surgical patients when allocating ICU beds (Kim et al. 2015; Shen et al. 2020). Hospitals also reserve some beds in inpatient units for high-revenue-generating patients (Song et al. 2020; Dong et al. 2019). Policymakers also influence the allocation of medical resources in hospitals. The designs of payment schemes can significantly affect hospitals' and physicians' patient admission and discharge decisions (Einav et al. 2018). Since multiple parties with potentially conflicting interests are involved when allocating hospital resources to patients, and their incentives are not necessarily aligned with that of the social planner, a market design perspective is particularly valuable for deriving realistic models and useful insights. Third, given the complex and often stressful environment of hospitals, the behavioral aspect of the decision-making, including the potential for human error, cannot be ignored in this context. In addition, patient outcomes unfold over time, which brings additional complexity to these decisions. Finally, hospital resources are interconnected instead of isolated; the allocation decision of one resource might affect others, generating chain effects throughout the entire system. Understanding the complexity of the allocation problem and designing desirable mechanisms in this market can potentially have significant impacts on patient outcomes as well as hospital performance and overall health care expenditures.

In this chapter, I use three examples to demonstrate some of the complexity of the resource allocation problem in hospitals and the need for more work in this area, especially from the market design aspect. The first example is physician's decision regarding which patients to admit into the intensive care unit (ICU) in the hospital. ICUs are specialized inpatient units which provide the highest level of care to patients with the most severe conditions. They are also one of the most expensive medical resources in a hospital, accounting for an estimated 15–40 percent of total hospital costs in the United States (Halpern and Pastores 2015). In addition, ICUs often operate near full capacity (Coopersmith et al. 2012; Halpern and Pastores 2010), which makes physician's decision of how to allocate such a scare resource crucial for its efficient utilization. Moreover, access to ICU beds has been shown to have significant impacts on patient outcomes and health care expenditures. Kim et al. (2015) find that access to ICU beds reduces adverse patient outcomes, including hospital readmission and length of stay (LOS) by 30–75 percent for high severity patients admitted through the emergency department.

Shen et al. (2020) study one behavioral aspect of physician's ICU bed allocation decision. They use data from 24 Kaiser hospitals and detailed patient-level information to study whether physicians are forward-looking when they allocate ICU beds. When each physician, or intensivist, decides whether to allocate an ICU bed for the current patient, several factors might be taken into consideration. First, the patient's own severity and needs.

Second, the current number of ICU beds available, which depends on the number of other ICU patients, including surgical patients whom many hospitals prioritize. Finally, the decision made by the physician for the current patient has intertemporal externalities on future patients. In other words, an ICU bed allocated to the current patient is one less bed available for future patients who might need ICU care. Shen et al. (2020) extend the standard dynamic discrete choice model (Rust 1994) to estimate whether physicians take the intertemporal externalities of their ICU admission decision into consideration. Shen et al. (2020) find that, on average, the discount factor over a two-hour period is 0.3, suggesting that physicians barely take into account bed availability for patients arriving two hours later. Shen et al. (2020) also find that there is large heterogeneity across hospitals within the same hospital system, with the estimated discount factor varying between 0.1 and 0.9. Similar findings of large heterogeneity in physician behavior have been shown in the literature for other diagnostic settings (Abaluck et al. 2016; Mullainathan and Obermeyer 2022). Using counterfactual analysis, Shen et al. (2020) show that more forward-looking behavior in physician's decision-making can substantially reduce congestion in high-occupancy ICUs, with the magnitude of the effect equivalent to adding one ICU bed or saving $1.1 million per year in ICU operating costs.

This study highlights the importance of taking into account physician behavior in matching medical resources with patients in need. It also provides interesting directions for future research in this area. For instance, it calls attention for researchers to identify effective mechanisms to facilitate more informed decision-making by physicians, perhaps through providing real-time patient census information or forecasting patient demand in the future. In addition, the large behavioral heterogeneity across physicians and hospitals also shows that more work is needed for designing guidelines and incentives to potentially reduce such heterogeneity and improve the efficiency of medical resource allocation. The role of artificial intelligence (AI) in assisting physicians' diagnostic decision-making is another exciting area for future research.

Given that many medical resources such as ICUs in hospitals are shared across different types of patients (e.g., medical vs. surgical), how such resources should be shared across different departments and different types of patients in the hospital is another under-studied area. More broadly, incorporating incentives and behaviors of all parties involved in hospital's resource allocation will also be valuable for future research. In other words, market design tools robust to behavioral distortion and human error will be particularly useful in this area of research.

The second example is in the context of allocating operating rooms (ORs) to cardiac surgeons. In most US hospitals, cardiac OR schedule is organized by blocks—i.e., one OR is assigned to one surgeon for an entire day. One of the reasons for this allocation scheme is that surgeons prefer block schedules, as it allows them to spend other days teaching and seeing patients. Such block schedules are typically fixed months in advance. As a result, when an urgent surgical patient arrives, the surgeons with OR blocks on that day are more likely to perform the surgery. However, such practice might also significantly increase a surgeon's daily workload. Using detailed cardiac surgery data from Columbia Hospital, Shen et al. (2021) find that adding one more case to a surgeon's daily workload increases OR time by 27 minutes per surgery and post-surgery ICU time by 21 percent, on average. In other words, inefficient OR allocation leads to surgeon fatigue, inefficient use of ORs, and poor post-surgery patient outcomes. The authors also demonstrate that a simple optimization—making minimal adjustments to surgeons' schedules to distribute their workloads more evenly across different days—can significantly improve patients' post-surgery outcomes.

These findings give rise to a series of follow-up research questions on the allocation of ORs in hospitals. Given the commonly adopted block schedules in most hospitals, designing mechanisms to incentivize surgeons not in schedule to share the workload when the number of urgent cases is high can be one possible way to mitigate the negative impact of surgeons' daily workloads. More accurate forecast of OR time by surgeons might be used to better allocate ORs to surgeons and surgeries. The matching of ORs and surgeons is also closely dependent on the matching between surgeons and patients, which has not been studied much in the literature. In addition, coordinating the schedules of specialists and staff members needed for each surgery and across surgeries is another opportunity to improve the overall matching efficiency. More broadly, coordinating the provision of care pre-surgery and post-surgery with the allocation of ORs might further improve the matching outcomes. These are all interesting directions for future research.

The third example considers the allocation of inpatient ward (floor unit) beds to patients admitted into the hospital. In most US hospitals, inpatient floor units are organized by medical specialties. For instance, a certain number of inpatient beds might be dedicated for the cardiology unit, which accepts cardiology patients who are admitted to the hospital. However, in practice, a cardiology patient might be admitted to a gastroenterology unit if the demand for cardiology beds is high. With high levels and fluctuations of demand for hospital resources, such off-service placements are common in most hospitals' daily operations (Song et al. 2020; Dong et al. 2019). This practice highlights the important role that network structure plays in studying the allocation of hospital resources: Hospitals are complex, interconnected systems where resources are shared across different care teams and medical specialties (Dong et al. 2023). Studies have also shown that some interconnections across units established by practices such as off-service placements can have a significant negative impact on patient outcomes

(Song et al. 2020), further complicating the design of mechanisms to match floor unit beds to patients.

To summarize, the examples in this chapter demonstrate the complexity of the challenges, and the value of further work to apply the tools of market design, in the area of matching hospital resources to patients in need. The involvement of multiple parties with potentially competing objectives, the importance of behavioral aspects in decision-making, and the interconnections among various hospital resources make this problem particularly challenging and exciting for market design researchers. As discussed in this chapter, future research should focus on developing allocation schemes that account for behavioral factors, incentive distortions, and human error when matching medical resources to patients in need. Additionally, incorporating real-time patient data, system data, and AI assistance into the decision-making process is an important avenue for further exploration. Finally, another promising direction for future research is enhancing decision-making processes by considering the interconnected nature of hospital resources. Understanding and leveraging the complex network of interdependencies between different units, teams, and resources within a hospital can lead to more efficient and effective allocation strategies. By addressing these network dynamics, researchers can develop more robust models that better reflect the real-world complexities of resource management in health care settings.

References

Abaluck, J., L. Agha, C. Kabrhel, A. Raja, and A. Venkatesh. 2016. "The Determinants of Productivity in Medical Testing: Intensity and Allocation of Care. *American Economic Review* 106(12): 3730–64.

Coopersmith, C. M., H. Wunsch, M. P. Fink, W. T. Linde-Zwirble, K. M. Olsen, M. S. Sommers, K. J. Anand, K. M. Tchorz, D. C. Angus, and C. S. Deutschman. 2012. "A Comparison of Critical Care Research Funding and the Financial Burden of Critical Illness in the United States." *Critical Care Medicine* 40(4): 1072–79.

Dong, J., P. Shi, F. Zheng, and X. Jin. 2019. "Off-Service Placement in Inpatient Ward Network: Resource Pooling Versus Service Slowdown." Columbia Business School Research Paper.

Dong, J., P. Shi, F. Zheng, and X. Jin. 2023. "Capacity Management in Networks: A Structural Estimation Approach for Hospital Inpatient Wards." Columbia Business School Research Paper.

Einav, L., A. Finkelstein, and N. Mahoney. 2018. "Provider Incentives and Healthcare Costs: Evidence from Long-Term Care Hospitals." *Econometrica* 86(6): 2161–219.

Halpern, N. A., and S. M. Pastores. 2010. "Critical Care Medicine in the United States 2000–2005: An Analysis of Bed Numbers, Occupancy Rates, Payer Mix, and Costs." *Critical Care Medicine* 38(1): 65–71.

Halpern, N. A., and S. M. Pastores. 2015. "Critical Care Medicine Beds, Use, Occupancy and Costs in the United States: A Methodological Review." *Critical Care Medicine* 43(11): 2452.
Kim, S.-H., C. W. Chan, M. Olivares, and G. Escobar. 2015. "ICU Admission Control: An Empirical Study of Capacity Allocation and Its Implication for Patient Outcomes." *Management Science* 61(1): 19–38.
Mullainathan, S., and Z. Obermeyer. 2022. "Diagnosing Physician Error: A Machine Learning Approach to Low-Value Health Care." *Quarterly Journal of Economics* 137(2): 679–727.
Rust, J. 1994. "Structural Estimation of Markov Decision Processes." *Handbook of Econometrics* 4: 3081–43.
Shen, Y., C. Chan, F. Zheng, and G. J. Escobar. 2020. "Structural Estimation of Intertemporal Externalities on ICU Admission Decisions." Available at SSRN 3564776.
Shen, Y., C. W. Chan, F. Zheng, M. Argenziano, and P. Kurlansky. 2021. "The Impact of Surgeon Daily Workload and Its Implications for Operating Room Scheduling." Columbia Business School Research Paper.
Song, H., A. L. Tucker, R. Graue, S. Moravick, and J. J. Yang. 2020. "Capacity Pooling in Hospitals: The Hidden Consequences of Off-Service Placement." *Management Science* 66(9): 3825–42.

9 The Provision of Information and Incentives in School Assignment Mechanisms

Derek Neal and Joseph Root

9.1 Introduction

For roughly a quarter of a century, economists have been publishing papers on centralized school assignment mechanisms. Much of this work has focused on the technical properties of competing mechanisms. Some mechanisms are strategy proof. If a mechanism is strategy proof, students find it optimal to report their true preference rankings over possible schools. Some mechanisms avoid justified envy. If a given mechanism produces school assignments that eliminate justified envy, then when any student assigned to school A prefers school B, the stated priorities of school B give this student weakly lower priority in school B than all students the mechanism assigned to school B. Some mechanisms are Pareto efficient with regard to student preferences. Efficient mechanisms produce assignments of students to schools such that there is no way to swap assignments among students and make some students better off while harming no students.[1]

Many education policymakers would gladly implement an efficient,

Derek Neal is the William C. Norby Professor in the Kenneth C. Griffin Department of Economics at the University of Chicago, and a research associate of the National Bureau of Economic Research.

Joseph Root is an assistant professor of economics in the Kenneth C. Griffin Department of Economics at the University of Chicago.

We thank participants in the NBER-Schmidt New Directions in Market Design Conference for their feedback. We thank Gadi Barlevy, Chris Campos, Ian Dew-Becker, Dunia Fernandez, and Parag Pathak for useful feedback. For acknowledgments, sources of research support, and disclosure of the authors material financial relationships, if any, please see https://www.nber.org/books-and-chapters/new-directions-market-design/provision-information-and-incentives-school-assignment-mechanisms.

1. See Abdulkadiroğlu and Sönmez (2003), Ergin and Sönmez (2006), Pathak (2016), and Agarwal and Somaini (2020a).

strategy-proof mechanism that eliminates justified envy, but Abdulkadiroğlu et al. (2009) stress that no single mechanism can satisfy all three criteria. Thus, a portion of the assignment literature explores welfare comparisons among mechanisms that possess different properties. For example, some papers compare Deferred Acceptance (DA) to Top Trading Cycles (TTC). Both are strategy proof, but DA avoids justified envy while TTC produces assignments that are efficient with respect to student preferences. An even larger set of papers compares DA to a system known as the Boston mechanism (BOS). BOS is not strategy proof, and because it induces strategic play, it produces allocations that are not efficient with respect to student preferences. Further, it does not avoid justified envy. However, the strategic play that BOS invites provides a channel for students to communicate the intensity of their preferences. As a result, one can create examples in which the set of assignments that BOS generates compares favorably to the assignments produced by DA.[2]

Pathak (2017) departs from much of the literature. Based on his experience as an advisor to numerous US school districts that have implemented various centralized mechanisms as well as documented accounts of similar efforts in other countries, Pathak concludes,

> Transparency is paramount . . . While hard to formalize, the idea that a mechanism is transparent and simple to understand plays as important a role in choosing mechanisms as the algorithmic properties of the mechanisms.

In large measure, Pathak's call for transparency is a plea to establish common knowledge that, ex ante, families need only report their true preferences to the mechanism, and that ex post, families should expect to receive a single, final assignment that does not create justified envy or raise concerns that the mechanism ignores the stated priorities of the school system in order to favor some families over others. Mechanisms that invite strategic behavior or involve chaotic after markets impose costs on families and may erode trust. Further, Pathak and Sönmez (2008) note that because resource-rich families may enjoy competitive advantages when interacting with mechanisms that involve strategic play or complicated after-market procedures, transparency likely promotes equity.

Pathak (2017) also discusses how transparent assignment systems built around DA may be useful tools for promoting competition among all

2. For example, imagine a setting where every student participating in a centralized mechanism has an outside option that involves paying tuition to attend a private school. For any allocation produced by the mechanism, we can define the compensating variation, CV, associated with each assignment as the maximum amount that each student would pay to keep his assigned school rather than leave the system and attend her outside option. The sum of the CV associated with each assignment produced by a mechanism is a measure of the welfare generated by the mechanism. Given this welfare measure, it is straightforward to create examples such that BOS beats DA. See Calsamiglia et al. (2020), Abdulkadiroğlu et al. (2011), and Kapor et al. (2020).

schools that receive public funds, in part because these systems generate useful information concerning how parents view the performance of different schools. Neal (2018) proposes a school choice system that illustrates this point. Imagine a system that funds authorized schools using a common funding formula. These schools may be traditional public schools, charter schools, or private schools, but they are all authorized in the sense that the public education authority deems them eligible to receive public funds. In the spring of each year, the school system would require each authorized school to post information about their school in an online portal maintained by the education authority. The information could include the educational philosophy of the school, testimonials from former students, schedules of student fees, descriptions of available transportation services, etc. On the information page for each school, the education authority would add academic performance metrics that describe academic outcomes for each school's recent students. During the month of May, each authorized school would hold open houses that give interested families an opportunity to visit the school and speak with faculty and staff. In June, each school would submit a seating capacity and a formula that determines priority rankings among students who apply to the school. In July, each student would either inform the education authority that she plans to remain in her current school or submit a rank-ordered list of N schools that she prefers to her current school. At the end of July, the education authority would assign students using DA, and then assign funds to schools based on their enrollments. As we discuss more in section 9.4, Neal also notes that the following spring, the education authority could award performance bonuses to participating schools based on various measures of school performance, and the authority could also make decisions about whether, based on their entire performance history, particular schools remain eligible to receive public funds.

Such a choice system clearly promotes competition among schools. Yet, both Pathak (2017) and Neal (2018) note that this type of school choice system also generates valuable information for education authorities. Consider the following scenario. School A is a K-5 school in a neighborhood that contains 500 kids ages 5–10, and there are no other elementary schools in the neighborhood. While reviewing the data submitted to the mechanism this summer, the education authority learns that only five students ranked school A among their top three choices. The education authority may need to investigate school A closely before renewing its authorization.

Yet, before we explore how education authorities could employ information about schools and their performance, we dig deeper into a different information concern that has recently received considerable attention. To date, the starting place for the analysis of most centralized assignment mechanisms has been the assumption that families can rank N different schools, where N is either the total number of schools available to a given student or the total number of available schools that dominate the student's outside option. However, results from several recent papers raise concerns about the information families possess as well as their willingness to acquire information about schools.

In the next section, we review several papers in the recent literature on how parents choose schools for their children. We pay close attention to papers that employ data from centralized assignment mechanisms and highlight papers that study how families respond when education officials provide families with new information about schools or about how school assignment mechanisms work. We then develop a simple model that explains why many parents who participate in centralized assignment mechanisms may be *rationally uninformed*, and we also discuss possible connections between Pathak's claim that *transparency is paramount* in the design of school assignment mechanisms and the conjecture in Wilson (1987) that some trading systems survive as stable institutions because participants find that making bids and offers that reflect their true valuations is an approximately optimal strategy and that outcomes are efficient when participants bid their valuations. We close by discussing challenges faced by an education authority that must decide what information to provide to parents and what performance metrics should inform accountability systems, e.g. rules concerning the accreditation of schools or the allocation of performance bonuses to high-performing schools.

9.2 Parents and Information

Systems that give parents more control over where their children attend school also often allow them to influence the level of public funding that specific schools receive. As a result, researchers and policymakers are keen to understand how parents choose schools for their children given different choice mechanisms. The literature on how parents choose schools largely addresses two questions: what do parents prefer, and what do parents know? Parents often make choices that reveal they place little or no weight on certain school attributes, but researchers find it difficult to discern whether parents do not value these attributes or simply possess no information about them. However, if choices reveal that parents place considerable weight on a particular school characteristic, it is often reasonable to conjecture that parents not only care about this characteristic but also understand it. We begin by reviewing results concerning one such school attribute.

Numerous studies find that, all else equal, parents want their children to attend schools that are closer to their homes. While no one should be shocked that parents would rather avoid having their kids spend extra time commuting to school, the strength of the evidence that travel distance matters for family preferences over potential school options is noteworthy. In fact, Agarwal and Somaini (2020*b*) note that the standard choice model in this literature employs quasi-linear preferences that express how parents compare two schooling options in terms of the additional distance a family would be willing to travel to secure the more preferred school.

In recent work on the New York City (NYC) high school assignment mechanism, Corradini and Idoux (2023) also report that parents care about the racial composition of the schools their children attend. All else equal, parents rank schools higher if they have higher fractions of students who share their race or ethnicity. This result is also less than shocking. However, Corradini and Idoux (2023) also conclude that self-sorting on racial preferences contributes to academic inequality since schools with large fractions of Black and Hispanic students tend to be less effective in terms of value-added performance measures.

Abdulkadiroğlu et al. (2020) examine the preference rankings that parents submit to the DA mechanism that assigns students to NYC high schools. They find that parents prefer schools that have historically enrolled high-achieving students, and these schools are more likely to excel at raising student test scores in the future and promoting future educational attainment. However, the authors find no evidence that, conditional on the quality of peers in a school, parents rank schools at the margin based on how effective schools are at promoting future achievement or attainment. Once again, there are multiple ways to interpret these results. It is possible that parents in NYC have considerable information about the levels of historical achievement at various high schools but lack precise information about the effectiveness of various schools in producing various short- or long-run outcomes.[3]

A number of papers document scenarios where parents choose schools that are not effective in promoting achievement growth. Abdulkadiroğlu et al. (2018) study parents who participated in the Louisiana Scholarship Program (LSP), a voucher program that targeted economically disadvantaged families enrolled in under-performing public schools. These parents used vouchers to find private schools for their children, and they reported high levels of satisfaction with these new schools. However, these voucher schools were not effective in fostering achievement growth, especially in math. Attending LSP voucher schools reduced math achievement by roughly 0.4 standard deviations. LSP did not provide voucher parents with value-added performance measures by school before parents selected LSP schools for their children, so parents might not have realized that the schools they chose were harming their kids academically. Or, parents may have been

3. During part of the sample period, the NYC schools provide parents with no measures of effectiveness. Further, the system never provided parents with the granular measures of school performance that Abdulkadiroğlu et al. (2020) create. Hastings and Weinstein (2008) conducted an experiment in Charlotte, NC. Among parents who did not receive school performance information from the district, they randomly gave some parents information about the average test score performance of students in different schools. Treated parents were 7 percentage points more likely to express a preference for a non-guaranteed school, relative to a baseline rate of 0.31.

willing to accept lower achievement growth to find schools where they felt their children were safer and happier.

Abdulkadiroğlu et al. (2018) also note that the design of LSP likely contributed to these negative outcomes. Low funding levels combined with significant administrative burdens attracted many private schools with declining enrollment, and the LSP accountability practices did not screen schools on value-added or some other metric of achievement growth. While the LSP system did give new schooling options to disadvantaged students enrolled in failing public schools, the architects of LSP did not design the system to guarantee that these new options would be effective schools. Rather, they designed LSP to make sure that these new options would be cheap, and it appears they got what they paid for.[4] We return to this topic in section 9.5. Yet, for now we note that design choices greatly influence the degree to which systems that expand parental choice generate reductions or increases in the inequality of academic outcomes.

Walters (2018) studies charter schools in Boston, MA. Many charter schools in Boston follow the No Excuses Model, which has a strong record of improving student achievement in disadvantaged urban areas.[5] Walters models application decisions, attendance decisions conditional on admission lottery outcomes, and the academic impacts of charter school attendance. He concludes that disadvantaged public school families who choose not to apply to any charter school would likely gain more academically from charter attendance than the students who do apply to charters and matriculate. Walters cannot rule out the possibility that disadvantaged parents who choose not to apply to urban charters are simply less motivated to secure better schools for their children, but he notes that disadvantaged families may fail to apply to these schools simply because they do not know that these charters are much more effective than local public schools.

Overall, there is little evidence that parents are able to figure out on their own which schools excel at promoting achievement growth or future education attainment. However, the results in Beuermann et al. (2023) are an exception. Beuermann et al. (2023) examine data on parental preference orderings and school performance in Trinidad and Tobago. Trinidad and Tobago employ serial dictatorship, a special case of DA where all schools have the same priorities, to assign students leaving elementary school to secondary schools. The authors find that secondary schools here differ substantially in their impacts on achievement growth and future outcomes such

4. In section 4 of chapter 5, Neal (2018) notes that the results in Table 11 of Abdulkadiroğlu et al. (2018), which reports estimates of LSP effectiveness by the tuition level of LSP schools, shows that among students who attend LSP schools that charge tuition equal to at least 75 percent of public school funding per student, achievement did not decline and may have risen slightly. However, the average LSP school tuition was only 57 percent of per-pupil spending in public schools, and many LSP schools spent less than half as much per student as public schools.

5. See Angrist et al. (2013), Fryer (2014), and Dobbie and Fryer (2015).

as arrests, teen births, secondary school graduation, and future labor market participation. Further, they find evidence that many parents care about many of these dimensions of school performance when forming preference orderings over potential schools.[6] Compared to other collections of parents that researchers have studied, parents in Trinidad and Tobego appear to have a much better understanding of the relative effectiveness of different schools on different dimensions. Future work is needed to understand why this is so.

9.2.1 Parental Responses to Better Information

One possible explanation for the patterns we observe in the literature on parental preferences over schools is that most parents desire schools that generate positive causal impacts on achievement growth, attainment, and post-secondary outcomes but few are able to discern which schools are most effective. This conjecture is an obvious place to start since most centralized choice mechanisms furnish parents with little information about school effectiveness.

Consistent with this conjecture, several studies find that parents respond when provided with additional information about the relative effectiveness of various schools. Ainsworth et al. (2023) examine parental preferences over high schools submitted to a serial dictatorship mechanisms that Romania uses to assign students to high schools. They run an information experiment that provides parents with value-added estimates of high school effectiveness and find that the children of treated parents end up in schools with value-added scores that are, on average, .2 standard deviations higher. The authors also conclude that parents care about school attributes other than value-added, but the size of the response that Ainsworth et al. (2023) document is consistent with the hypothesis that many parents would rank high value-added schools more favorably if they possessed better information about the relative effectiveness of different schools.

Corradini (2023) finds that the introduction of school report cards changed the way parents ranked high schools in NYC. The letter grades assigned to high schools served as coarse measures of school effectiveness. This change shifted parental preferences toward schools that promote achievement growth, and this shift was more prominent among Black and Hispanic students. Corradini (2023) concludes that these differential responses contributed to a narrowing of racial achievement gaps. These results, like many we have already discussed, support the idea that parents have imperfect information about school effectiveness, and this lack of information may be particularly acute among disadvantaged parents.

Campos (2023) describes a similar information experiment in Los Angeles,

6. The parents of high-achieving students appear to place more weight on the academic performance of schools.

CA. Students who live in Zones of Choice (ZOC) neighborhoods in Los Angeles participate in a centralized mechanism that assigns students to high schools. Campos (2023) treated randomly selected parents with information about both the historical achievement levels of entering students and rates of achievement growth for each high school in the ZOC. Campos (2023) concludes that treated parents are more willing to incur travel costs for placement in a school with higher achievement growth, but he also reports that this effect is driven by treated parents in middle schools with a high fraction of treated parents. He argues that much of the treatment impact he observes arises not because the treatment makes parents better informed but rather because the treatment makes achievement growth more salient for parents. However, this conclusion rests on strong modeling assumptions, and this pattern may not be present in other settings. The ZOC system is quite small, and even parents in the control group, who receive no information, appear to place more weight on expected achievement growth than expected peer achievement levels when ranking schools.[7]

As a whole, the literature we review here suggests that many parents who submit ordered rankings of schools to centralized assignment mechanisms do not possess detailed knowledge of the attributes of the schools in their choice set. However, a recent paper from Chile suggests that many parents do not even know what schools are in their choice set. Chile uses a centralized DA mechanism to assign all students who attend schools that receive public funds, whether the schools are public or private. The mechanism allows students to rank as many schools as they desire, and Chile allows students to interact with the centralized choice platform for roughly one month before they submit their final list of schools. Further, the platform provides easy access to information about the locations of schools, their enrollments, their governance, curricula, fees, and other basic information. Nonetheless, Arteaga et al. (2022) show that the average student submits only three schools to the platform. Further, 30 percent of students submit preferences to the mechanism that imply at least a 30 percent probability that they will receive no placement, and a non-trivial number of students face non-placement risks of more than 50 percent.[8]

Arteaga et al. (2022) conduct several information experiments. They find that a significant portion of students who initially submit risky lists will re-enter the mechanisms and add one or more schools to the list if warned of the risk and encouraged to act. However, far more than half who receive

7. Cohodes et al. (2022) report the results of a series of experiments that provided information to the parents of middle school students about the graduation rates in different high schools. All three interventions reduced enrollment in high schools with low graduation rates.

8. Some of these students are enrolled in a school within the system and have the right to return to their current school if they do not receive a new placement. However, even among new students or students who must find a new school because they are matriculating to a new schooling level, many accept significant risks of receiving no assignment in the first round.

warnings do not change their lists. Arteaga et al. (2022) also conduct a detailed survey of parents who enter the mechanism, and they use the results of the survey to form hypotheses concerning why many initial lists are so short and why a significant fraction of those who receive warnings do not add schools to their list. Arteaga et al. (2022) present compelling evidence that many families overestimate their placement chances, but in our view, the most important survey results involve levels of parental knowledge about schools and their perceived costs of search. When asked about a randomly chosen nearby school, only 17 percent reported that they knew the school well. When asked why they did not add more schools to their list, 30 percent respond that there are no more schools around, even though this is typically not true. Finally, when asked about the steps required to know a school, many parents provided a long and costly list of actions including in-person visits and interviews with school staff.

The fact that many parents who initially submit risky lists respond to warnings by adding schools is consistent with Arteaga et al. (2022)'s claim that many parents do not understand the system that well and are overly optimistic about their placement chances,[9] but we see the overall reluctance to list more schools as equally important. Chilean families believe that participating in the assignment mechanism is quite costly, and most models of school assignment ignore these costs.

In the next section, we present a simple model that explores the consequences of these costs, but before turning to our model, we note that the results in Arteaga et al. (2022) are not unique to Chile. There are over 500 high schools in NYC, and the city provides a dense network of public transit options. Nonetheless, according to Abdulkadiroğlu et al. (2017), the behavior of participants in the NYC high school assignment system is similar to the behavior Arteaga et al. (2022) document in Chile. In NYC, students may list 12 schools, but only 20.3 percent use all 12 slots, and almost 40 percent list 6 or fewer. Further, over 17 percent receive no placement in the main round. In the next section, we highlight reasons that these outcomes may be expected. We then discuss potential policy responses.

9.3 A Simple Model

Arteaga et al. (2022) report survey evidence consistent with the claim that many families find search for schools quite costly, and many families give weight to the real possibility that, even if they search and find a great school for their child, there is no guarantee that their child will receive a placement in that school. For any given family, costs of search, beliefs about the likeli-

9. Kapor et al. (2020) and Ajayi et al. (2020) describe environments where parents who are submitting lists to mechanisms that invite strategic play are often poorly informed concerning strategies that work well.

S1 a * * * b * c * * * d S2

Fig. 9.1 13 Locations, 4 Students, 2 Schools

hood of receiving an assignment, and beliefs about the difference between the expected quality of the school assignment that results from adding one more school to its ranked list and the expected quality of an assignment secured in the after-market processes should all impact the decision to investigate more schools and submit a longer list of school choices.

Here, we present a simple model that highlights these considerations. The model is highly stylized. However, the appendix demonstrates that our key results remain in a setting that does not involve the exact parametric assumptions we employ in the simple examples we work through here. Figure 9.1 describes the environment. There are two schools, indexed by $j \in \{1, 2\}$, at the ends of a line. Both schools have a capacity of two. There are four students indexed by $i \in \{a, b, c, d\}$. For a student i and a school j, $d(i, j)$ is the distance i needs to travel to attend j. For example, $d(b, 2) = 7$. Each school j has a quality $\theta_j \in \{0, 5\}$. These qualities are drawn independently and each value is equally likely. Both students learn the quality of the school closest to them at the beginning of the game. Students can pay a cost of 0.5 to learn the quality of the school that is farther away. Students also decide how to report to the centralized DA mechanism as a function of what they learn. They can submit a full ranking, list only one school, or choose not to submit a preference at all. Distance determines priorities. Each school ranks students according to how close they are to the school. Students who are not assigned by the DA mechanism are administratively assigned to the nearest school with empty seats.

A student i assigned to school j gets a payoff of

$$u_i(j) = \theta_j - .5d(i, j) - .5m_i,$$

where m_i is one if they choose to learn the quality of the other school and zero if not.

Students' strategies are as follows. Each student decides whether to search as a function of the value of the local school. They also simultaneously choose a plan for how to submit preferences to the centralized match given the information they learn. This results in a Bayesian game between the agents. We search for pure strategy Bayes-Nash equilibria.

First, we note that there is no equilibrium with search in this game. To see why, imagine that an equilibrium with search could be found. Clearly, this equilibrium will not involve search in the state where the quality of both schools is high. In this case, all students want to attend their local school where they enjoy priority. Thus, an equilibrium with search must involve a student i who chooses to search when the quality of her local school is low. However, this search cannot prove beneficial unless her non-local school is high quality, and in this case, students who have priority at this school can and will adopt strategies that exhaust the capacity of their school. As a result, student *i* can never benefit from search when she observes that her local school is low quality.

Furthermore, there is a Bayes-Nash equilibrium of this game in which all players follow the same strategy: if a student observes that her local school quality is high, she does not search and submits a preference list to the mechanism that contains only her local school, but if she observes that her local school quality is low, she not only chooses not to search, but in addition, does not bother to submit a list to the mechanism. To understand why this is an equilibrium, we start by assuming that *c*, *d*, and *a* play this strategy and show that the strategy is a best response for *b*. In our setting, suppose *b* could search for free and observe the quality of both schools before submitting her preferences to the mechanism. Here, even in the state where she observes $\theta_1 = 0$, and $\theta_2 = 5$ she would gain nothing from listing school 2 first since school 2 is always filled with local students, *c* and *d*, when $\theta_2 = 5$. Thus, choosing not to pay for costly search is always optimal for *b*. Choosing not to search is always optimal for *a* regardless of the strategies that others play since the maximum possible gain from an improved school match is less than the sum of the search cost and the additional travel cost required to access school 2, i.e., $5 < .5 + .5 * 10 = 5.5$. Further, students *a* and *b* lose nothing from refusing to submit a list when they observe that their local school is low quality. In this state, *c* and *d* will never want to attend *S*1, and *a* and *b* will be assigned to *S*1 whether they list it or not, since administrative assignments place students in the nearest school with empty seats.[10]

9.3.1 Horizontal Differentiation

So far, we have only modeled vertical differentiation in school quality. Here we consider the opposite case where all match qualities are idiosyncratic. Let $\theta_{i,j}$ denote the value of the match between student *i* and school *j*. For every *i* and *j*, $\theta_{i,j}$ takes values in $\{0, 5\}$. These draws are independent and each value is equally likely. Now, the strategic considerations are more interesting. It remains true that *a* and *d* still refuse to invest in search, since the extra travel costs associated with attending a non-local school exceed any possible gain in match quality. However, we need to do more work to find equilibrium strategies for *b* and *c*. Suppose *b* and *c* adopt the following strategy: as before, if the local school match quality is high, do not search and submit only the local school to the mechanism. If the local school match

10. In this example, it is not an equilibrium for all students to simply refuse to submit lists regardless of what they observe. If *c* and *d* play this strategy, then the best response for *b* is to pay the cost of search whenever she observes $\theta_1 = 0$ knowing that there is a one-half chance that she will learn that $\theta_2 = 5$ and pay an extra travel cost of 1 to gain five units of match quality. This $.5 * 4 = 2$ expected gain from search exceeds the search cost of .5. Students near good local schools list them to avoid losing them.

quality is low, search. If the match with the non-local school is high, list the non-local school first and the local school second. If it is low, again submit a list with only the local school. Here, if b searches when $\theta_{b,1} = 0$, there is a one-half chance that $\theta_{b,2} = 5$ and there is a one-fourth chance that both $\theta_{c,2} = 0$ and $\theta_{c,1} = 5$. This means that there is a .125 probability that she will gain 5 in match quality for an extra travel cost of 1, and therefore the expected gain from search is $.125 * 4 = .5$ which is exactly the cost of search. Since a symmetric argument holds for c, we have found an equilibrium involving search. However, if we increase the cost of search slightly, e.g. to .51, no equilibrium of the game involves search.

Next, set the cost of search to .51, but imagine that, in addition, we move c one unit to the left so that $d(c, 1) = d(c, 2) = 6$.[11] The no-search equilibrium remains the only equilibrium because the private returns from search are negative for b, even if c were to search when $\theta_{c,2} = 0$. However, this equilibrium is inefficient. A planner who maximizes the sum of utilities would prefer both b and c to search when they observe low match quality with their local schools. With these strategies, the expected search costs are the following: with probability one fourth both b and c will search. With probability one half, only one will search. So the expected costs from search are $.25 * 1.02 + .5 * .51 = .51$. The gains from search occur when both search and trade assignments as a result. This outcome occurs with probability one sixteenth. So, the expected gains from search are $[(5 - 1) + (5)] / 16 = 9 / 16 > .51$.

This result is not simply a knife-edge case given our choice of parameters. It is possible to create many examples with asymmetric returns from search where the private equilibrium involves inefficiently low levels of search. Since centralized assignment mechanisms do not allow transfers among participants, this result may not be surprising. In the appendix we analyze a similar environment with two symmetric students and two schools. Once again, each student directly observes how she matches with her local school, and as above, she may pay a cost to see how she matches with a non-local school. In many cases, the private equilibrium involves no search in states where the planner wants both students to search. This result reflects, in part, the fact a student who relinquishes a slot in her local school receives no compensation from the student who fills this open slot, even if the incoming student benefits greatly from the assignment.

Taken together, the examples above and the material in the appendix illustrate several important lessons. First, if school match qualities primarily reflect vertical differentiation, there are strategic reasons to expect that students will be reluctant to pay substantial search costs to learn about a school where they do not have high priority. They know that even if they discover that this school is high quality and rank this school as their first choice, the

11. Even though c is half way between the two schools, we still assume that c views school 2 as her local school since she has priority two in school 2 and priority three in school 1.

mechanism is almost surely not going to assign them to this school, since students with high priority are likely to exhaust the capacity of a high-quality school. Second, horizontal variation in match quality creates more scenarios where students may find it optimal to pay search costs to learn about more schools and submit longer ranked lists to the mechanism, but there still exist combinations of search costs, priority rules, travel costs, and rules for administrative placement such that individual students rationally choose to forgo search, submit short lists, and accept non-trivial probabilities of administrative placement. Finally, in many settings, the planner can improve welfare by mandating or subsidizing search, but details matter. In our example above, the planner does not want to pay additional costs to subsidize search for *a* or *d* since information about other schools is not valuable to them. This reality suggests that in many settings, interventions that lower search costs likely dominate interventions that seek to provide full information at no cost to all students. While the levels of search present in decentralized equilibrium are likely too low, the social returns from efficient levels of search vary among students as a function of their preferences, their characteristics, and the priorities chosen by the education authority, and there is no reason to believe that a social planner would, in general, fully subsidize all search activities for all students.

Arteaga et al. (2022) conclude that some parents submit ranking lists that are too short because they over-estimate their placement chances, and this conclusion is likely correct. In any given year, many families who participate in the mechanism are participating for the first or second time. They have little past experience that would have allowed them to learn about placement probabilities through experimentation, and any one family would find it prohibitively expensive to acquire all the information that the Smart Platform uses to calculate the likelihoods that specific students will receive no assignment. However, other Arteaga et al. (2022) results are equally important. Many families know little about the schools that are available to them, and obtaining the information required to place an additional school in a ranked list is costly. Therefore, the logic of the model presented above implies that some families knowingly accept a non-trivial risk of receiving no school assignment in the first round because the costs of search are greater than the expected gain in final school quality associated with ranking one additional school. These expected gains may be small because there is no guarantee that the quality of the next school that a family investigates will be greater than the quality they expect to receive from after-market mechanisms, and even if this investigation results in the family adding one more school to the ranking it submits, the family may still receive no school assignment from the mechanism. The costs of learning about one more school are roughly known. The gains are not, and the logic of the scenarios we describe above suggest that these uncertain gains may often be small in expected value.

In the next section, we discuss various ways educational authorities can provide information to parents. However, before turning to these details, we take a moment to discuss possible points of connection between the focus in Pathak (2017) on transparency and observations in Wilson (1987) about trading rules that survive as equilibrium institutions.

9.3.2 More than Transparency

Wilson (1987) argues that some trading rules, e.g. the double auction, survive as institutions because they create an environment where participants believe that simply bidding their true valuations is an approximately optimal strategy, and further, when participants do bid their valuations, market outcomes exhaust potential gains from trade. Wilson does not offer a specific reason that an equilibrium would exist in which all agents ignore strategic considerations and simply bid their values, but when the number of participants is finite but large, and participants find it quite costly to acquire even imprecise estimates of the distribution of valuations among other participants, it is reasonable to conjecture that each participant would find that the best response in a market when other participants are bidding their values is to simply bid one's own value.

As a result, we see overlap between Wilson's conjecture and Pathak's emphasis on transparency. Pathak argues that school assignment mechanisms are more likely to survive as institutions if families believe that there is no gain from engaging in strategic behavior. Gaming activities likely amplify inequality and may produce inefficient outcomes that create justified envy. On the other hand, any education authority that convinces all families to truthfully report a complete ranking of schools to a DA mechanism eliminates the resource costs associated with strategic play and produces the student optimal match among the set of assignments that avoid justified envy.

Nonetheless, there is an important difference between the problems that Pathak and Wilson consider. No one is required to bid in any particular auction, and the participants in most auctions are a highly select sample of individuals. When the US Treasury holds a T-bill auction, almost all bidders have participated in many similar auctions, and for most bidders, a key task in their day jobs is the creation of estimates of their valuations for different securities. Wilson is arguing that certain trading rules that minimize gains from strategic behavior survive as institutions because they produce efficient outcomes when all participants simply bid their valuations, and this conjecture is compelling, in part, because it seems reasonable to assume that all participants in these markets know their valuations. Pathak is correct to highlight the value of convincing parents to report their true rankings over schools, but the papers reviewed in section 9.2 suggest that many parents cannot provide a meaningful ranking over a substantial number of schools because they just do not know enough about the schools available to them. A given parent who is not wealthy enough to afford private schools that refuse public funding may be forced to choose between incurring a significant risk of administrative placement or paying substantial search costs with no guarantee that information acquired through search will allow her to secure better ex post school quality for her child.

Traders in markets know their valuations or know a great deal about them because they trade frequently. Families interact with these school assignment mechanisms a few times in their whole life. So, they have little information, and the model above suggests that they may be reluctant to pay significant costs to acquire it. This observation suggests that education authorities that design and operate centralized assignment mechanisms could improve the performance of the match if they share information about schools with families. Next, we consider options for the information provided and the way that it is communicated.

9.4 Providing Information

We argue that researchers who work on the design of centralized assignment mechanisms should also move beyond the design of the algorithms that produce assignments and explore the design of systems that provide information to parents before parents are asked to submit rankings. Here, we discuss topics that are likely central to this research agenda, and we offer some conjectures about several features of optimal information provision.

9.4.1 Ordinal Information

Education authorities are able to provide considerable information about schools that parents value and comprehend. Most education authorities that design school information portals for parents can easily provide school locations, enrollments, average class sizes, historical average test scores, graduation rates, etc. Further, they can easily allow individual schools to add information about the education practices and philosophies that guide each school.

However, measures of achievement growth and many other metrics of school performance that education researchers create may be difficult for non-researchers to interpret. For example, value-added performance measures are standardized averages of deviations from statistical benchmarks. Since many students and parents may find it hard to understand what it means for school A to earn a value-added score of .05 in reading while school *B* earns a score of .03, it may be more useful to report that school A ranks 35th in reading value added while school B ranks 40th in reading value-added. We return to this topic in section 9.5 when we discuss the provision of incentives, but for now we note that whenever researchers use complex statistical methods to create performance metrics, education authorities that place a premium on transparency may choose not to report the metrics directly but instead report the ordinal performance rankings implied by these metrics.

Along these same lines, an education authority that creates multiple performance metrics for schools, e.g., reading growth, math growth, standardized measures of graduation rates, etc., may choose to report separate rankings of schools on each dimension of performance and abstain from creating or producing a single ranking of overall school quality. The NYC public schools and many other education authorities have, at different times, produced school report cards that contain rankings of schools based on some metric of overall quality, and some parents may value these reports. However, these composite rankings raise transparency concerns. Any attempt to create a one-dimensional ranking of school quality requires those involved to make numerous choices about how to scale and weight the various performance metrics used to create an overall measure of quality. As a result, an education authority that reports overall rankings of school quality may find it difficult to explain to parents what these rankings mean.

Finally, while value-added measures of school performance are ubiquitous in education research and policy discussions, reports of these measures or rankings of schools based on these measures may raise important conceptual questions for some parents. Consider two high schools. School A is an elite exam school that places high priority on math and science scores when ranking prospective students. School B is a neighborhood high school in an extremely disadvantaged area that serves mostly kids who tested far below grade level in math during middle school. Now, suppose that the local education authority reports that school B ranks higher than school A on math value-added between the beginning of high school and the end of 10th grade. Informed parents may ask what it means to rank school B as a higher performer than school A given that the math faculty at the two schools were likely not doing the same job. The ninth and tenth grade faculty at school B were likely focused on remedial pre-algebra work, while their counterparts at school A were teaching advanced geometry, trigonometry, and even calculus. Since these two groups of educators were doing quite different jobs, does it make sense to report to parents that one group performed better than the other? The hidden assumption behind the claim that school B performed better than school A is the decision by value-added researchers to treat units of scale scores as meaningful welfare measures. When researchers use value-added models (VAM) to create performance metrics for educators, they are assuming that helping a student move from a score of 120 to a score of 130 requires the same skills and creates the same value for society as helping a student progress from 420 to 430. VAM advocates defend this approach by arguing that policymakers and parents demand universal school quality rankings, but it is not obvious that education authorities should provide answers to nonsensical questions. In our example above, the math faculty at school A is doing a different job than the math faculty at school B, and it therefore makes no sense to ask which faculty did a *better* job.

Barlevy and Neal (2012) propose an alternative performance metric that makes different performance growth comparisons among schools. Returning to our example above, suppose that the education authority is able to place each entering high school student in a math league based on the history of each student's past performance in math and the average performance of other students entering her school. Then, at the end of tenth grade, the authority can assign a percentile rank to each of these students within her own league based on her tenth grade math score. These percentile ranks are invariant to any re-scaling of the tenth grade test scores that preserves ordering, and they have a natural interpretation. If Sue's within league percentile rank is .6, Sue scored better than 60 percent of students who began high school in her cohort with comparable records of elementary school math achievement and comparable peer-achievement levels. Further, Barlevy and Neal (2012) note that average within league percentile rank over all students in a given school is a Percentile Performance Index (PPI) that reports the average within-league winning percentage of students in that school. In our example, knowing that school A receives a math PPI of .7 and school B receives a math PPI of .8 tells us nothing about the relative performance of these schools because the students in these schools do not compete in the same leagues. However, if school C is another neighborhood high school that serves disadvantaged students, and school C receives a math PPI score of .5, we know that entering students in school B are, on average, earning higher within-league percentile scores in tenth grade than comparable students from school C.

If education authorities report PPI performance measures for schools as well as the baseline achievement levels and background characteristics of entering students, they can explain clearly to parents what PPI scores mean. In our example, a PPI score of .55 means that tenth grade students in a given school perform better than 55 percent of students who entered high school with comparable expected math achievement and similar peers. Parents may find this type of information quite useful. The parents of a child who struggles in math should not care about the performance of elite exam schools when choosing a high school for their child. Parents should be most interested in comparisons among schools that serve many students who are comparable to their own children in terms of past achievement.

Education authorities should consider creating performance indices that capture how well schools promote non-academic skills that are vital for future success in school and the labor market. A growing literature demonstrates that some schools and teachers excel at promoting socio-emotional development among students or at helping students develop strong work habits, and these skills are also important for adult outcomes.[12] The ordinal content of such metrics can be used to create additional PFP contests

12. See Rose et al. (2022), Beuermann et al. (2023), Petek and Pope (2023), and Jordan et al. (2024).

among schools, and parents should be interested in how schools rank on these dimensions of performance.

9.4.2 Hidden Action and Multitasking

In any environment where a school benefits when students rank it higher on their lists of submitted schools, the public provision of information on school quality creates multi-tasking concerns. The logic of Holmstrom and Milgrom (1991) warns that once an education authority constructs any particular measure of school quality and then shares it publicly, schools will almost certainly search for low-cost ways to improve their measured school quality even if these strategies produce no real improvements or degrade true school quality.

Neal (2011, 2018) catalog several simple steps that education authorities may take to avoid some rather ubiquitous hidden action problems that arise when students take tests that create high stakes for educators. To begin, education authorities can enlist third parties to administer high-stakes assessments. Events during the No Child Left Behind (NCLB) era revealed that, in high-stakes settings, some educators are willing to give students answers, change students' answers, and engage in other forms of explicit cheating if given the opportunity. There are important potential drawbacks to reporting proficiency rates for schools. Proficiency standards are quite manipulable, and there is considerable evidence that during NCLB, many schools reported increases in the fractions of their students who scored above the proficiency threshold in math or reading primarily because actors in state testing agencies made a series of scoring decisions over time that compromised proficiency standards. Using data from Chicago, IL, Neal and Schanzenbach (2010) also demonstrate that when education authorities build accountability systems around proficiency standards, some educators respond by devoting less attention to students who are far below grade level and therefore not able to become proficient in the near term.[13]

An additional set of multi-tasking concerns fall under the broad heading of *gaming the system.* Recent controversies concerning the influential US News and World Report (USNWR) rankings of colleges provide one example. Critics of these rankings have long complained that because students pay close attention to these rankings, colleges and universities distort their educational practices to earn higher rankings. For example, Yale Law School recently refused to supply data to USNWR, in part, because their ranking system counts graduates as unemployed if they accept fellowships to work in public interest organization or enter PhD programs, regardless of how prestigious the fellowship or graduate program may be. Yale announced that it would rather not participate in the USNWR rankings than limit its

13. Chapter 2.6 in Neal (2018) catalogs much of the sizable literature on incentive alignment problems created by accountability and incentive programs for educators that involve high-stakes student assessments.

support for students who desire a career in public interest work. Other prestigious law schools joined the boycott, and USNWR announced changes to their scoring system.[14]

USNWR has long known that law school and colleges manipulate their practices and reporting procedures to improve their USNWR rankings without improving and while possibly harming the quality of instruction they provide. Yet, the fact that USNWR has tolerated these behaviors while building a successful ranking service does not imply that public education officials should tolerate similar actions. Education authorities and USNWR are pursuing different goals. USNWR is trying to produce rankings that readers value. If their methods induce all or most schools to engage in the same wasteful gaming activities, the rankings USNWR produces ex post will still likely be highly correlated with the true rankings that readers desire. Thus, as long as the gaming costs are not so large that schools refuse to participate, USNWR cares little about the resources that schools waste trying to manipulate the metrics they submit to USNWR. However, an education authority cares not only about producing valid ranks; it also cares about the efficient use of public funds allocated for the education of children. If education authorities produce performance rankings using metrics that are manipulable, they invite schools to allocate public funds to wasteful gaming activities. Since these wasted resources could be allocated to productive instructional activities, an education authority that invites wasteful gaming may well harm learning outcomes.

Many of the most studied gaming behaviors fall under the headings of *coaching rather than teaching* or *teaching to the test*. We return to these behaviors in section 9.5, but first, we discuss information policies that have received much less attention from education researchers.

9.4.3 Face-to-Face Encounters

The results presented by Arteaga et al. (2022) indicate that many parents are not going to feel comfortable ranking a particular school if they have not had an opportunity to interview teachers and administrators from the school. Therefore, education authorities may entertain creating school fairs that allow parents to speak with teachers and administrators from many different schools in one place. For example, numerous researchers have studied various aspects of the high school assignment system in NYC, but school officials in NYC have likely not explored holding an annual high school fair in a large hall in the Javits Center. Officials could invite each high school in the city

14. Before implementing these changes, USNWR released a set of rankings that still ranked Yale Law first. See "Dean Gerken: Why Yale Law School Is Leaving the U.S. News & World Report Rankings," Yale Law School, November 15, 2022, https://law.yale.edu/yls-today/news/dean-gerken-why-yale-law-school-leaving-us-news-world-report-rankings, and "Despite Boycott, Yale Still Tops U.S. News Best Law School Rankings," Michael T. Nietzel, April 12, 2023, https://www.forbes.com/sites/michaeltnietzel/2023/04/12/despite-boycott-yale-still-tops-us-news-best-law-school-rankings/.

to staff an information booth with current students, former students, faculty, and administrators who are prepared to answer questions about the school.

Many economists and policymakers may respond to this idea by noting that many high schools already hold open house events for prospective students, and some may even argue that, in a world where large school fairs are valuable to parents, we expect private actors to organize such events and charge admission to families seeking information about schools. Yet, two rejoinders are obvious. First, some schools may not participate in such school fairs unless they are compelled to do so. A public school that expects to be over-subscribed simply because it is located in an area with many children and few other schools may have little incentive to participate in such events. Second, the model we present above suggests that, in this setting, market mechanisms may fail to provide efficient levels of information for parents. When deciding whether to attend such a fair, family A does not consider the possibility that if they discover a new school that works well for their child, they may open up a slot in their default school that turns out to be a great match for a different student.[15]

As school systems design the mechanisms they use to provide information for parents, they must remember that when they lower the costs that families pay to acquire information about schools, the response will be greater if they can simultaneously convince parents that other parents are also acquiring more information. Our model illustrates that lowering search costs may not be enough to create an equilibrium where all parents actively acquire information and submit complete ranking orderings over schools. Parents need to believe that other parents are also searching and thus opening up slots in other schools.

So far, we have discussed information interventions that may improve the value of the assignments produced by centralized assignment mechanisms holding the quantity and qualities of existing schools fixed. However, as we illustrate in our simple model above, the gains from centralized assignment are limited in settings where vertical quality differentiation is the primary source of school heterogeneity. Given numerous potential rules for assigning priorities, many parents may have little to gain from participating in a centralized assignment mechanism if there is an acute shortage of high-quality schools. Further, this may remain the case even if the school district provides parents with detailed information about all schools. In the next section, we therefore consider how education officials may embed accountability and incentive mechanisms within centralized assignment mechanisms. Successful assignment mechanisms must not only help parents make informed choices but also provide parents with options worth choosing.

15. We learned from Dunia Fernandez of the Los Angeles Unified School District that ZOC program hosted this type of school fair prior to 2018. However, when faced with funding cuts, even this small program abandoned this approach. We know of no large centralized system that hosts an event that allows parents to speak with faculty and staff of all schools in their choice set.

9.5 Shaping the Supply of School Quality

The centralized school choice mechanism in Chile likely facilitates competition between public and private schools, and since funding levels for schools in both sectors are tied to enrollment, schools have incentives to compete in ways that increase parental satisfaction with schools. Further, providing parents with better information about schools may enhance the value created by this competition, but several of the papers we review above raise the possibility that information provision alone may not guarantee the outcomes that advocates of school choice systems expect.

Recall the description in Abdulkadiroğlu et al. (2018) of learning outcomes for students participating in the LSP voucher plan and the conclusions in Walters (2018) concerning the potential gains for students who never apply to charter schools in Boston. School choice mechanisms create incentives for schools to provide what parents demand, but both papers raise concerns about the decision rules that some parents use to choose schools for their children. As a result, policymakers cannot be certain that the competitive pressures generated by the introduction of centralized school choice will generate significant improvements in the distribution of academic quality among schools. Further, there is no guarantee that policymakers can design information platforms, school fairs, and other mechanisms that will induce all parents to acquire the information they need to make informed schooling choices for their children. Even in a hypothetical world where all parents knew everything about the academic performance of different schools, there is no guarantee that all parents would make school choice decisions that served their children well. Some parents might place inefficient weight on factors like convenience, the beauty of a school's campus, or the success of a school's sports teams.

For these reasons, the competitive pressures created by school choice may not guarantee that all schools operate efficiently. Therefore, education policymakers may find it helpful to create explicit incentives systems for educators that provide additional accountability pressures.

We have already discussed how PPI performance measures provide useful information for parents and students. Barlevy and Neal (2012) describe a Pay for Percentile (PFP) incentive system that rewards schools based on their PPI scores. PFP works as follows: for each grade-subject combination, place each student in a league at the beginning of each year based on the student's past record of achievement and summary measures of the past achievement of her classmates. At the end of the year, calculate each student's winning percentages within her different leagues, and then calculate PPI scores at the school $*$ grade $*$ subject level. Finally, reward each school with a set of performance bonuses that are proportional to its vector of PPI scores. Barlevy and Neal (2012) characterize the bonus rates that induce teachers in all schools to allocate efficient effort to all tasks that promote achievement among students. If the education authority can correctly place students in leagues, PFP elicits efficient effort from educators under quite general conditions.[16]

PFP also allows an education authority to reward educators for improving measured student performance without creating incentives for educators to coach students on test-taking strategies that raise scores without improving student mastery of the tested subject. Neal (2013) explains how the test-development procedures that modern psychometricians use to create scale scores for results from different test forms in an assessment series necessarily make test items predictable in ways that make coaching rather than teaching profitable. However, PPI scores require only ordinal information about the relative performance of different students on a given exam. Therefore, education authorities can implement PFP using a series of exams that do not repeat questions, follow predictable formats, or meet other development criteria used to create most modern test score scales, and in this scenario, the best response for educators would be to teach for mastery rather than coach students on test-taking strategies.[17]

We have already noted that parents do not possess perfect information about the schooling options available to them. However, parents do possess important information that policymakers may not. Parents know if their child is eager to go to school. Parents often know if their child feels safe in school. Parents observe whether their child is developing important social and emotional skills in school. Thus, the rankings that parents submit to centralized assignment mechanisms likely contain information that is valuable for education authorities. However, future research is needed to determine the optimal method for extracting performance information from these rankings.

Education authorities cannot use these rankings to create additional PPI scores. Even when choice is organized around mechanisms that induce par-

16. A number of researchers have tested PFP in field experiments. See Loyalka et al. (2019), Chang et al. (2020), Gilligan et al. (2022), Fryer Jr et al. (2022), and Mbiti et al. (2023). These experiments implemented several different variations on PFP. In each study, some version of PFP generated significant improvements in academic outcomes for a significant population of students. Forming leagues correctly would be an important challenge for any education authority that attempts to implement PFP on a large scale. One approach is to estimate the conditional distribution of year-end scores controlling for a rich set of controls that characterize each student's past achievement, the past achievement of their peers, the size of their class, student demographics, etc. Given this estimated distribution, each student's year-end score can be converted into a conditional percentile. Derek Neal's home page, https://voices.uchicago.edu/derekneal/, provides a User's Guide (see bottom link to "A User's Guide to the Percentile Performance Index Software," Ian Fillmore and Eric Nielsen, November 15, 2011, https://bpb-us-w2.wpmucdn.com/voices.uchicago.edu/dist/6/3381/files/2023/12/A-Users-Guide-to-PPI.pdf) for an R package that computes PPI scores using this method. The package is available upon request.

17. The A-level leaving exams in the UK are an example of high-stakes exams that have historically been created without the strict item development requirements that make modern Item Response Theory (IRT) scales possible and coaching on test-taking strategies profitable. See Wheadon (2013).

ents to submit truthful rankings, most parents rank few schools. Thus, we cannot give each school a set of percentile scores that reveal how each student ranks the school relative to all other schools. Further, even if all parents ranked all schools truthfully, education officials would likely find it difficult to create desirable leagues that contain large numbers of schools. School location is a primary concern for parents, and most schools are not located within a short distance of a significant number of competing schools that serve the same grade levels. Thus, how would one create a league of schools that compete on a level playing field for a common set of students?

Nonetheless, education authorities can glean important information from the lists that parents submit to centralized assignment mechanisms. Each year in Chile, NYC, and other cities, some portion of the students entering a centralized assignment mechanism are already attending a school in the system and could continue in the school during the next academic year. However, they are participating in the mechanism because they believe they may be served better by another school. Thus, education authorities can measure the fraction of students in each school who are searching for better options. Further, they can examine the lists submitted by these students and see how many of the listed schools would require parents to incur additional travel costs. More work is needed, but if education authorities observe that a high fraction of students in school A seek assignments in different schools and also observe that significant fractions accept new assignments that require additional travel costs, they likely need to investigate school A.

9.5.1 Shaping the Choice Set

Researchers should also turn their attention to the design of rules that determine the eligibility of schools to receive public funds through centralized mechanisms. Some advocates of school choice may note that centralized choice systems, e.g., the current system in Chile, allow parents to decide which schools receive public funds. Any school that does not receive sufficient demand through the assignment mechanism will not be able to cover the fixed costs of running a school and be forced to close. However, Gallego (2013) argues that historically, local governments in Chile have subsidized municipal schools that face declining enrollment. He claims that in 2002, voucher revenue accounted for only 70 percent of funding for public schools in Chile. Further, in the United States, some school districts find it politically difficult to close low-performing public schools that have many empty classrooms.[18]

In competitive markets for consumer goods, firms may exit the market if only a portion of consumers understand that they are producing low-quality products. If a firm facing declining demand for its products finds that it

18. See Fay (2017) for a description of the political backlash that followed the closing of almost 50 Chicago schools that were grossly underutilized.

can no longer cover its fixed costs, it can limit its losses by shutting down. However, failing public schools often possess political clout that insulates them from similar pressures.

In addition, we note above that parents who participate in the LSP voucher program expressed high levels of satisfaction with the voucher schools they selected for their children, even though many of these children experienced stunning learning losses as a result. It is possible that similar outcomes would not occur in systems that provided parents with better information about the academic performance of different schools, but we see no reason to assume that better information alone would produce sets of parental choices that would force the closure of all low-quality schools.[19]

These observations suggest that researchers working on the design of centralized choice systems should tackle the following questions: (i) How should education authorities evaluate the applications of organizations that wish to open a new school that receives public funds? and (ii) How should education authorities form decision rules that map the history of parental demand for a given school as well as the school's history of performance on numerous dimensions into a determination concerning the school's eligibility to continue receiving public funding?[20] These are challenging problems, and even if researchers discover the optimal rule for deeming schools eligible for public funding, policymakers may be unwilling or unable to adopt it. However, these questions are first order. The best centralized assignment systems cannot guarantee effective schooling for all children unless they are paired with mechanisms that shape the quality of the menu of schools available to students.

9.6 Conclusion

Over the past quarter century, researchers have learned a great deal about the design of school assignment mechanisms and how different design choices impact student welfare. We agree with the claim in Pathak (2017) that centralized assignment systems are more likely to be effective and politically stable if they are transparent. Yet, we contend that recent research suggests that transparency alone does not create informed choice. Many parents lack information about the schools in their choice set, and better information provision may not only improve efficiency but also enhance equity since several studies have shown that advantaged parents often possess superior

19. Given the high levels of parental satisfaction, we realize that these LSP schools were likely doing some things well. However, we contend that schools that reduce math achievement by .4 standard deviations in one year are likely low-quality schools.

20. Neal (2018) notes that any school system that adopted a PFP scheme would also need to adopt procedures for reseeding competition among schools over time. The details required for dynamic implementation of PFP remain for future research, but the optimal dynamic system almost certainly involves a rule for deeming low-performing schools ineligible to receive public funds based on some summary measure of their historical performance.

information about the schools available to them and how assignment systems work.[21]

Future research should also confront the task of designing mechanisms that shape the menu of schools offered to students. For example, it may be possible to improve the quality of schools offered to students in historically disadvantaged communities by combining school choice, centralized assignment, and a PFP scheme that offers exceptionally high bonus rates to schools that operate in disadvantaged communities. Systems that pay bonuses to educators who operate high-performing schools in disadvantaged areas may fruitfully engage and serve parents who would otherwise see choice systems as mechanisms for providing better options for other people's children, i.e., children from families who face lower transportation costs or already live in areas with numerous high-quality schools.

Shi (2015) discusses how the centralized assignment mechanism in Boston restricts choice menus in ways that seek to grant more equitable access to the best schools. The rules are complicated, but the motivation for the rules is clear. In Boston and other cities, a disproportionate share of the most highly ranked schools are in the most advantaged parts of the city. Thus, a system that allows all families to rank all schools would privilege the privileged, since they would be able to create longer lists of highly ranked schools that are close to their homes. To address this concern, the rules in Boston contain limits on the number of schools that a family may include in its ranking that are both highly ranked and nearby.

If parents believe that a choice system is not expanding the supply of high-quality schools available to their child or that they do not possess the information they need to participate effectively in the mechanism, they are less likely to support it. Public school leaders in Chicago are now considering proposals to restrict school choice. Advocates of these proposals argue that the centralized assignment mechanisms that allow students from across the city to apply to charter schools, magnet schools, and selective admissions schools harm neighborhood schools, especially schools in historically disadvantaged areas that may see the best students in their neighborhoods enroll elsewhere in the city.[22]

The efforts to limit choice in Boston and eliminate choice in Chicago are not surprising. Public sector unions have long opposed systems that create competition among schools, and not all families benefit equally from the adoption of any centralized school choice mechanism. We argue here that

21. See Pathak and Sönmez (2008) and Corradini and Idoux (2023).

22. See "Chicago Public Schools Leaders Want to Move Away from School choice," Reema Amin and Becky Vevea, December 12, 2023, *Chalkbeat Chicago*, https://www.chalkbeat.org/chicago/2023/12/12/chicago-public-schools-moves-away-from-school-choice/. To date, these proposals to limit choice offer no explicit strategies that provide additional rewards for educators who operate excellent schools in disadvantaged areas or new sanctions for educators who fail to serve disadvantaged students well. Instead, these proposals lean heavily on the assertion that neighborhood schools will perform well if they simply receive more resources.

better ex ante information provision to families may create more robust parental engagement in school choice mechanisms that improves student welfare. Yet, in both Chicago and Boston, the potential gains from improvements to centralized assignment mechanisms are constrained by a limited supply of excellent schools. Neal (2018) argues that researchers need to focus on how education authorities can use the information gleaned from both traditional accountability systems and the rankings that parents submit to assignment mechanisms to reward excellent schools and to deem persistently low-performing schools ineligible to receive public funds. Market design researchers should take up the task of designing centralized assignment mechanisms that provide parents with clear and relevant information about schools while providing schools with clear incentives to serve students well.

Appendix

Theory

In this section, we construct a model that highlights the features described in the examples above. We restrict to a very simple environment with just two schools and two students. This simple model allows us to investigate how the set of equilibria change with the model parameters.

Model

There are two students a and b and two schools 1 and 2. Each school has capacity 1. At the beginning of the game, student i's value for school x denoted θ_{ix} is drawn i.i.d from the uniform distribution on [0, 1]. Students are matched to schools using the deferred acceptance algorithm. School 1 prioritizes student a over student b while school 2 prioritizes student b over student a. We refer to school 1 and 2 as the "local school" for students a and b respectively. Each student learns without cost their value from the local school but can only learn their value from the other school at cost $c \geq 0$. We assume that students only rank schools for which they know their value and that, when they know both values, they rank schools truthfully. Pure strategies are measurable maps $\sigma_i : [0, 1] \rightarrow \{0, 1\}$ which indicate whether or not an agent decides to learn when the value from the local school is $\upsilon \in [0, 1]$. We look for symmetric pure strategy Bayes-Nash equilibria.

LEMMA 1. *In any symmetric equilibrium, there is a value υ for which a learns when $\theta_{a1} \leq \upsilon$ and b learns when $\theta_{b2} \leq \upsilon$.*

PROOF. We prove this for student a since the analogous result for student b is entirely symmetric. Suppose that student b learns when θ_{b2} is contained in a (Borel) set A. Let

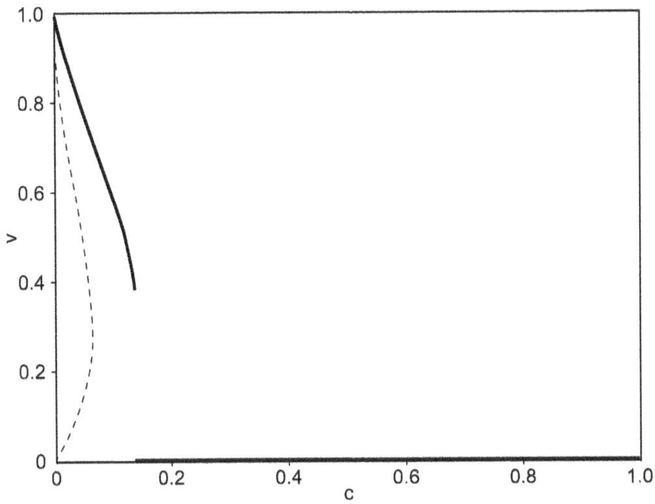

Fig. 9A.1 Equilibrium and efficient v as a function of cost

$$A' = \{(\theta_{b2}, \theta_{b1}) : \theta_{b2} \in A \text{ and } \theta_{b1} > \theta_{b2}\}.$$

The marginal payoff for agent a from learning θ_{a2} when $\theta_{a1} = x$ is given by

$$m(A')\int_x^1 (\theta_{a2} - x)d\theta_{a2} - c.$$

where m is the Lebesgue measure on $\mathbb{R}^2$. Note that $m(A')$ is the probability that b will top-rank 1 given that they search when θ_{b2} is in A and the integral measures the expected marginal utility when a learns that $\theta_{b2} > x$. This expression can be simplified to

$$m(A')\left(\frac{x^2}{2} - x + \frac{1}{2}\right)$$

which is a strictly decreasing function over [0, 1], so that if it a weak best response for a given type x to search, it is a strict best response for all lower types to search.■

In general, this game has multiple equilibria as it is a game of strategic complements. For example, the strategy in which neither student ever learns is an equilibrium. For any interior v which constitutes an equilibrium, we must have that

$$\left(\upsilon - \frac{\upsilon^2}{2}\right)\left(\frac{\upsilon^2}{2} - \upsilon + \frac{1}{2}\right) - c = 0$$

since this is the marginal value from learning the utility of the other school at the cutoff. The pairs $(c, \upsilon) \in [0, 1] \times [0, 1]$ satisfying this equation are shown in figure 9A.1 with the dashed line. We see that for sufficiently high c

there is no equilibrium with search. For low levels of c, however, there can be multiple equilibria.

There is a potential inefficiency to these equilibria. When either agent learns about the other school, there are two effects. First, they increase their options in the case where their non-local school is high value. Second, they open up the possibility of trade with the other student. This second effect is not fully internalized by the student, so a planner might want to encourage search. We can formalize this by asking what level of υ would the planner choose to maximize social welfare.

Welfare $W(\upsilon, c)$ is given by

$$\int_{\upsilon}^{1}\int_{\upsilon}^{1}(\theta_{a1}+\theta_{b2})d\theta_{a1}d\theta_{b2}+2\int_{\upsilon}^{1}\int_{0}^{\upsilon}(\theta_{a1}+\theta_{b2}-c)d\theta_{a1}d\theta_{b2}$$

$$+\ 2\int_{0}^{\upsilon}\int_{0}^{\upsilon}\int_{0}^{\theta_{b2}}(\theta_{a1}+\theta_{b2}-2c)d\theta_{b1}d\theta_{a1}d\theta_{b2}-\int_{0}^{\upsilon}\int_{0}^{\upsilon}\int_{0}^{\theta_{b2}}\int_{0}^{\theta_{a1}}(\theta_{a1}+\theta_{b2}-2c)d\theta_{a2}\,d\theta_{b1}d\theta_{a1}d\theta_{b2}$$

$$+\ \int_{0}^{\upsilon}\int_{0}^{\upsilon}\int_{\theta_{b2}}^{1}\int_{\theta_{a1}}^{1}(\theta_{a2}+\theta_{b1}-2c)d\theta_{a2}\,d\theta_{b1}d\theta_{a1}d\theta_{b2}.$$

The first expression calculates expected utility when both students learn that the value from the local school is at least υ. The second term measures the expected utility when exactly one of the students observes a value lower than υ at their local school. Since this is symmetric across the two agents,

$$\int_{\upsilon}^{1}\int_{\theta}^{\upsilon}(\theta_{a1}+\theta_{b2}-c)d\theta_{a1}d\theta_{b2}=\int_{0}^{\upsilon}\int_{\upsilon}^{1}(\theta_{a1}+\theta_{b2}-c)d\theta_{b2}d\theta_{a1}$$

and the sum of these two terms is twice the first.

In the third term, we have the expected utility when both agents see a value at their local school less than υ but one of them gets an even lower value for the non-local school so that there is no trade. Since this is symmetric across the agents, this term has a weight of two. However, this double-counts the region where both agents get an even lower value from their non-local school, so the fourth term corrects this. Finally, the last term is the expected gains from trade.

This expression simplifies to

$$-\frac{1}{6}\upsilon^5+\frac{5}{6}\upsilon^4-\frac{3}{2}\upsilon^3+\upsilon^2-2c\upsilon+1$$

For each c, we can calculate the υ^* which maximizes this expression. These values are shown in figure 9A.1 by the solid line. As we can see, the planner always prefers more search than will arise in equilibrium.

For a concrete example, when $c = 1/16$, the equilibrium with the most learning occurs when $\upsilon = 1-(1/\sqrt{2})$ which is approximately 0.3. For the same cost, the planner prefers υ of approximately 0.7. This results in a roughly 4 percent increase in welfare.

References

Abdulkadiroğlu, Atila, Nikhil Agarwal, and Parag A. Pathak. 2017. "The Welfare Effects of Coordinated Assignment: Evidence from the New York City High School Match." *American Economic Review* 107(12): 3635–3689.

Abdulkadiroğlu, Atila, Yeon-Koo Che, and Yosuke Yasuda. 2011. "Resolving Conflicting Preferences in School Choice: the Boston Mechanism Reconsidered." *American Economic Review* 101(1): 399–410.

Abdulkadiroğlu, Atila, Parag A. Pathak, and Alvin E. Roth. 2009. "Strategy-Proofness Versus Efficiency in Matching with Indifferences: Redesigning the NYC High School Match." *American Economic Review* 99(5): 1954–1978.

Abdulkadiroğlu, Atila, Parag A. Pathak, Jonathan Schellenberg, and Christopher R. Walters. 2020. "Do Parents Value School Effectiveness?" *American Economic Review* 110(5): 1502–1539.

Abdulkadiroğlu, Atila, Parag A. Pathak, and Christopher R. Walters. 2018. "Free to Choose: Can School Choice Reduce Student Achievement?" *American Economic Journal: Applied Economics* 10(1): 175–206.

Abdulkadiroğlu, Atila, and Tayfun Sönmez. 2003. "School Choice: A Mechanism Design Approach." *American Economic Review* 93(3): 729–47.

Agarwal, Nikhil, and Paulo Somaini. 2020a. "Revealed Preference Analysis of School Choice Models." *Annual Review of Economics* 12: 471–501.

Agarwal, Nikhil, and Paulo Somaini. 2020b. "Revealed Preference Analysis of School Choice Models." *Annual Review of Economics* 12: 471–501.

Ainsworth, Robert, Rajeev Dehejia, Cristian Pop-Eleches, and Miguel Urquiola. 2023. "Why Do Households Leave School Value Added on the Table? The Roles of Information and Preferences." *American Economic Review* 113(4): 1049–1082.

Ajayi, Kehinde F., Willa H. Friedman, and Adrienne M. Lucas. 2020. "When Information Is Not Enough: Evidence from a Centralized School Choice System." Technical Report. Cambridge, MA: National Bureau of Economic Research.

Angrist, Joshua D., Parag A. Pathak, and Christopher R. Walters. 2013. "Explaining Charter School Effectiveness." *American Economic Journal: Applied Economics* 5(4): 1–27.

Arteaga, Felipe, Adam J. Kapor, Christopher A. Neilson, and Seth D. Zimmerman. 2022. "Smart Matching Platforms and Heterogeneous Beliefs in Centralized School Choice." *Quarterly Journal of Economics* 137(3): 1791–1848.

Barlevy, Gadi, and Derek Neal. 2012. "Pay for Percentile." *American Economic Review* 102(5): 1805–1831.

Beuermann, Diether W., C. Kirabo Jackson, Laia Navarro-Sola, and Francisco Pardo. 2023. "What Is a Good School, and Can Parents Tell? Evidence on the Multidimensionality of School Output." *Review of Economic Studies* 90(1): 65–101.

Calsamiglia, Caterina, Chao Fu, and Maia Güell. 2020. "Structural Estimation of a Model of School Choices: The Boston Mechanism Versus Its Alternatives." *Journal of Political Economy* 128(2): 642–80.

Campos, Christopher. 2023. "Social Interactions and Preferences for Schools: Experimental Evidence from Los Angeles." Available at SSRN 4352040.

Chang, Fang, Huan Wang, Yaqiong Qu, Qiang Zheng, Prashant Loyalka, Sean Sylvia, Yaojiang Shi, Sarah-Eve Dill, and Scott Rozelle. 2020. "The Impact of Pay-for-Percentile Incentive on Low-Achieving Students in Rural China." *Economics of Education Review* 75: 101954.

Cohodes, Sarah R, Sean P. Corcoran, Jennifer L. Jennings, and Carolyn Sattin-Bajaj. 2022. "When Do Informational Interventions Work? Experimental Evidence from

New York City High School Choice." *Educational Evaluation and Policy Analysis* p. 01623737231203293.
Corradini, Viola. 2023. "Information and Access in School Choice Systems: Evidence from New York City." Technical Report, Working Paper.
Corradini, Viola, and Clemence Idoux. 2023. "Overcoming Racial Gaps in School Preferences: The Role of Peer Diversity on School Choice." Technical Report, Working Paper.
Dobbie, Will, and Roland G. Fryer. (2015). "The Medium-Term Impacts of High-Achieving Charter Schools." *Journal of Political Economy* 123(5): 985–1037.
Ergin, Haluk, and Tayfun Sönmez. 2006. "Games of School Choice Under the Boston Mechanism." *Journal of Public Economics* 90(1): 215–37.
Fay, Jacob. 2017. *School Closure and Abnormal Justice*. PhD thesis, Harvard University.
Fryer Jr., Roland G., Steven D. Levitt, John List, and Sally Sadoff. 2022. "Enhancing the Efficacy of Teacher Incentives Through Framing: A Field Experiment." *American Economic Journal: Economic Policy* 14(4): 269–99.
Fryer, Roland G. 2014. "Injecting Charter School Best Practices into Traditional Public Schools: Evidence from Field Experiments." *Quarterly Journal of Economics* 129(3): 1355–1407.
Gallego, Francisco. 2013. "When Does Inter-School Competition Matter? Evidence from the Chilean Voucher System." *B.E. Journal of Economic Analysis & Policy* 13(2): 525–62.
Gilligan, Daniel O., Naureen Karachiwalla, Ibrahim Kasirye, Adrienne M. Lucas, and Derek Neal. 2022. "Educator Incentives and Educational Triage in Rural Primary Schools." *Journal of Human Resources* 57(1): 79–111.
Hastings, Justine S., and Jeffrey M. Weinstein. 2008. "Information, School Choice, and Academic Achievement: Evidence from Two Experiments." *Quarterly Journal of Economics* 123(4): 1373–1414.
Holmstrom, Bengt, and Paul Milgrom. 1991. "Multitask Principal-Agent Analyses: Incentive Contracts, Asset Ownership, and Job Design." *Journal of Law, Economics, and Organization* 7 (Special Issue): 24–52.
Jordan, Andrew, Ezra Karger, and Derek Neal. 2024. "Early Predictors of Racial Disparities in Criminal Justice Involvement." Technical Report, BFI Working Paper.
Kapor, Adam J., Christopher A. Neilson, and Seth D. Zimmerman. 2020. "Heterogeneous Beliefs and School Choice Mechanisms." *American Economic Review* 110(5): 1274–1315.
Loyalka, Prashant, Sean Sylvia, Chengfang Liu, James Chu, and Yaojiang Shi. 2019. "Pay by Design: Teacher Performance Pay Design and the Distribution of Student Achievement." *Journal of Labor Economics* 37(3): 621–62.
Mbiti, Isaac, Mauricio Romero, and Youdi Schipper. 2023. "Designing Effective Teacher Performance Pay Programs: Experimental Evidence from Tanzania." *Economic Journal* 133(653): 1968–2000.
Neal, Derek. 2011. "The Design of Performance Pay in Education." In *Handbook of the Economics of Education*, edited by Eric A. Hanushek, Stephen Machin, and Ludger Woessmann. Elsevier.
Neal, Derek. 2013. "The Consequences of Using One Assessment System to Pursue Two Objectives." *Journal of Economic Education* 44(4): 339–52.
Neal, Derek A. 2018. *Information, Incentives, and Education Policy*. Harvard University Press.
Neal, Derek, and Diane W. Schanzenbach. 2010. "Left Behind by Design: Profi-

ciency Counts and Test-Based Accountability." *Review of Economics and Statistics* 92(2): 263–83.

Pathak, Parag A. 2017. "What Really Matters in Designing School Choice Mechanisms." *Advances in Economics and Econometrics* 1(12): 176–214.

Pathak, Parag A., and Tayfun Sönmez. 2008. "Leveling the Playing Field: Sincere and Sophisticated Players in the Boston Mechanism." *American Economic Review* 98(4): 1636–1652.

Petek, Nathan, and Nolan G. Pope. 2023. "The Multidimensional Impact of Teachers on Students." *Journal of Political Economy* 131(4): 1057–1107.

Rose, Evan, Jonathan Schellenber, and Yotam Shem-ov. 2022. "The Effect of Teacher Quality on Adult Criminal Justice Contact." Technical Report, Working Paper.

Shi, Peng. (2015). "Guiding School-Choice Reform Through Novel Applications of Operations Research." *Interfaces* 45(2): 117–32.

Walters, Christopher R. 2018. "The Demand for Effective Charter Schools." *Journal of Political Economy* 126(6): 2179–2223.

Wheadon, Christopher. 2013. "Using Modern Test Theory to Maintain Standards in Public Qualifications in England." *Research Papers in Education* 28(5): 628–47.

Wilson, R. 1987. "Game-theoretic analyses of trading processes." In *Advances in Economic Theory: Fifth World Congress*, edited by T. F. Bewley, 33–70. Econometric Society Monographs. Cambridge University Press.

Author Index

Subject Index

Page numbers followed by "f" or "t" refer to figures or tables, respectively.